Robert and Sheila

ove

Crab's Odyssey

Malta to Istanbul in an Open Boat

Penny Minney

taniwha press uk

Published by taniwha press uk

Title: Crab's Odyssey: Malta to Istanbul in an Open Boat

Type: Travel. Non-fiction. Sailing. Memoirs. Ancient sailing vessels. Roman history. Greek history. Mediterranean history. Adventure.

ISBN: 978-0-9954699-2-1

Printed & Bound by CMP (uk) Ltd.
Poole, Dorset BH12 4NU

Preface

It was on a holiday in the Mani with my friend Polly - a general's daughter to the end - that I got marching-orders to write an account of this Greek journey, made more than fifty years previously in an open boat. I had met Polly at Taormina as we worked our way up the east coast of Sicily, and both she and her husband became good friends. I was to clear both time and space in my life, she said, track down the log of the four trips, and write as factual and accurate account as I could. She, a gifted artist, would illustrate it with drawings to liven it up (this she did not live to do). And so began a re-living of those four summers of snail's-pace travelling. On several occasions people's memories did not correspond to the record, and I always gave precedence to the ship's log, which was written day by day.

Crab was a seventeen-foot lifeboat, clinker-built, six foot in the beam, unconverted. When we got her she had a ten-foot mast, a dipping-lug mainsail and minute jib, both of heavy red canvas, a rudder, and five oars. We later added an extra six inches of solid oak keel running the whole length of the boat, and acquired a fair-weather jib and mainsail, both about twice the size of the original ones and of lighter canvas, and put an iron plate onto the bottom of the rudder, which otherwise had a tendency to come out of the water. We also changed the mast for one four feet longer. With these alterations she did not make too much leeway, and it was possible to beat satisfactorily out of harbours, although passage-making against a head wind still took too long to be worthwhile.

We were not at first aware that we would have to get her registered. When we returned after our first crossing to Sicily we were met at Customs by the Registrar of Ships, shaking his fist and shouting, "You should not have left Malta! YOU SHOULD HAVE COME UNDER MY POWER!" Apparently he had nearly sacked the whole of his staff for letting us leave Malta without being registered as a sea-going vessel (although this was only compulsory for vessels of over fifteen tons).

In the nineteen-fifties it was almost impossible for British people to holiday in places like Greece and Egypt, because the annual currency allowance was limited to £50 p.a. So Egypt and Greece were places of mystery - hence the widespread interest in the books of writers like Lawrence and Gerald Durrell, and Patrick Leigh Fermor. But on *Crab,* using local produce, we lived off about £3.6s. per week per head, and so were able to travel for up to four months on end.

Homer's *Odyssey* describes Odysseus' long-drawn-out journey homewards. But in travelling to Malta and then venturing across the Mediterranean we were trying to get away from home, surely? I had first started to try and learn Ancient Greek at the age of seven, taught by my older brother, and from the beginning the culture held a magical attraction for me. At university I became fascinated also by this country which had cradled the early years of Christianity. After growing up in the utilitarian drabness that was Britain in the long post-war years, we were longing to go off in search of our British culture's remoter origins - of the invading Romans who when withdrawing were begged to stay; of the conquered Greeks whose culture, in time, conquered Rome. As with Odysseus, our aim was a returning.

Seeking news of our shipmates, I found that several could not be traced. Others had died. But the end piece, "Trips Round the Survivors" has reminiscences from six who sailed with us, as well as from the co-owners - my father (who sailed twice), Robin Minney (three times), and Sally Humphreys, skipper.

Acknowledgements

Thanks to all my shipmates, and to kind and generous friends in Malta who helped us equip after the shipwreck, especially Erroll Bruce (sadly no longer with us) and his family, for ongoing support. Thanks to those villagers on the south coast of Sicily who hosted us for nearly a week when we were stormbound so many years ago. Thanks especially to the skipper, Sally Humphreys, for the two log books, the ship's papers, and a wealth of lively letters written to her parents; and for the reunion of old shipmates in Oxford that she organised in 2010. Thanks to my husband Robin for his support, his colour slides and photos, carefully listed, and to Roland Wedgwood and Richard Davy for their photos, and John Hope, who was especially supportive as I struggled to write the opening chapters. Thanks also to my sons Tom and Hugo Minney and to my grandchildren Alex and Francesca Minney. Thanks also to Dominic Wells, for guidance and time-consuming help. Thanks also to Dr Kerem Oktem for tracing the article published almost sixty years ago in *Hurriyet*. Thanks to the widow of David Edwards, who sent us David's travel-diary, and to my brother Owain, whose diary-essay I have also used. And finally, huge thanks to Shelagh Aitken, who as an editor has been a joy to work with, to Peter Skelton for cleaning up the old photos, to Richard Davy, Ian Morin and Sally Humphreys for proof-reading, to Rod Heikell, and to Elinor Cole, who also pushed and prodded this book into shape.

Contents

Illustrations

(unless otherwise stated, photos are by Robin Minney)

List of maps

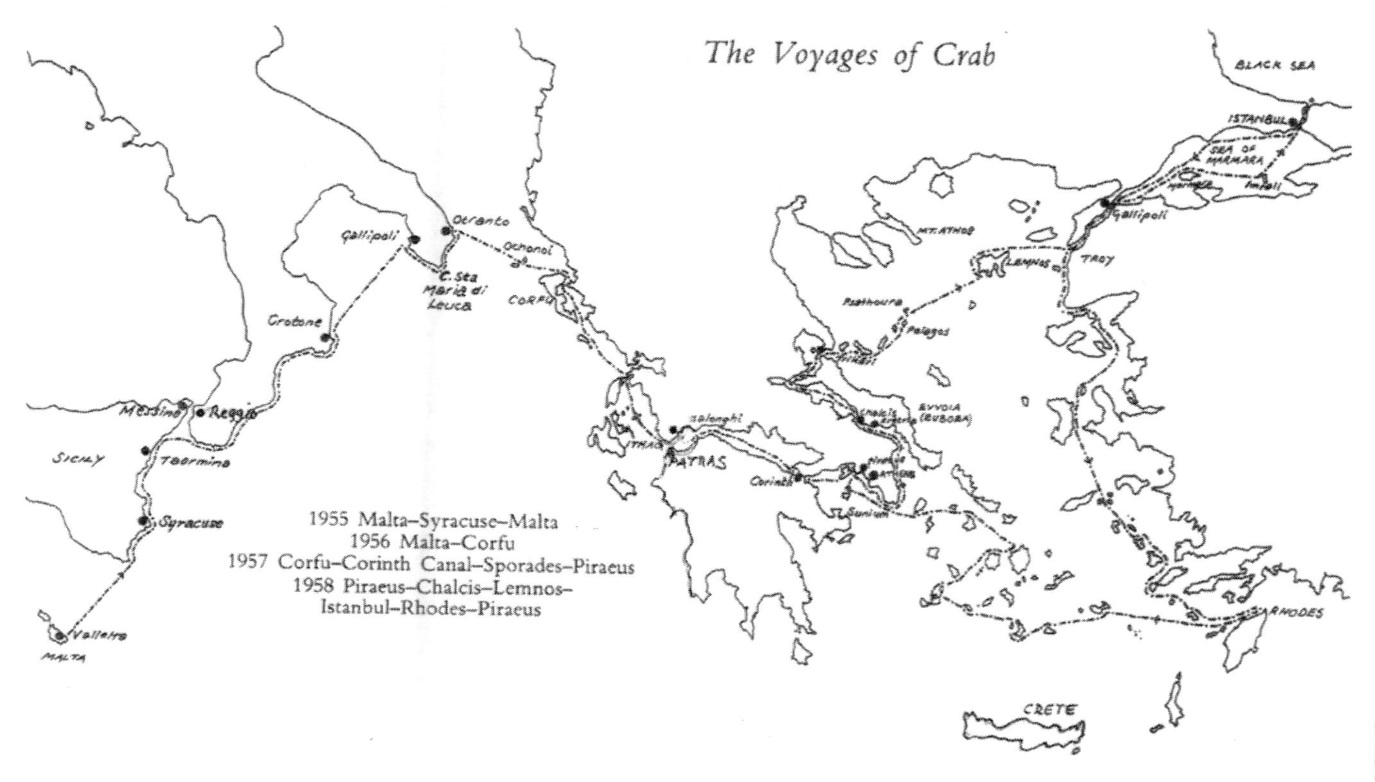
The Voyages of Crab
1955 Malta–Syracuse–Malta
1956 Malta–Corfu
1957 Corfu–Corinth Canal–Sporades–Piraeus
1958 Piraeus–Chalcis–Lemnos–
Istanbul–Rhodes–Piraeus
BLACK SEA
ISTANBUL
SEA OF MARMARA
Gallipoli
MT. ATHOS
LEMNOS
TROY
Psathoura
Pelagos
EVVOIA (EUBOEA)
Corinth
Sunium
PATRAS
RHODES
CRETE
Otranto
Othonoi
C. Sta Maria di Leuca
CORFU
Gallipoli
Crotone
Messina
Reggio
SICILY
Taormina
Syracuse
Valletta
MALTA

Prologue

I remember it as one of those windy spring days when shadows of clouds were sweeping across the grass of the college quad. The wind was tugging the young leaves on the big chestnut in the centre of the quad. I was wishing there was enough time to get down to Port Meadow to the Yacht Club.

I walked to the hall to collect my mail. In my pigeon-hole with the notes from friends in other colleges and missives from college administration, was an unfamiliar sight - a blue airmail envelope. Strangely, it had an English stamp, not a foreign one, but it was post-marked OHMS. I turned it over and over as I walked back through the quad to my room. I decided Sally and I would open it together.

It was from a Captain Naish, R. N., stationed in Malta:

Dear Miss Hughes,

You wrote to me some time ago, to enquire whether it might be possible to purchase an outworn naval whaler, such as we use in training our cadets. You mentioned that my son Jeremy gave you my address, and I would be happy to help you. I would not recommend such a purchase, however, because by the time the Royal Navy has finished with a whaler, it is no longer to be reckoned seaworthy. But I have an alternative suggestion…

He had noticed two small ship's lifeboats for sale in the forecourt of the filling-station. The proprietor told him that they had been built for a certain MV *Juba* only the previous October. The owner of *Juba,* Naish gathered, had gone bankrupt and fled, leaving them behind as payment of an outstanding debt. In his letter Naish offered to have them surveyed, to choose the sounder of the two, and then to arrange the sale for us. They were being offered at £90 each.

I remember vividly the day we had decided to write to Captain Naish. It was early March, and another windy day. After lunch we were revising hard together for fifth-term exams, sharing Sally's coal fire. We wanted to go sailing, we desperately wanted to go sailing, and make use of this rousing wind. Instead we found ourselves grabbing swimsuits and cycling into the teeth of the wind down to the river for a swim - it would be so much quicker than all the hassle of taking a boat out. Rapidly we stripped and waded into the river. It was almost paralysing - the shock of encountering the cold water felt like being caught in a rat-trap. We managed to swim across the river and back, dressed on the riverbank, and struggled homewards, feeling as if a layer of ice encased our skin. An hour after getting back to our room, we were still so cold, we could only lie in front of the fire wrapped in eiderdowns.

Lying there, still shivering from time to time, we had conceived the idea of sailing in the Mediterranean - if possible in the Greek islands, where I had sailed briefly during my gap year. We discussed taking my father's elderly five-ton Bristol Channel pilot cutter through the French canals, and down the Rhone to the Mediterranean. Non-starter - the Rhone had too-powerful a current.

As we held Captain Naish's airmail sheet between us, it was clear that, all of a sudden, instead of a fanciful daydream we had a real possibility.

"Sally, I have fifty pounds available from when I sold two short stories to *Argosy* in my gap year - and that's it," I said.

"I know. And I have £50."

"From winning the *Vogue* Talent Competition. What a thing to do!"

"Not from the *Vogue* thing - from a scholarship. But we're going to need twice the purchase price to cover survey fees, and registration, and insurance. Can we possibly...? Let's go and talk to friends!"

There followed two days of frantic cycling and leg-work, contacting our network of friends in other colleges to ask them if they would like to be co-buyers. We suggested that for £5 a year they could buy themselves a timeshare - the right to join us on the boat for a fortnight or more. As soon as we had collected enough shareholders we took the plunge and responded by cable, asking Captain Naish to pick for us the better of the two boats.

Sally realised she would have to write to her parents about our fledgling plans:

Our summer holiday is at last fixed up. Penny got a letter from a father of a friend of hers in Malta, saying he could buy us a ship's lifeboat complete with sails for £90 - ideal for us, really small slow and uncomfortable but absolutely safe and seaworthy, meant for use in gales. The idea is to go out and sail about Malta till we know the climate pretty well, then try and get to Sicily (70 miles, which would only take about 24 hours) if we feel confident enough.... ...So I've got a banker's order from Barclays here and am sending it off to Maidstone at the same time as this, so if they ring you up (which I suppose they might, with my being a minor) to say is it alright my sending £100 to Malta please say it is...

For my part I contacted both my father (who was self-employed), and a friend of my brother's named Robin Minney, ex-Oxford and working for Shell in East Africa, the only one of my friends who actually had a job at the time. I asked if they would like to join as co-owners, and meet us in Malta or Sicily during the coming summer. Robin Minney cabled agreement from Nairobi, my father replied that it was a good idea, he should be able to find the money - and maybe later he might even come.

*

When Sally's parents in Kent got the letter from their daughter they felt seriously alarmed. They had sent Sally as a teenager to learn to sail on summer courses abroad, at her request, and they knew she had already crewed a yacht crossing to Normandy. They were aware some sort of Mediterranean boat-travel was being dreamed about, but had assumed that my parents would block it - only to find my parents had actually given it pretty active encouragement. I can only ascribe the discrepancy in attitudes to parenting to the fact that my parents had five children, whereas Sally's had only one. In fact my parents not only approved of the boat-purchase scheme, but had even agreed to my taking the working mainsail off my own fourteen-foot boat in North Wales, even though it was supposed to be for general family use.

Worse still from Sally's parents' point of view was that my father had agreed to lend me not only his nautical instruments, but also his old Seagull outboard engine. To try to mollify her parents, Sally pointed out that Malta, at that time still a British Crown Colony, was an ideal place for us to purchase and base a boat. A major British naval base, the island was then in the sterling area, so there would not be much trouble with Customs over the purchase.

Naish's letter had warned us that this boat had no decks - just the thwarts for the oarsmen, and the eighteen-inch-wide benches which ran along each side from stem to stern - and as a result had nowhere safe for stowing valuables. Rigged as a lifeboat with lug-mainsail and jib, she had minimal sailing powers. She was, however, certified to carry 12 people, was equipped with buoyancy tanks from stem to stern below the benches, and with oars, rowlocks, anchor and a rudder.

*

Nearly three months had passed. I was on the train from Harlech to Paddington, nervous and excited. It was a swelteringly hot July day. The precious Seagull engine and my sailing-dinghy's mainsail were travelling with me in my luggage.

When I clambered off the train I was hit by the airless heat of London, so different from my estuary in North Wales. I found a porter and made my way to the Parcels Office. From there I collected a wooden crate, forwarded by the manufacturers of Seagull, packed the engine into it, and went by taxi to Victoria Station.

As I found my seat on the boat train, Sally's figure appeared outside on the platform, studying her seat reservation.

"Look, there's Martin and David," she pointed out when she joined me, "either they came together to the station, or they've found each other. It's good we have two people who already know each other. Sorry there was no chance for you to meet them beforehand."

I scrutinised them, trying to guess what they would be like as close companions on this crazy venture to Malta. Each was carrying a substantial suitcase, and I wondered where they hoped to stow these on a boat the size of our ship's life-boat.

The Channel crossing was refreshingly cool after two hours of sitting in a sweltering carriage. Afterwards the train lumbered southwards hour by hour. We shared out bread and cheese and fruit, and slept sitting upright for a second night. By the time we reached Naples my thighs were sticking to each other and to the varnished wooden bench we sat on. I muttered to Sally that if even the Italians in the carriage were fanning themselves and complaining, perhaps this temperature was unusual, a heat-wave.

Arriving at the ferry-port on the toe of Italy in the evening and boarding the ferry to Messina, we found the air was still hot and sticky, and the rising moon was almost hidden in a heat-haze. When we reached Syracuse and boarded the *Star of Malta*, was it because of the heat-wave, and in consequence officials working at half speed, that we were told to leave the crate containing the engine on the quay, to follow on the next boat, once the papers for it had been processed?

1 Between Malta and Sicily (1955)

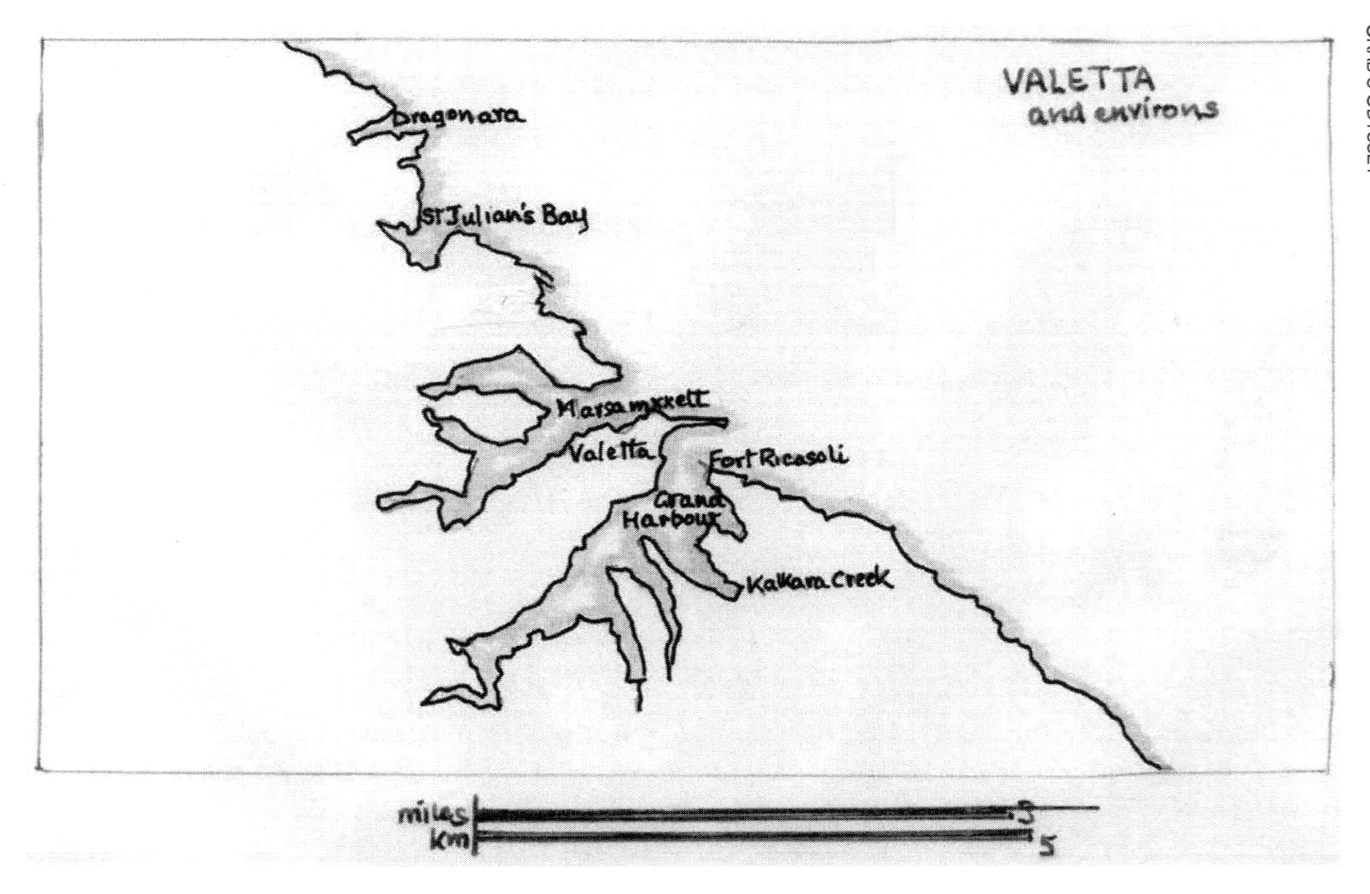
VALETTA
and environs
Dragonara
St Julian's Bay
Marsamxett
Valetta
Fort Ricasoli
Grand
Harbour
Kalkara Creek
miles
km
5
5

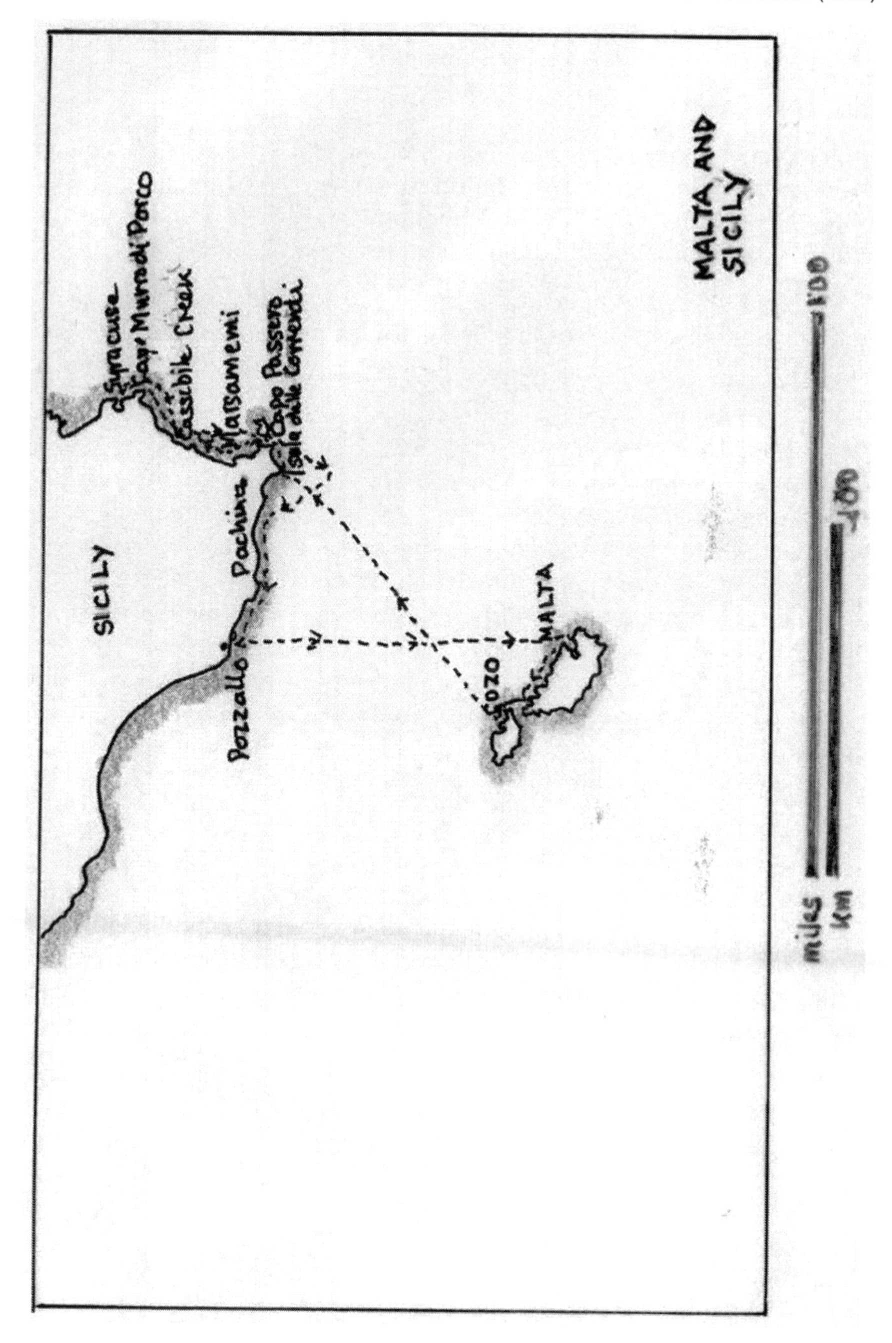
SICILY
Syracuse
Cassibile Creek
Marzamemi
Capo Passero
Isola delle Correnti
Pachino
Pozzallo
GOZO
MALTA
MALTA AND SICILY
miles
Km
100
100

1. Hitting Malta

Friday July 29th

When you are travelling, there is a moment when you are suspended between travelling purposively and the unknown. We were in the saloon of the *Star of Malta,* our knapsacks and suitcases piled together on the deck. We should have arrived thirty minutes before.

Thick fog surrounded us. Outside the windows of the breakfast saloon nothing was visible. It was as if we were suspended in porridge. The slow purr of the engines, running at half speed, vibrated the floor under our feet.

"If we come back from Sicily in a fog like this in our lifeboat we'll have a really difficult job even to hit Malta," Sally said anxiously. We found a table in the ferry's breakfast saloon. As we contemplated our fried breakfasts, there was a sudden grinding noise, a strange shuddering – had the vessel tried to go into reverse? I froze. The floor of the saloon reared up. I was tipped backwards, my handbag slid off my lap, replaced by a plateful of sausages and baked beans. Water poured through the doors. I struggled to free myself from plates and cutlery, to get a foothold against the waterfall. From above, a hand reaching out to me. I looked upwards. The hand's owner hauled me free. I used the table legs – which were screwed to the deck – as ladder rungs, while Martin gave Sally a hand also.

The morning heat was already building up. As we searched for a footing with the ship lying on her side, we were joined by David, the fourth and last of our party. He was trouserless, ready to swim away. But with no landmarks visible, he had no idea in which direction to swim. He began to think he had been too melodramatic – it was becoming clear the ship was in no hurry to sink.

The stern was almost submerged. The afterdeck had been stacked with open trays of ripe peaches, now beginning to be dislodged and float away. The ship was heeled over at more than forty-five degrees, so we stood wherever we could find footing. All around us men, trouserless like David, were busy taking photographs. The purser was trying to organise the launching of the life-rafts, which were tightly roped to the deck. Without hesitating, he dived and disappeared below deck. He emerged a minute later with a cook's knife between his teeth.

By now the sea was full of floating peaches. The woman next to me tugged my sleeve and pointed downwards. I saw, not more than ten feet down, a ledge of rock. The ship must be hard aground on it!

"Where are we? Do you know?"

She shook her head.

Water continued to flow in. The ship settled a bit more. We were standing on the wall of the saloon, now horizontal: top view had become side view. It was so odd to see the ship's dark, slimy flanks exposed, gleaming with barnacle-shells like the rough side of a cheese-grater. I wondered how secure she was, heeled over on her point of rock. Any minute now she might slip off her rock, swamped as she was, and suck us down with her.

"Most of the crew have dived overboard and swum away," I heard a man mutter to his wife.

Around us, life-rafts began plopping into the sea. They hit the water with a satisfying smack. People started to call out, "Women and children first!" That meant us two girls. We were in light summer skirts and eyed the barnacled surface we would have to slide down with apprehension, but there was no alternative. I sat down with legs straight, telling myself firmly that I was in a children's playground, going down a slide. On second thoughts I bunched as much of my skirt under me as I could, and pushed off.

It was a relief to be in the water, which was warm and welcoming. We swam to a life-raft and clambered on board. But it turned out there were no paddles. Some people took off one shoe to use, freeing the other hand to reach for the peaches bobbing all around us. We munched as we moved forward. One or two people were strong enough to take apart the wooden trays with their bare hands. They handed out slats of wood to use – they proved more effective than shoes. And so the flotilla of life-rafts moved shore-wards through the all-encircling mist.

As the sun rose above the horizon, light suddenly gleamed, brightening the high ground. A palace floated above us, about four hundred yards away. It was an extraordinary moment. Drifts of fog obscured it again. As our life-raft approached the shore the sound of children's voices greeted us, magnified by the fog. When we were within six feet of the rocks, children materialised and helped us scramble onto dry land. Not an adult in sight. There must have been twenty or thirty of them standing on the rocks, gathering salty peaches and welcoming survivors. We four travellers found each other and stood wondering what to do. A boy of ten approached me: "Excuse me, Miss. Would you like to come to our house for a cup of tea?"

As we walked with him and his younger brother, he told us that they had heard a strange bang and then distant shouts floating up to their window through the fog. They had rushed downstairs: "Dad, there must be a shipwreck!" But their parents were about to start breakfast. Their father had merely said: "How could there be a shipwreck when it's flat calm? Leave us to finish our breakfast!" So the children had gone down on their own through the fog to the water's edge to see for themselves what was going on.

It was strange to make our way through these foreign, but oh-so-English, streets. David had kicked off his sandals when the ship had heeled over, and I had lost the sandal I had used to paddle with. I found myself peg-legging along the scorching tarmac.

"Martin, how come you got out of your chair ahead of Sally and me, when the ship rolled on her side?"

"I happened to be watching the ship's purser, a man older than the others, who was standing by the food-hatch. When we heard that grating sound I saw his face go grey. I leapt up out of my chair and got myself a good foothold."

I reflected that it was good to have someone so super-observant with us – Sally had picked him well.

We had arrived; the children reached up and rang the bell. The front door swung open. The children's parents registered not the faintest vestige of surprise. They invited us sodden visitors in, found us dry clothes and invited us to join them for a second breakfast.

After, both Martin and David were able to produce rather damp visiting cards. Our host produced his: Major Newbury, in charge of army stores on Malta.

"Where are we?" I asked him.

"Sleima. You must have run aground on Dragonera Reef, below Dragonera Palace. Two to three miles short of Grand Harbour! Running aground isn't exactly the expected way of arriving in Malta! Has it rather affected your plans?" asked the Major.

Where to begin? We explained as briefly as we could that we had bought a ship's lifeboat which was awaiting us and that we had hoped to start living on board straight away. Major Newbury asked with interest about the boat itself: how we had found it and what it was like. Whether it had an engine. And shelter from the elements.

How we had found it was too long a story. Shelter from the elements? The one-word answer was No. An engine? Yes.

"We shall have a Seagull outboard motor belonging to my father," I responded. "The reason why it didn't go down with the rest of the luggage was that unloading it from the train at Syracuse was delayed. We were told it would be following on the next ferry-boat, in three days' time. We are lucky. It would have been ruined!"

"And what do your parents think of this project?" asked Mrs Newbury. "Warmly in support?"

Sally admitted that hers were dubious.

"They assumed that mine would be against it," I explained, "and they were miffed when they heard that my Dad was giving it whole-hearted support. My Mum hated the idea, though on land she was an adventurous person, but my father reckoned that as she didn't like boats, that disqualified her from having a say in the matter. Also, my parents have five children, so I am much more dispensable. Sally is the only one in her family!"

"I agree with your father," Mrs. Newbury said. "I'm all for it! I sailed racing dinghies as a young thing, before I met Bob. Bob doesn't get seasick, but he cannot abide being on a sailing-boat all the same."

Clearly Mrs Newbury wasn't a run-of-the-mill Army wife. I warmed to her greatly, for her support.

"The Seagull outboard will be useful when there's a flat calm," Sally interjected, "but not much use, I'm afraid, in a swell, because in a rough sea the propeller will hardly ever be under the water. An engine that is only useful in a flat calm is better than nothing, of course". Tactless as her remarks were, after all the trouble I had had getting the engine to Paddington train station and then getting it crated, Sally certainly had a point. The engine's limitations were to determine our future pace and our future route. Three times, indeed, the engine was of no use to us in heavy seas. We were lucky to have come through to tell the tale.

The Major pressed us now as to our immediate plans. Sally answered: "First we'll have to go and cable our parents to say we are safe, in case they hear about the shipwreck on the news. Parents are terrible worriers even at the best of times..."

"And buy new toothbrushes," said the Major's wife, "... and go to the office of the *Star of Malta* and give them a contact address..."

"And register that we have lost our passports," Sally added. "And buy some clothes, we only have these you have lent to us. The first thing will be to get some money out of Barclays Bank – I don't have a cheque-book any more, neither does Penny."

"You'll have to book into a hotel, at least for the first few days, so that they can contact you," added the Major. "The Meadowbank Hotel is not too expensive – organised for having Service families while they are waiting for married quarters to be ready. We can telephone them."

The Major came with us to the Meadowbank Hotel. When we parted on the doorstep he brushed away our thanks, inviting us to come back and see him as soon as the boat was ready to live on. He said he was able to lend us protective clothing and camping equipment from his Quartermaster's Stores.

As we trudged along the street under the midday sun, we realised that things could hardly get any worse for us, and we felt an odd sense of freedom in knowing that. The kindness and generosity of the Newbury family overwhelmed us. All of us were feeling cheerful. Martin and David teased Sally mercilessly because on the ferry she had refused bacon and eggs at breakfast to save money – on account of the shipwreck, they pointed out, *no-one* had had to *pay* for their breakfasts!

We spent that day getting to know Malta's capital, as we went about doing what had to be done. Valletta itself is crowded together on the promontory fortified by the Knights of St John in the sixteenth century. North of it is Marsamxett Harbour and Sliema Bay. South of it is Grand Harbour, on the southern side of which are a series of creeks, the innermost occupied at that time by the naval dockyard. The next, Kalkara Creek, was reserved for British forces. On the outermost headland, Fort Ricasoli, now semi-ruined, was at that time in use by the British Navy.

We were impressed by the sheer scale of the fortifications and by the golden-yellow stone from which they were built. Sally said it reminded her forcefully of the fortifications at Dover, where she had been born and her father had a medical practice. She told me that when the war came Dover was heavily bombarded by the German Luftwaffe, and she had been sent, at the age of barely five, to live in Uppingham School with her mother's sister's family, who were wealthy enough to have a nanny for their four children. It was very young to have to live away from home.

We somehow got money out of Barclays Bank that first day. At the Meadowbank Hotel there were only two items on the evening menu: fish and chips and baked beans. And only a pot of tea to drink. Prospects did not look cheerful. Ahead of us stretched long days of waiting to send cables and see insurance agents, waiting to get our passports and all our equipment back, waiting to claim insurance and find out what the insurance agent's verdict would be.

It was time to telephone Captain Naish to tell him our whereabouts. It was he who had found us the boat and had her surveyed.

Sliema (August 1st to 3rd)

Some good news: Captain Naish phoned to say that the transfer of ownership papers for the boat was signed. He had also asked around and found that a naval quay in Kalkara Creek known as Hay Wharf was currently unused. He had arranged for the boat to be delivered there and put into the water immediately the sale was completed.

We also got back our passports, which had been together in the purser's office at the time the *Star of Malta* ran aground.

Captain Naish collected us in his car from the Meadowbank Hotel, and drove us round to Kalkara Creek. Our boat lay alongside. I almost laughed out loud when I first looked over the edge of the wharf and saw her. She looked so small. We had named the boat *Crab* because she was described as having a new coat of "crab-fat", the name for regulation naval grey paint.

We spent the morning puzzling out how things worked, and where to put things away. A bundle of twelve oak pegs puzzled us. We gave up wondering and had some lunch. When we had eaten our bread and cheese, I looked at Sally expectantly.

"O.K., then," she responded.

We had already stepped the stumpy little mast which had been lying on the lengthwise bench, so as to get it out of the way. We identified the little gaff, and laced the top edge of the storm mainsail to it. There was no boom. Apparently the sail was loose-footed. The sail was still new, and deep red – it even smelt of redness – heavy, and stiff as a starched shirt. We rove the halyards, and hoisted the main and the storm jib. The rudder was already in place. We noticed that on top of the rudder-stem an eye was fixed, so that the rope attached to the loose foot of the sail could be cleated aft. We set out under sail for the harbour mouth, Sally in the bows on look-out, and me at the helm. She got irritated because I did not obey her instruction to sail closer upwind; it soon became clear that it wasn't my fault – it was just that the preferred course for our round, flat-bottomed little boat was sideways. Several modifications were going to be needed. It was also clear that without someone permanently on look-out in the bows, there would be interesting collisions: the mast was so low that the helmsman could not see under the mainsail.

At about five o'clock the wind abruptly died away. We were still outside the harbour – we would have to row back. There was a fine strong pair of oars, but where were the rowlocks? David suggested that the oak pegs we had found were to be used as thole-pins. They fitted into the rowlock-holes perfectly. Rowing home, we broke three – we realised then why there was such a stock of them. We got back about 6.00 pm, after an hour's rowing – too late for the Meadowbank's teatime.

Next morning we took back the borrowed clothes to Mrs Newbury. The Major told us that he had read in the newspaper that two people below deck had drowned in the shipwreck, but everyone else had been on deck and got safely to shore. The ship had been three miles off course and the captain asleep, leaving someone else in charge. The captain survived the disgrace, nonetheless. Apparently several passengers had written to the *Times of Malta* praising the conduct of the ship's purser. When they interviewed him, he said he had been in a shipwreck several years previously, so he knew what to do. Perhaps beginning with a shipwreck was an experience which would turn out to be useful to us one day.

The Major had some disheartening news. He told us he had heard that the ferry company already owed money to the Naval Dockyard and so could not afford to ask the Navy to bring lifting equipment to raise the ferry so that the passengers' possessions could be rescued. Instead, the company would probably use a Scandinavian salvage firm, which meant delay. He suggested that we could live alongside our little boat, however, while we waited for the return of our luggage and the arrival of the outboard engine.

Major Newbury took us straight to his stores. The Ship's Notebook lists items such as a petrol-burning pressurised stove, billycans and four outsized cotton Arctic camouflage suits, which he suggested we could sleep in at night.

Thus equipped, we left the Meadowbank Hotel, and started to live on *Crab.*

2. Life "Downstairs" The Gains of Waiting

Sally and I were both twenty-year-old, competitive students of Classics (Latin, Greek and Ancient History) and close friends, united in our love for sailing. We sailed twelve-foot Firefly dinghies in the Thames alongside Port Meadow through the Oxford University Yacht Club.

Sally's parents were not confident either boat would be sound. They had other worries too. I don't know the question (perhaps it concerned the attitude of the college authorities to such a plan) - but Sally wrote in answer, "There will be nothing immoral or unchaperoned in a boat that size with four people on her, anyway!"

Girls at Oxford were outnumbered five to one and there was no shortage of male friends and fellow adventurers. Our tutor, Isobel Henderson, herself spent much of the long summer vacations driving through Greece and Italy on the hunt for more understanding of the history she was teaching and researching. In the Oxford crucible, anyone who told young women students "you can't possibly do that on your own" was throwing down a challenge that simply had to be taken.

In those post-war years, troubled Greece still fired my imagination as much as it had the Romantic poets, such as Byron. The cost of the war had been huge: Germans relentlessly requisitioned and extracted resources and food. In Athens alone 40,000 civilians starved to death; by 1944 famine and malnutrition were thought to have cost 300,000 lives. An estimated 70,000 Greeks were killed by Nazis, Bulgarians and Italians in anti-partisan reprisals, including mass executions and the burning of villages and fields, wiping out 879 towns and villages completely and leaving a million Greeks homeless.

Greece had produced one of the most effective resistance movements against fascism, which began in April 1941 and lasted until British troops liberated Athens in October 1944. Civil war followed from 1946–49, between the Democratic Army of Greece, which included many heroes of partisan war resistance and fought for socialism and communism, and the Greek government army backed by Britain and the United States, even though it included many Nazi collaborators. By the early 1950s, many Greeks had died and the economy was shattered. The politics would remain unstable for another two decades.

When I set off in my gap year, I was almost completely unaware of this or any other Greek history after the days of classical historian Thucydides (460–395 BC) and his great accounts of sea battles. I was to work from February to August 1953 as an *au pair* and companion to a grand family in Athens. A short sailing trip on a hired *caique* with two English friends, Penny Hooper and Margaret Luttrell, from Rafina on the east coast of Attica to the island of Zea fired a desire to sail as much of Greece as I could. I had probably not picked up much of the recent history even then: by the second year at Oxford, my research and interest was firmly in classical times, tempered with growing interest in religion and religious life. Sally was honest when she wrote in 1955 to her parents that she only intended to sail *Crab* from Malta to Sicily and back, but my sights were already set for farther horizons and our increasing confidence in the summers that followed gradually made my dreams come true. We dressed up our adventures as serious research into merchant shipping and got to know intimately the sea approaches, harbours, markets, mountains and pathways of many of the places that we read about in university textbooks.

Kalkara Creek (August 3rd to 4th)

The harbour where we now began to live "downstairs" (as the Maltese referred to the waterfront), Kalkara Creek, belonged to the navy and was completely deserted apart from a single supply ship, *HMS Duquesne,* moored in the middle of the creek. On the far side were some working naval dockyards, but our quay was abandoned and overgrown with weeds. At night we slept on the floor of an empty waterside shed we had been lent. Otherwise we lived under the open sky. And at night the harbour was spangled with reflections of street-lights. Exotic. Breathtaking.

Our first brief foray outside the harbour in *Crab* had shown us that the mast was too short, the rudder was too small, and the keel not deep enough. While we waited for the outboard engine to arrive and our luggage to be returned to us, we had a chance to fix such things. We left David to guard the boat and went in search of a chandlery. David quite enjoyed being on guard. People struck up a conversation out of curiosity. Martin had a talent for fixing things, and a nose for where to find exactly what was needed.

We found the chandlery at last, and from the yard behind it we bought a plate to be fitted to hang down from the rudder, to give it greater depth and grip, and a twelve-foot tapering pole to replace our ten-foot mast. When we got back to the boat, David told us that he'd had a visit from a journalist on the local paper, the *Times of Malta.* He said he had had quite a long interview. I was furious, indignant that the newspaper would certainly get facts wrong and distort the truth as I knew it. The others were phlegmatic - what is truth? We had little inkling of what the effect of the publicity would be.

The second day of living on the boat we had a *sirocco* - a scorching wind which blew from the Sahara, becoming moisture-laden and sticky by the time it reached Malta. It blew in powerful gusts, darkening the water as it ruffled the surface. By the afternoon we could no longer stand having our clothes sticking to our bodies, and the flying grit. We took a bundle of postcards and pens and struggled up the hill to the air-conditioned lounge of the celebrated Phoenicia Hotel. It was in this very hotel, requisitioned by the Navy, that towards the end of 1942 the invasion of Sicily was planned.

In the evening we received a message from a Commander Wigg that the Navy would like us to move away from their wharf to St Julian's Bay, about three miles distant: "Please be ready to accept a tow at twelve o'clock". Once outside Grand Harbour the launch towing us turned left, crossing the mouth of an even bigger expanse, which we learnt was Marsamxett Harbour, and brought us to St Julian's Bay, where there were other small boats. Commander Wigg helped us find a place to moor. We were well content with the move and liked our new anchorage.

St Julian's Bay (August 5th to 7th)

We visited a nearby chandlery and there fell into conversation with a Major Borda, who told us he was Commodore of the Malta Yacht Club, in Sliema Bay, not so far from St Julian's Bay. He urged us to come and call, now that we were moored so close. As the afternoon grew cooler we sailed down the coast, entered Marsamxett Harbour, and climbed up the steep path to the yacht club.

By this time our story had appeared on the front page of the *Times of Malta.* Within the first few minutes in the yacht club, we were being offered a handsome brass bilge-pump, charts and even a copy of Volume 2 of the *Mediterranean Pilot,* at that time the only easily available guide to the coastal waters of the Mediterranean. Major Borda gave us an old jib sail off his 30-metre boat, which we were to use as a spinnaker in light winds. We were both dumbfounded at people's kindness.

When we said that we hoped to sail to Sicily and back within the next few weeks, no one ridiculed the idea. They advised us to sail north-west up the coast to Gozo and start from there so as to shorten the length of time out of sight of land. We should start at about 3.00 am so as to have the maximum daylight hours, in case of a change in the weather, which we were warned would become more and more unsettled. We were enrolled as members for the rest of the year, for £1.

We were notified that the engine had arrived but had to be valued so as to calculate import duty. While we were waiting we made several short trips up and down the coast of Malta, to practise our sailing and coastal navigation, taking fixes with the hand-bearing compass on three prominent points of land, and using the readings to work out our position. It took a lot of practice to get a passable reading with the hand-bearing compass on our wobbly little boat.

Somehow the *Times of Malta* had given the impression that we were destitute as a result of the shipwreck, and had been forced against our wills to survive on board *Crab* till we got our possessions back. The following day the padre of the local mission to seamen offered us help from his mission, and we had a gift of an egg and two tomatoes, left by two small boys too shy to talk to us, who hopped onto the boat and left their gifts in the stern.

Sally wrote to her parents from St Julian's Bay:

c/o Barclays Bank, Valletta, August 4th:..Still no luggage – but hopes that we may have it soon...We are sleeping on the boat in moderate comfort and excessive publicity. A crowd gathers as soon as we come alongside the quay and all the local rowing boats are running trips round the survivors, as a change from trips round the wreck (we are in the next door bay to it now). In a way very useful, as we can use everyone's lavatories and telephones, and get free water (haven't had to pay for it anywhere) and paraffin and things. We got into the local papers due to David getting friendly with a ship agent at the Custom House Quay in Valletta Harbour while the rest of us were shopping. He had a brother working on the Times of Malta so now everyone knows about us! The whole thing is very funny. All the small children adore us, and there is great competition to get a survivor to take home. I'm not sure the parents are so keen!

Today Penny and I went to the Yacht Club who were also most friendly and helpful and are letting us have charts and Mediterranean Pilots and pumps and all sorts of useful things, besides good advice and lifts by car to ships' chandlers – really we have got a great deal of good out of this shipwreck!

We should have a lovely time sailing round Malta – which everyone agrees is within our power. Valletta is fascinating – immense fortifications, walls and moats of the anti-Napoleon Dover Castle type, only made of buffish yellow stone, as everything is. Most attractive with blue sea and sky...The boat looks so comic with such a tiny mast in comparison to its size, and red storm sails, and us all in sort of explorers' clothes, looking as if we had been to the North Pole and not seen land for months.

I'm just going to have a brandy and go to bed. We have a tame café here – the proprietor's two sons were on the Star of Malta too – and use it as our lavatory, bathroom and drawing room – the boat is kitchen and bedroom.

In the next few days we started making friends with local families. People still had vivid memories of the hardships of bombardment during the war, when Malta was a British garrison. They had gone through months on end when there were serious shortages of fuel, long hours in underground shelters and the danger and dust caused by the air bombardment. They told us the story of the three ancient Gladiator biplanes that had taken on the Italian air force alone for three weeks until reinforcements could be sent and the dramatic story of how the oil tanker *Ohio* was towed into Grand Harbour awash and with a hole in her side, but still with enough oil on board to ward off having to surrender Malta to the Italians.

So far as we ourselves were concerned, people had put two and two together and made five. The story had now become: These young people had been on the *Star of Malta* when she foundered. They are living on a small lifeboat. So they must have barely escaped with their lives, on board this very lifeboat. Everyone showered us with kindness. Maltese bread was rationed, though sliced white bread was freely available. We were always allowed to buy the Maltese bread, which was delicious, tasting a bit like sourdough.

A policeman whose job it was to patrol the quays at St Julian's Bay became my admirer and declared he was determined at all costs to marry me. When I told him that next summer my father might possibly join the boat for the first part of the journey, he said he would put his request to him, as was right. But when I told him that we were looking forward to visiting Gozo, the fertile island north-west of the main Malta landmass, his scorn knew no bounds. "They Gozo boys... They country fellers!" My policeman was immensely proud, however, of the George Cross awarded to the people of Malta in April 1942 by King George, whom he greatly admired. "King George he jolly good fellow!" he confided. I found his extreme loyalty to Britain a little disconcerting, because at that time I had transferred patriotism from England to Greece - Greece my dream and, hopefully, our destination.

*

St Julian's Bay (August 7th to 10th)

We celebrated our second Sunday in Malta by taking four small Maltese boys as far as the conical buoy marking the entrance to St Julian's Bay. They were very excited to come with us, but in that short time three of the four were seasick - not a good prognosis for how we as a crew would feel out in the open sea.

In the afternoon we performed a buoyancy test with the help of the small boys, whose weight we needed. Storage space on board was almost nonexistent and the obvious solution was to get rid of some of the buoyancy tanks, if that was possible. We emptied the boat and then filled her with water using the canvas buckets. We found that with all the tanks in place and with all four crew and all four small boys standing in her, she floated with water just below the thwarts. If we removed one tank to create more storage space, the boat became unstable and if we removed two, so that she was balanced, and continued filling her with water, she floated with only three inches of freeboard amidships. The decision was obvious - if we wanted an unsinkable boat, all the buoyancy tanks would have to stay. By shunting them up, we could make a space large enough to stow away the billycans, the primus and the basic navigational equipment. But personal luggage would have to be cut right down. In future all that would be allowed was one pair of long trousers, one of shorts, one shore going outfit and only one pair of footwear. We had brought four sleeping-bags from England, but when these were submerged with the rest of the luggage we did not bother to replace them. I bought a little red notebook, measuring three inches by four and a half, in which to keep a record.

The wind was freshening. By nightfall it was coming in fierce gusts, and after a largely sleepless night we decided we must borrow extra jerseys from our yacht club friends. We would also take advantage to wash clothes that would benefit from being ironed by the wind.

My log in the little red notebook mentions a north-east gale. This wind direction, known as the *grigale,* had a signal code of its own flown from the weather station because it blew unchecked straight in through the mouth of Grand Harbour and was a special hazard for small boats. Even in St Julian's Bay, eating and sleeping in the open on a small boat in the now choppy harbour was a new and uncomfortable experience.

It took us three days to get the engine valued so that we could pay import duty, and a similar amount of time to get the wherewithal to grease the gearbox. The northeaster continued to blow, and we decided to move away from St Julian's Bay so as to be in the shelter of an oil fort we had noticed opposite the chandlery shed, which was in a recess of Grand Harbour, near where the *Dusquesne* was anchored.

Kalkara Creek (August 11th to 14th)

The next day was more than a little better. An officer rowed over from the *Dusquesne* to invite us to drinks on board after supper with the four officers who made up the duty watch. We had drinks on deck, under a ship's lifeboat not unlike ours, which seemed incredibly small.

On our third Sunday we took an outing with naval families. Sally wrote:

Yesterday a day's outing to the other end of Malta with a crowd of families from one of the ships in this harbour, and spent the day on the beach. It was the first time we had been away from the boat. We just left her moored alongside this large ship for the navy to look after, where she was quite safe. And looked very funny. In the evening we went to a cinema show on another boat – invited by a chap in the yacht club.

In this "survivor" life we had made new friends, and accepted what they offered, sometimes amazingly useful things like charts, sometimes just the chance to share watching a bad film on board ship to while away an evening.

We moved back to St Julian's Bay. Our bags had been under water for the better part of three weeks. Eventually passengers were invited to come to the office of the *Star of Malta* to reclaim their baggage. The smell rising from the collective contents was like a combination of rotten eggs and vomit. I'll never forget that smell! When Martin opened his case, his white shore-going shorts had been imprinted with the patterns of the ties he had laid neatly on top. On the other hand, the fair-weather sail which I'd brought and the two tins of expensive antifouling paint were almost unharmed.

St Julian's Bay (August 15th to 16th)

The next two days were spent washing and boiling and rewashing, trying to get rid of the stink from our clothes. We could not afford to just throw them away. We cleaned tools, primus and billycans. Major Borda visited and took to pieces the still-functional prismatic compass, so that he could wash its mirror. The range-finder was useless and had to be thrown away; the books were swollen but still usable. That evening we were invited to a lovely bad film on the *Dusquesne* and were offered three boxes of naval flares.

We were no nearer to setting off for Sicily, being still busy trying to buy gear. We tried in vain in the chandlery shops to buy a stock of "hard tack", as ship's biscuits were called, as a precaution against being blown off course and running out of food. We were told ship's biscuits had gone out of use because they were so prone to weevils.

Many people now dropped by out of curiosity. One visitor, however, at first put all four members of *Crab's* crew on edge. He approached unannounced, immaculate in white shirt and shorts, and introduced himself as Commander Erroll Bruce, Official Receiver of Wrecks. He said he had heard about *Crab*, and was coming to size her up with a view to a likely future encounter. My hackles rose defensively. He was slightly offhand about our plan of going to Sicily.

"Oh yes, what fun! Take about ten days' food in case you get off course. You are bound to hit land within ten days."

As we talked, Erroll Bruce became more friendly. He described a slightly comic incident the previous week. Called out to rescue a motor boat which was out of control and drifting onto the rocks, he managed to approach quite close but at first could not get anyone's attention to catch a rope and attach it so that he could tow them to safety. When he taxed them with it afterwards they said: "What do you expect? We all had our eyes shut. We were praying!"

We explored up and down the coast, fishing and practising taking fixes to work out our position. Mastering the art of working out our precise position on the coast was a big challenge because it was difficult to get accurate compass readings on such a small boat. Using my father's hand-bearing compass, we took it in turns to try and get an accurate bearing on a prominent landmark, and drew lines from three landmarks lightly on the chart. Our position must be somewhere within the triangle where these three lines met. The compass readings were not easy to get but it would be essential to have a fairly clear idea of our position once we were out of familiar waters and their easily recognised landmarks.

Next morning *Crab* was taken out of the water with a crane to have an extra six inches bolted onto her keelson and a coat of antifouling on her bottom. Our possessions were stored in an RAF shed nearby, and we continued to live alongside the boat. All week the weather was cloudy and threatening, to David's frustration: he was trying to brown himself well before his now imminent departure for England.

Tuesday (August 23rd)

Before we could leave for Sicily there had to be a changeover of crew. The two who were coming next, Donald Hope and Robin Minney, both friends of mine, could hardly have been more different from each other, although they shared a talent for wit and laughter. Donald was the first to arrive. He had been two years ahead of me at Oxford and was now at the Slade School of Art in London. His father headed up Hopes Metal Windows, already a big firm, and he had hoped his son would join the business. It was a disappointment when Donald opted for the Slade instead. Donald had never sailed, but was a good travel companion and had some proficiency in Italian because his family had had an Italian cook after the war, as he was growing up. We met Donald off the plane from London. I remarked censoriously in the log *skin very pale* – not much of a welcome.

Thursday (August 25th)

The weather did not give Donald much of a welcome either. The dawn sky the following day was flecked with clouds like the cotton-flowers that grow in marshland. By eight o'clock there was thunder, followed by heavy rain. We sheltered under the piece of awning to eat our lunch. *Crab* lay covered with a tarpaulin while we waited the chance to antifoul. We had a second visit from Erroll Bruce, this time to bring us the Italian customs papers and offer us dry beds and meals. I said stiffly there was nothing at all we wanted, except ship's biscuits. This embarrassed Sally, who did not like us asking for things. "But I could have asked for oysters," I complained, "I was being very modest." Looking at the papers Erroll Bruce had brought us, we found that the Italian customs wanted to know the accommodation for and status of the crew, our gross and net tonnage, and the colour of our funnel. Our new crew members were listed as "Donald Hope, Ship's Painter and Interpreter" and "Robin Minney, Chief Engineer".

Once we realised how little storage space there was, we began to see the hazards of venturing out of sight of land. We could only carry fresh food for two days, although tins of emergency rations were stashed in the extreme recesses of the pointed bow and stern. Water was rationed by the fact that it had to be dipped out of the water tank with a one-gill dipper, standard practice in lifeboats. Our water supply, even so, would last us comfortably only three days. After that we would have to start rationing it. We could only carry enough petrol for about thirty miles. There could be strong currents in the straits between Sicily and Malta. They were not tidal and predictable, but dependent on winds and local conditions. So, besides the risk of being blown or carried off course, there was the risk of being becalmed out of sight of land. But *Crab's* crew were optimists.

Friday (August 26th)

Martin spent his final day helping Sally fit the box compass securely in position where it would be visible to the helmsman. We saw him and David off on the ferry in the evening.

Robin, whose role was to be ship's engineer, was overdue. We received a cable to say that his plane from Nairobi had been cancelled, but he might come the following day.

"What is Robin like?" asked Sally, "Our paths never crossed in Oxford."

I told her that he was the opposite of his father, a writer and journalist who seemed to work a twenty-four-hour day, but was so impractical he could hardly boil an egg. At Oxford, Robin had spent most of his time rowing on the river rather than working at his studies. He was a good person for fixing things. He was now working in East Africa as a salesman for Shell, after being trained in the intricacies of combustion engines.

The weekend Robin was due was the annual Regatta. Sally and I spent the day competing in races, leaving Robin to find his own way from the airport. We even went out to supper with friends, abandoning our newly arrived crew with orders to go to Medina and do some sightseeing. We got back to the boat at Hay Wharf at 10.30 pm, only to find there was no boat. *Crab* had disappeared without trace.

Were we dreaming? Looking round, we noticed that the door to the shed where we kept our equipment was ajar and found Donald there, asleep on the table and not too friendly. He said he thought Robin had mentioned rowing the boat across to the other side of the harbour and sleeping there. It had never occurred to us that anyone would want to row *Crab* singlehanded but we then realised that, since Robin rowed in the Balliol College First Boat, it would seem as easy to him as carrying the shopping. We were beside ourselves with worry. "Borrowing" a rowing dinghy ourselves, we set out through the darkness in search of our home.

We searched the dark harbour fruitlessly for any sign of *Crab* till 11.45 pm. When we got back, we found *Crab* tied up neatly and Robin sound asleep.

Captain Sally woke him and gave a good shouting, but he failed to see her point of view – he had not had any intention of sleeping on the other side of the harbour. Since it was nearly midnight, we pulled the white Arctic camouflage-suits from their bag, explaining to Robin their use. We changed into long trousers and sweaters, pulled on the baggy Arctic suits and slept on board with no more words said.

We had plenty to worry about. It was now the last week in August – originally we had hoped to be heading back from Sicily by now. Around now it was likely that the weather would change. Instead of the summer northerlies, predictably light in the early mornings and at dusk, there would be winds from the south, possibly gales.

Monday was spent preparing our new crew for the voyage ahead – paring down the luggage. Commander Wigg had kindly offered to store spare clothes. We also had a useful session with Major Borda, learning the flow of currents through the Comino Straits. When Robin had overhauled the engine, we were ready to get our final registration to depart for Sicily.

3. Setting Off Via Gozo

St Julian's Bay (August 29th to 30th)

We set off so early that at 8.45 am we were already starting to fill in forms at the Water Police Station in Valletta, and by 12.15 pm the registration was finished. This was apparently because it was the lunch hour and senior staff had gone home. "But I never make a registration so quick in my life!" the water police clerk protested. At the Customs House, where we needed a Bill of Health, we were told that we must first go to the Master of Shipping and be registered as a seagoing vessel. The Master of Shipping's office was kind and helpful, however, and by 1.00 pm we had also cleared Customs. It was too late to leave that day, so we sailed back to St Julian's Bay. There we spent some time working out where everything was to be stowed. My entry in the little diary that doubled as log: *Donald refuses to leave behind a loose-leaf file he has brought for writing poetry. Loose-leaf file must double as asbestos mat.*

St Julian's to St Paul's Bay (August 31st)

At last, at 8:45 am the following day, we sailed out of the harbour and headed northwards up the coast, en route for Gozo. By teatime we had reached the bay where St Paul was reputed to have been wrecked, and anchored there for the night. Ahead of us lay the Comino Straits, the narrows between Malta and Gozo.

When we took stock that evening, we realised we had left our box of spare shackles and all our flags in the shed at Kalkara Creek. Donald, who had not sailed before, said, "I don't know what shackles are - sounds sinister". Once we had explained that they were just small metal hooks with a safety catch, he nobly offered to go back to Valletta by bus for them. He was to rejoin us in Gozo at Marsalforn, a good harbour on the north coast of the island.

St Paul's Bay to Marsalforn, Gozo (September 1st)

We saw Donald off on the 7.00 am bus, and left St Paul's Bay under engine half an hour later. By twelve o'clock, the wind had freshened. Seas began coming on board in the straits between Malta and Gozo and we had to bale constantly. The seas became so short and sharp that the rudder-plate snapped off. Fortunately, we had a lifting line attached and we were able to pull it on board.

In the Comino Channel the three of us had our first taste of being chilled by the wind as it dried us, again and again, between being doused by waves. Its effect was to make us drowsy and weak, rather than consciously cold. When we passed Ramla Bay, with its wide stretch of ochre sand, I was so cold that all I wanted was to stretch out on that warm sand and sleep. Reputedly it is where Calypso had her cave: *The cave was sheltered by a fragrant copse of alders, aspens, and fragrant cypresses, which were the roosting place of feathered creatures, horned owls, and falcons, and garrulous choughs, birds of the coast, whose daily business takes them down to the sea. Trailing around the very mouth of the cavern, a garden vine ran riot, with great bunches of ripe grapes.*[1]

With the binoculars we could see a crevice halfway up the cliff which would certainly have had a fine view over the bay.

At 1.00 pm, somewhat dazed, we limped into Marsalforn, the harbour for the main town of Victoria which lay inland, up in the hills. We took the rudder-plate to a garage to be mended and took our salt-soaked clothes to a tap on the quayside. Robin said he would dismantle and clean the engine ready for the crossing ahead. When we came back to spread our clothes to dry he was still busy, with dark-brown shoulders hunched over the engine and pebble-glasses intent on the job. Donald rejoined us from the afternoon bus just as the sun was setting, yellow as a fried egg.

At 9.00 pm, as we were getting ready to sleep, we were taken by surprise by a thunderstorm. Large, warm drops of rain assaulted us, soaking us to the skin. We should have realised that the bright yellow sunset that evening was a forewarning. We found shelter nearby till it eased. When we lay down for the night, end-to-end on the thwarts, we carefully spread the awning over us.

Marsalforn (September 2nd to 3rd)

When we got up next morning we found so much water in the bilges that our navigation locker was awash. The wind was still gusting across the harbour, and seas were crashing against the harbour wall. No question of leaving until the wind calmed down a bit.

---

[1] Homer, *Odyssey* Bk V, translated by E. V. Rieu.

We found a slightly sheltered place where we could spread the sails out to dry. At 4:30 pm there was another heavy thunderstorm. It was Sally's and my turn to stay on board until everything was stowed away, while Donald and Robin went off to find shelter for themselves. Just as we completed the stowing the rain eased, and we sat down to draw breath. A small girl approached us, and told us shyly she had been sent to fetch us to the Convent Orphanage. Both of us were in oilskins that had seen better days. Under her oilskin, Sally was wearing only a swimsuit and shirt. We hoped this would not shock the nuns. Welcomed to the convent, we were sat down alone and given clean towels and tea with bread, butter, jam and white table-napkins. With the tea came two combs - a clear hint. They were not shocked by what we were wearing, but by the salt-stiffened state of our hair. After we had eaten, a nun beckoned us to a window and showed us Donald and Robin wandering below - clearly wondering where we were.

Next day it was again stormy and we realised we would have to spend another night in harbour. We clearly did not expect it to be very comfortable, as much of that day was spent on an expedition to a government surplus store for army blankets and two really watertight boxes. We slept on board nevertheless, pulling the awning round us. At intervals during the night I woke to feel the rain pattering on it.

On Sunday September 4th, in the early morning, the *Crab* at last set sail for Sicily.

4. The Open Sea

Marsalforn to Isola delle Correnti, Sicily (September 4th to 5th)

The wind was forecast to be light and variable, between NNE and NNW - against us. We left the entrance to Marsalforn under sail, close-hauled on the starboard tack. Sally set the course and we headed north - or rather moved northwards in suitably crablike fashion. At 8:30 am we took a three-point fix to work out our position, and found that in nearly two hours we had progressed one and a quarter nautical miles. After four hours, we were only three miles from Marsalforn. Finally, after six hours Sally succumbed to persuasion, and agreed to use the engine, but keep the sails up. At 1:30 pm we were still only five and a half miles from Marsalforn. Around 3.00 pm the wind veered and strengthened, so that it was no longer heading us, and we were able to lift the engine inboard, and proceed at a respectable speed.

All through that day we headed steadily northwards towards Sicily, and gradually Malta receded behind us. On this northerly course the fair-weather sail did little to provide shade. It did, however, provide a screen if one wanted to use the bucket in the forepeak. As the day wore on the bucket in the forepeak got good usage. Sally and I were used to using it, but the newcomers not so, and it was a source of embarrassment, still remembered fifty years later by one of our fellow sailors.

Supper was a simple stew, part-cooked before we left. Reheating it was an uncomfortable affair. It was Donald's job to look after the primus, so that my hands, as cook, could be kept free of the taste of paraffin.

"When I pump you, you bastard, all you do is spill meths and vomit paraffin everywhere! Now just behave and get started!" Donald shouted at the primus. The primus must have been deaf: it was almost dark by the time he managed to get it alight. Donald held it on the central thwart while I held the billycan in place, stirring with the other hand.

At dusk, the air became deliciously cool and clear, then darkness fell. Behind us the skyline of Malta disappeared. We trailed our fingers in the water to watch the sparks of phosphorescence stream from them. Ahead was darkness, and empty sea. It was an extraordinary feeling to be in the middle of such emptiness, with big lazy waves ambling past on a diagonal course, humping first the stern, then the bows. Only eighteen inches of planking protected us against whatever that sea might throw at us out of the darkness.

The night was divided into two-hour watches. Because the wind was light, the person at the helm would be alone, with an assistant sleeping on the thwart nearby. The course was so nearly due north that it was possible to steer by lining up the top of our little, stumpy mast with the Pole Star. The sea was no longer rough, but waves slapped playfully against *Crab's* side, and every few minutes a dollop of spray dropped on board.

Sally was already asleep. I was at the helm for my watch.

"Robin," I asked tentatively, "how did you learn to sail?"

"On the Stour Estuary friends said I could borrow their boat, whenever I wanted it - and that was how I learnt to sail. When you are alone you work things out bit by bit. I hate being told what to do."

Donald, asked the same question, was thoughtful. "I suppose the closest I've come to an expanse of water before this summer was being taken fishing by my cousin Thomas. I was praying all the time I wouldn't catch a fish, because I had no idea how to deal with it, if I did. I just came because I liked you - and Sally of course."

"Entrusted yourself to a girl skipper?"

"In *Swallows and Amazons* it was the girls who were the capable ones, not the boys. I assumed that was how it usually was!"

Our laughter woke up the skipper and we were in trouble.

The other three lay down to sleep. For the first time I had the little boat in my hands and was alone, steering by the Pole Star. The moon had not yet risen. On such a night one picked one's way through the waves more by listening than by using one's eyes - the sound of the creaming, curling foam clearer than the white plume in the darkness. I felt immeasurably happy. Alone, perched on the gunwale so as to listen and to see as far ahead as possible, I found that even though my body moved constantly in response to the movement of the boat, I was soon so drowsy that it scared me. How easy just to fall asleep and drop overboard, probably taking the precious tiller with me! I rolled up my sleeve and bit my arm, so that the pain would stir me out of drowsiness. Sally took over at midnight. The night sky was thrilling for someone from northern latitudes, accustomed to the presence of a veil of cloud or smog. No other experience can compare to lying stretched out at night surrounded from Mediterranean horizon to Mediterranean horizon by a cloudless sky in which the stars are so bright you can almost read by their light.

I was back at the helm at 4.00 am. Dawn brought a hazy skyline to the north with Sicilian mountain peaks showing in the distance. Everyone began to stir. As the sun rose Donald pulled the primus out of its case and held it up by the neck. "Good morning!" he said to it, in a menacing tone. For once it cooperated, and we had hot tea. I looked at the tooth marks in my arm and tried to recall how they got there.

For a second day running we sailed all day, broiled like lobsters by the sun. We seldom spoke. I reflected on my lack of qualifications for my role as First Mate. I used to say that I was a very useful person to have on a boat because in my childhood years of living on the edge of an estuary with a tidal rip, I had made more mistakes, and survived them, than most people twice my age. What I knew had been worked out on a basis of trial and error, augmented by advice from my Dad.

My father, Richard Hughes, or "Diccon", was a distinguished writer and novelist who loved nothing more than an adventure, preferably involving high winds and wild seas or mountains. My mother, Frances Bazley, was a painter and as such a rebel, adventuring far from her respectable Gloucestershire family. Our childhood years involved repeated moves, including Norfolk, where we had lived in a huge sixteenth-century house inadequately modernised, and Laugharne Castle in South Wales, with Dylan Thomas as neighbour and friend. Eventually we settled at Mor Edrin, a large white house near Harlech in North Wales, on the shore of the beautiful Dwyryd estuary. The house lay across from Portmadoc and Portmeirion; the horizon ringed with mountains to north and east, spelling mystery and adventure.

We were five children, roughly divided into sailors (elder brother Robert, me and youngest brother Owain) and horse riders (Frances and my sisters Lleky and Kate). Diccon frequently travelled, including some post-war service with the Admiralty in London, and sometimes Frances too. We were sent off like parcels to boarding schools.

Adventure seemed second nature for all of us. At the beginning of my first Long Vac, heading home for holidays, I and two invited friends got off the train fifty miles early and walked the rest of the way, sleeping in barns or under the sky. The following year Robert commandeered me and some of his friends for a holiday in Italy living in a small van.

My sailing experience was mostly on the *Amy*, a fourteen-foot gunter-rig dinghy, on the Dwyryd estuary. Between our house and Portmeirion, I learnt the vagaries of winds and rip tides, sand banks and small boats. My only experience of the open sea was at twelve years of age. Just after the war, my father had been invited by a friend to join his yacht and sail across the Irish Sea to Dublin. He had asked if I could come too, as there was a very small bunk available in the foc'sle, before the mast. The owner, Patrick Blackett, was a summer neighbour and good friend of my father. He had won the Nobel Prize for his work as a nuclear physicist, and had spent his prize-money on a small second-hand yacht, in 1946 an unheard-of luxury. Two other sailing friends came also, and the conversations about the politics of keeping the peace fascinated me. I would sit and listen to the grownups, hoping I could store it all in my memory till such time as I would be able to understand it properly. And the same went for picking up the basics of navigation – I watched and stored up in my mind everything I saw them doing, in the hopes that I would understand it later.

Sally had picked up much more sailing experience, crewing in dinghy races at Burnham-on-Sea with a friend, and once getting the opportunity to cross the Channel in a friend's yacht. She had been taught to sail by a naval commander, Douglas Dixon, who ran a sailing school for teenagers, and had been on two sailing weeks abroad. Because she knew a little more than the other teenagers, both times she was put in charge of her group, and gained much valuable experience from that.

How did Sally and I get on so well together – two young lunatics, joined by love of sea and adventure and a craving to explore Greek waters, relishing hardship and excited by the vast and heady new horizons opening for women in the 1950s? We were such opposite personalities. Sally was bossy and irritable, but always intelligent and good company, making her a great skipper, good at sticking to schedules, forcing discipline as regards luggage, and cutting short our leisurely swims in paradise bays. I am a peacemaker and too inclined to compromise, but I loved cooking, especially under difficult circumstances, and for this reason was useful. Sally and I both also had the mental strength somehow to hang on to the tiller and keep the boat straight to the waves for hour after hour until we nearly fell overboard from cold and exhaustion.

We made slow progress towards the coast of Sicily. By evening we were not far from land, and we thought we could identify Isola delle Correnti, an island connected to the mainland of Sicily by a low, narrow isthmus. If we were right, we were now only about three miles short of Capo Passero, where the coast of Sicily turns dramatically northwards. On the island's eastern side was a small natural harbour where we found anchorage before dusk. No need to set watches - we could all four of us stretch out and sleep. Bliss! We must have slept for a good ten hours - our first uninterrupted night's sleep for two days. As soon as we were awake we sent Donald, the only one who spoke Italian, to find someone and confirm where we had made landfall. It was good to know we were right: this was definitely Isola delle Correnti.

Isola delle Correnti to Syracuse (September 6th)

We left harbour at 9.00 am. An hour later we rounded Capo Passero, with its prominent lighthouse. Should we go ashore and try and buy petrol? There seemed little sign of habitation, apart from the lighthouse. Since the wind was fair we decided to push on towards Syracuse. Hour by hour we sailed northwards, keeping less than half a mile from the shore, so that we could recognise landmarks and pencil in our progress on the chart. About three o'clock we were alarmed to find our way apparently barred by tunny nets, marked by small black cork bundles at ten metre intervals. To our relief, we found that by raising our rudder we could pass over the hawser supporting the nets without touching it. We set our course again for Syracuse, and towards evening in the distance we could see a spread of white houses covering a hillside. Syracuse, according to our calculations.

At 7.30 pm, as the sun set on our left, we identified Capo Murro di Porco, a headland close to Syracuse - Syracuse, the most important and brilliant city of the Ancient World, according to Cicero. We could see storm clouds gathering over the mountains behind the city, and dusk came early, but Sally had memorised the lights leading us in, and we successfully found our way across Great Harbour to an anchorage for the night in the canal that links Great Harbour with the small one, the Porto Piccolo, on the north side of the city.

We had crossed the open sea! We were in a different country! There were hugs all round, causing the little boat to wobble dangerously.

"Sally, when I was being coached before Oxford by Diana Zvegintzov, she was always talking of how able you were – I really hated you!"

"Did you? And I really hated you too, till we actually met! I hope it is the basis of a good long friendship."

Syracuse (September 7th to 9th)

We slept like logs. In the morning we motored back to the Great Harbour, to the Port Commandant's office, and found alongside the quay two yachts – one a gleaming fifty-ton two-master, the other the *Samuel Pepys,* a little R.N.S.A. ocean racer, and Erroll Bruce with his wife Daphne and two of their children on board, plus one or two naval ratings as crew. He seemed surprised and pleased to see us, and there were warm greetings on board. In his cabin we also met the local British Consul, Warden Baker. The consul at once offered us his yacht to sleep and eat on for the duration of the time we were in Syracuse, since the anchorage for yachts in Great Harbour was exposed, and its short choppy seas, which we had already experienced, would make life on board our little *Crab* uncomfortable. We declined his offer, since we could not leave the boat unguarded overnight, nor were we confident that the mooring-lines we had were enough to keep her safe from harm unattended.

He also invited us to join him next day as he supervised a team of local divers searching for amphorae from ships wrecked in the bay. We gladly accepted the second offer. Warden Baker was one of the first to follow Jacques Cousteau's lead and use divers for underwater archaeology. He told us about the visit in 1953 by Jacques Cousteau to the wrecked Roman merchant-ship found off Anti-Kythera in 1900 by sponge-fishermen, and about rumours that Cousteau would soon be excavating it.[2]

He had a team of divers working along the western shore of Great Harbour, under rocky cliffs. He told us that in the great sea battle against the Syracusans in the harbour in 413 BC the Athenians had beached most of the triremes and scrambled ashore, trying to escape. Some of the ships, he added, had been driven onto the rocks and wrecked. These were the wrecks his team was particularly looking for, though they brought up everything they laid hands on.

---

[2] It was not until 1976 that Cousteau was able to come back to the site with a full team of divers and the support of the Hellenic navy. They retrieved more than 300 artefacts.

Our third offer was from Erroll Bruce - he could lend us an extra mooring line. We accepted with alacrity, and secured it on board a next door Italian navy boat, the *Antoinette*, since the holding ground was poor, and there was danger of dragging anchor. During the whole time we were in Syracuse the Bruces extended generous hospitality to us, letting us use their showers and lavatory, and giving us useful guidance as to where to find things ashore. They became more and more friendly, and eventually offered us beds and baths when - and if - we got back to Malta. Best of all, they offered us vital help with getting our ship's papers into proper order. We had certainly been naive about registering *Crab*. As Erroll now explained to us, as a seagoing vessel, *Crab* had to be registered at Lloyd's. This was a process that, done properly, even with his help, would have taken weeks, and would have precluded going to sea our first season.

We spent all that day having hot baths, seeing museums and re-stocking our supplies. In the evening we visited the consul on his yacht. Its gleaming copper, rich glow of well-kept varnish, its scrubbed deck-boards, and perfectly coiled manila ropes - everything was such a sensual pleasure to us. The consul told us that Erroll had sailed the *Samuel Pepys* in the 1951 Bermuda Race, and again in 1952, when he had been placed fifth of the sixty-four entrants, at that date the highest placing ever for a non-American yacht. We questioned our host about his yacht, which seemed to us far too small to compete in the Bermuda Race. He told us that indeed the safety rules had had to be changed to allow a yacht so small to compete in such a long race. He told us that Erroll Bruce's friend Adlard Coles' yacht, *Cohoe II*, was fitted with a false prow in order to reach the minimum length of twenty-four feet! Despite her small size the *Samuel Pepys* had weathered a hurricane and proved her ability at sea. Later that day we tried to draw him out on these exploits. "I'm one of those people who suffer from insomnia," he said offhandedly, "and while I lie awake I try to work out in detail exactly what I would need to do in such and such an emergency, in a Transatlantic race."

During our two days in Syracuse Robin absented himself at all hours, exploring with his camera. He recalls being in the huge open air Greek theatre in the moonlight. He was amused when Sally reproached him for looking exactly like a tourist. "But I *am* a tourist!"

Immediately after our evening visit to the consul's yacht, we went to a fish restaurant to celebrate Sally's twenty-first birthday. The following morning, Thursday, September 8th, in a flat calm, at 6.00 am, we went on board the consul's yacht, as instructed. With us in the yacht was a photographer from the local press. Warden Baker was directing operations with a copy of Thucydides in his hand. Alongside was a launch with several divers. He was using naval divers, connected to an air supply on deck, and using a prototype aqualung.

The shapeless chunks they brought up were roughly washed, and then gently cleaned of mud and encrustations of shellfish. These shapeless chunks were from amphorae that had gone to the bottom of the harbour when ships sank. What really interested Sally and me was that these weren't trying to be Fine Art, but were artefacts connected with ordinary everyday life - cheap and cheerful amphorae for storing supplies for daily use. In fact, they were probably later than the Siege of Syracuse, and not connected with the triremes. By and large, the wrecks of merchant ships were more often found well-preserved than the wrecks of triremes. The weight of their cargo meant that merchantmen tended to be embedded much more deeply in the all-protecting mud than triremes would be.

"This south wind is stirring things up, the water is so cloudy the visibility is down to three metres," the man in charge of the divers told the consul, disappointed at how little they were finding. A wind from the south was bad news for us also. The anchorage would be choppy, but worse than that - it was time we set out for the return journey, and we would be trying to sail into the teeth of the wind when we set out to return to Malta.

"This has been a useless day as far as finds are concerned," said Warden Baker, adding candidly, "'the presence of the press distracted the divers, and still more the presence of you two girls. I hadn't foreseen that." We thanked him warmly for the unique experience we had had, and made our way back to *Crab*. It was still only 11.00 am.

That same afternoon we were brought a note from the consul.

"The Port Commandant is going to stop you from leaving, as UNSAFE."

Clearly he had warned us to leave quickly. But could we? In the early morning we had had flat calm, but the wind was rising. By midday outside the entrance to the harbour there were big seas running. The anemometer on *Sam Pepys* was recording gusts of 50 m.p.h. We talked with Erroll Bruce, and decided to leave at dawn and get as far as we could before the wind blew up, then take shelter and wait till dawn next day. We knew that the *Samuel Pepys* was also about to head back to Valletta.

5. Stormbound in Sicily

Syracuse to Casibile Creek (September 9th)

Before dawn next day, September 9th, we left our mooring in Syracuse Great Harbour. We were proceeding under engine because there was a flat calm. As we looked back we could see the first rays of the rising sun setting ablaze the distant windows of the houses on the hillside. The return journey to Malta was going to be a game of Grandmother's Footsteps - leaving before dawn and getting as far as we could as fast as we could, before the wind blew up towards midday each day.

We passed a largish bay with sandy beaches which was probably Casibile, the natural harbour recommended to us by Warden Baker, and some five miles further on passed the outlet of a river that may have been the river Casibile. But off Capo del Cane the wind suddenly both freshened and headed us. It was Robin and Donald's first taste of rough weather. Heeling hard over, *Crab* was soon thumping her way through short steep seas, and following each thump a shower of spray came on board. It was too rough to try and use the engine. We would have to try and reduce sail, changing to the storm rig. Robin and Donald manned the oars to keep her head to wind while we took down the mainsail and hoisted the stiff little dark red storm mainsail, which together with the storm jib had a sail area of fifty-one square feet. Deciding that we ought to look for shelter, we turned back in the direction from which we had come. Shipping the oars, we surfed downwind towards the river mouth we had passed fifty minutes earlier. By 11.45 am we were inside the creek and in smooth water. We anchored in the lee of the rocky headland and took stock. We reckoned it was probably Casibile Creek. Further in, a fishing boat was drawn up on the shore. About half a mile away the only other sign of habitation was a farmhouse or shed, visible through a screen of bamboo clumps and prickly pear.

"Donald, what made you agree to come with us on *Crab*'s maiden voyage, when you'd never even sailed before? Are you beginning to regret it?" I asked, impressed that Donald was taking the rising wind so stoically.

"I'd have come with you to darkest Africa or the wastes of Antarctica, wherever ... but as it was, to the beautiful Mediterranean, *mare nostrum* – what could be more tempting?"

I wondered whether Arthur Ransome had given me the idea that, when it came to handling small boats, girls were always at least as competent as boys, if not more so. Sally was beginning to fit the bill nicely as Captain Nancy. But which of his characters was I?

After lunch Robin and Donald set off to try and buy petrol. They fell in with shepherds, who took them to the hut. One of them decided this was going to be a party and he wanted to read Robin his poems, which he had with him in his pocket.

At dusk, the fishermen approached and suggested they helped us draw *Crab* up the beach for the night. They told us they would be back at 3.30 am and would help us push off again. We declined quite such an early start. They advised us to dig a hole in the sand and completely bury the anchor as a precaution against it dragging in the night, since the wind was strong.

Supper was not uneventful that night. We were cooking on the primus in the stern, and had to stand it on the floorboards instead of on the thwart to shelter it from the wind. Some methylated spirits spilled on the floorboards and flames sprang up. Sally, in her haste to extinguish the flames, seized the lid of the billycan that lay to hand on the thwart to scoop up seawater, tossing out into the water four raw eggs which were waiting to be cooked. I berated my skipper for so cavalierly tossing our supper overboard, but she called out that their whites were gleaming phosphorescently as they began to sink. We passed her a mug and in no time she had retrieved three out of the four just before they sank.

I remember the evening still. After supper Robin began to feel cold, so he stepped ashore over the bows and lit himself a small fire. The shepherds he had met earlier must have noticed the gleam, for they brought their goats down to the water's edge to talk again. Sally and Donald and I went ashore to join them. It grew dark, and we sat round the fire, the shepherds reciting and singing. Afterwards, Sally and I went back to sleep on board *Crab*, but Robin and Donald slept on the sand, each hollowing out a comfortable niche for himself.

Sally said to me before turning in, "I wonder whether by now *Sam Pepys* is ahead of us. It has almost become a race to see which of us is going to get back to Malta first to spread wicked stories about the other."

Casibile Creek to Marsa Memi (September 10th)

The fishermen came at 5.30 am to help us push off, and we set off again. We were still a long way from Capo Passero. In the early morning we made good progress, and when we breakfasted at 7.00 am, Capo Passero was near enough for us to be able to steer for it. It was now less than 48 hours until Robin's flight back to East Africa left from Valletta. He had hoped to get back to Malta in *Crab*. Now he was beginning to think he would have to go on the ferryboat from Syracuse to Malta if he was to avoid missing his plane.

At 10.45 the wind suddenly veered round to the south and blew up strongly.

Battling against the wind, it was not till midday that we reached Capo Passero. The lighthouse was flying the storm signal for a gale from the south-west. We anchored for shelter by the tuna factory on the offshore island, among the fishing boats that had taken refuge. From one we heard that the *Sam Pepys* had passed through ahead of us that morning.

The fishermen told us we would be able to buy petrol and cash travellers' cheques in Pachino, two miles south west of Marsa Memi, a bus journey inland. Sally and Robin went to the police station to sign Robin off as crew and find out about transport.

Suddenly, Robin was back on board, hastily cramming his possessions into a kitbag. He waded ashore, no time for goodbyes, and left the bay on the back of a stranger's motorbike. I watched as the motorbike wound its way up the hillside and disappeared from view, the erratic put-putting audible long after it had disappeared.

So now we were without our ship's engineer.

Marsa Memi to Pozzallo (September 10th to 11th)

We decided to attempt to go on during the night, hoping for an offshore wind that would help us along. We weighed anchor and set off, the three of us.

Dusk fell. Instead of the hoped-for offshore wind, we had to chug southwards under engine. The night was divided into two-hour watches - Sally and I on watch, with Donald within waking distance should help be needed. There was a considerable swell, so that as *Crab* rose on each wave the Seagull's propeller would be raised out of the water. The snoring noise that resulted was ten times the volume of any human snorer. At last, at 10.00 pm, a light wind began to blow, ranging from south to south west or even west, and throughout the night we tacked under fair-weather sails. Yet somehow the light on the eastern extremity of Isola di Capo Passero never seemed to get any further away.

When daylight came we found we were only seven miles away from Capo Passero, and the size of the seas suggested there was a strong south wind on its way to us. We did some calculations: to cross straight to Valletta from Capo Passero was a distance of some fifty-eight miles, whereas if we sailed westwards along the Sicilian coast to Scalambri, the passage from there to Gozo would be only forty-four miles. We opted to change course and make for Scalambri. There was an ominous haze over the land, and dark clouds. We bowled along, with the wind abeam, and by afternoon had covered twenty miles or so. The wind blew stronger and stronger. This south coast of Sicily consists of long sandy beaches – the last thing we needed with an onshore southerly wind. We studied the chart and decided to abandon the idea of getting to Scalambri, and take shelter in Pozzallo.

At 3.00 pm, a prominent, square, ruined tower one hundred feet high was identified through the storm haze by Sally as Pozzallo's Torre del Conto di Modica. We shortened sail so as to come in more slowly, because what we could see ahead baffled us. We could make out fishing boats drawn up on the sloping beach, but the shore seemed to be all rock strewn, and impossible for beaching a boat in a storm. By now we had taken in all our sails except the storm jib. The wind was behind us, pushing us forward fast, and ahead of us great rollers were breaking on the shore. We were now close enough to hear the roar as a wave broke, and the clitter-clatter of pebbles as the wave sucked back again. There seemed to be a crowd rapidly gathering. People were waving their arms and shouting at us, but what they said was inaudible because of the roar of the breakers. There were a good number of fishing boats drawn up on the shore, so there MUST be a way in – but where was it? Visibility was poor because of the driving spray. The three of us scanned in vain for signs of perches or marker buoys. Then we saw two of the men in the crowd strip their clothes off. In underpants they swam out to us, climbed on board and took the helm from Sally, pointing out a sand bar that we could now see was taking the worst of the swell. Behind the bar was a small, concrete landing slip. As soon as we were in the shelter of the sandbar things felt easier. They took the oars and began to row us towards the landing slip, while we hastily gathered in the storm jib.

As we approached the beach, more men waded into the water. There were hands all along the gunwales. They turned *Crab's* stern to shore and dragged her up the beach. Stiff with cold, shaky, bewildered, we stood by the boat, and people began feeling us all over, patting our hair, and all talking at once, in a dialect that seemed quite incomprehensible. We tried to indicate that we were basically OK. All we wanted just then was sleep.

Stormbound (September 11th to 15th)

Sally's letter home continues the story:

... we have beached the boat at this place with the help of local fishermen, and moved all our belongings into the house of the local mechanic, after being rained out last night in the most terrific thunderstorm I have ever experienced – continuous lightning for at least half an hour, and absolute cloudbursts of rain. This hospitality is very embarrassing as their house is full of our wet belongings and they insist on feeding us (lovely café au lait this morning for breakfast) and [the mechanic] driving us everywhere in his car and so on. However we really couldn't manage without because apart from the wind and the rain such crowds of small children surround us whenever we move outside that we should go quite berserk if we didn't have a refuge. Even in the house is bad enough since he seems related to ¾ of the town.

... At the moment there is a howling gale from the south and lots of rain, so we are now quite in their hands as it will take most of the village to launch the boat again, and anyway we will have to wait until the sea goes down before we can launch, and until there is a northerly wind before we can get to Malta. They say this weather will go on for 3 or 4 days and they will tell us when it is safe to go. If the worst comes to the worst we shall just have to leave the boat in Sicily...We have just sent off a telegram telling Erroll Bruce we are safe and not to send out search parties. This means we shan't catch the boat on the 16th. I know there is one on the 26th, or we may be able to get an earlier one. It is just a great inconvenience and misfortune and Isobel Henderson will have to put up with us not having done any work.

I wrote a postcard to my parents from Pozzallo, describing our scary entry into the harbour, and added "such fingering of our fair hair! Pozzallo windy town, with huge cheese factory, 6 palm trees and a flight of steps they said were built by Mussolini. Dialect seems to be half Greek. Donald very good interpreter – witty Italian."

Apparently even then Pozzallo was a reasonable-sized town, with a population of 12,000, but as often happened in Greece also, the town had grown up at quite a distance from the sea - presumably because of the constant threat of pirates in earlier times. Pozzallo is now one of the principal ports of Sicily, with a massive artificial harbour and a high speed ferry to Malta. But these structures were started in the 1980s and not finished until well into the 1990s. The first structure, a pier for petrol products, was not built until 1960, five years after *Crab's* visit. The railway looped south to the sea at this point, but the only road to the harbour village where we were stormbound was a small rough track. Even now, Donald remembers that scary moment when we could see no possible way in through the breakers to gain the safety of the little fishing harbour, and the two who stripped off their Sunday best and swam out to take over the helm and guide us in.

While the wind continued to batter the village, the engineer who had taken us in and his mother insisted that we stay with them, and fed us, day after day. He was a gifted mechanic, an extremely important person in the economy. Unfortunately he had some stomach problem that confined him to a diet of raw eggs and neat olive oil, which he drank from a glass. His mother made up for her frustration that she could not cook for him by cooking us enormous meals of spaghetti.

Crab was still drawn up on the shore, high and dry, and we were prisoners until the majority decided it was really safe for us to go, because we needed about twelve pairs of hands to launch her. While we waited for the wind to drop, the mechanic took Sally and me in his car with him every day when he went to mend the water pumps on country estates. Even now Sally still remembers the ornate gateways that seemed to be in the middle of nowhere. Sally wrote a second brief letter to her parents shortly before we left (September 14th):

Lots of talk with our mechanic about how he goes round the countryside mending people's engines and gets eggs, fruit etc. in return, and how 'il papa mio e dottore' and does the same. This pleased them all a lot. He makes you parents sound very rich by telling people that I have a father who spends his holidays in Spain.

It was not till nine days after we had left Syracuse that the villagers allowed us to set off. They gathered and heaved *Crab* down the beach into the sea, and waved as we left.

"This boat of ours does seem to make people undeservedly friendly and kind to us," Donald remarked thoughtfully.

*

We arrived in Valletta just in time to see the September 16th ferry for Syracuse leaving her berth. We had been hoping that Donald, at least, would be able to catch her, but we were too optimistic. Donald must have been longing to return to life on land by then, after more than two weeks of living on *Crab*. The three of us had become very close. Donald was never at all confident when at the helm, but he created for himself the role of court jester, defusing tension by his wit - and of tension there was plenty.

We made our way to the Customs House to register our return. My letter to Robin described an encounter with the Lloyd's Register of Shipping Malta Agent which boded ill for the following year:

As we tied up at the Customs, a furious little man who was from the Registry of Shipping came and shook his fist at us and said, "You should never have gone. YOU SHOULD HAVE COME UNDER MY POWER."

This encounter with the Lloyd's agent was a warning: we would have to get all our papers in order if we hoped to be able to set out the following year. We had an uncomfortable interview in his office. We realised he had the power to stop *Crab* setting sail the following summer - and most certainly would do so, unless she was properly registered.

6. Taking Stock

Kalkara Creek to Ricasoli (September 16th to 21st)

After this awkward time with the Registrar of Shipping, we headed back to Kalkara Creek, the deserted quay belonging to the British Navy where we had first lived on the boat. Taking stock of our first ventures into crossing water in an open boat, I wrote to my parents from Hay Wharf:

Home again and very happy. Sea swallows on the voyage were such pleasant company...

CRAB we have become very fond of: all the worst discomforts such as hitting your head, and roasting your face off in the galley, and the smell of the bilge, Crab has not got. By moving the spars and oars into the middle of the boat at night we have room and to spare to sleep, and now have so many sails we need few blankets. She is the only boat I have sailed in where you can take the helm without getting out of bed if you are Watch Below and suddenly needed! She is a surprisingly dry boat, and when waves do flop on board they come over the beam [amidships], where the buoyancy tanks are, and don't come into the lockers. Charts and Mediterranean Pilot [the Admiralty guide to harbours and lighthouses] we keep in odd-shaped bags we have made out of the sleeves of a deceased oilskin jacket, and they have survived this season fairly well. The engine lives in the well [the bilge], lashed down with its head on a life-jacket, and if run at half-throttle takes us along happily at three and a half knots for fourteen hours on end, when becalmed.

The next day Erroll Bruce came to insist we use empty barracks at Ricasoli Point as our quarters instead of Hay Wharf. He was immensely generous and hospitable, offering to look after the Seagull engine for us for the winter, and also to sort out our registration at Lloyd's. From him we heard that the Port Commandant in Syracuse was disappointed to find he had missed impounding us, but he had succeeded in stopping the fifty-ton yacht.

Sally and I saw off Donald on the next ferry to Syracuse, and stayed to lay up the boat. Captain Naish was away from Malta, but had asked his friends Commander and Mrs Wigg to keep an eye on us.

My letter home goes on to describe socialising, first in a context that went fair to turning our heads, then with naval friends:

Today is Sunday. Somewhere we lost a day, because after a long conversation on the crossing we decided it was Thursday, when in fact it wasn't. In Italy we did not know the names for the days of the week, so we would not ask, and I think we lost that day somewhere between Syracuse and Pozzallo.

We are very glad to be back home, much welcomed by Jose and Ferrugia, the boatmen here. We were invited to a Christening Party by our ship chandler, the Christening party of his sixteenth grandchild, where we kept meeting friends from Marsalforn, and cousins of Maltese yachtsmen we knew, and being introduced to more and more of his sons and daughters, who regarded us with such surprise and respect I feel as if I am not Me anymore.

We went to see Commander and Mrs. Wigg in the afternoon, who questioned us long and very interestedly about everything we had acquired and done, till Comm Wigg said, 'I must say I shouldn't like to deal with either of you two now if there was anything in this flat you wanted!' which made us laugh a lot. We shall probably be intolerable at home, having been 'capitani' out here for so long.

With Sally in Wateringbury (September 20th to October 4th)

The ferry took us to Syracuse. From there by rail and ferry we travelled back to Dover. Sally's father met us with the bigger of their two cars at Dover. He complained he had hardly recognised us, we were so burnt black by the sun - only the squalor of our luggage had served as an indication that we were the people he was looking for. He told us that when Sally's telegram from Malta had been delivered, her mother thought this was an unnecessary extravagance. Only two hours later a neighbour came to the door with the evening paper, which had a large front page picture of the *Star of Malta* shown lying on her side, straddling the submerged reef, her stern under water. Then they took in why we had indulged in the extravagance of sending a telegram.

I sat in the back of the car, Sally in the front with her father. After a mile he stopped.

"Do you mind, Sally, I'm going to put you in the back - you've had three days sitting up in trains, and apparently no chance to wash."

*

In two weeks time we would be back in Oxford and the autumn term would be starting. For the whole month of August we were happily being spoiled by the English community in Valletta, unconcerned that we had no books to do the required Long Vac reading, due to a convenient shipwreck. Now the day of reckoning was approaching. I accepted

Sally's invitation and stayed at her house so as to work together, instead of going home to North Wales as planned.

Determined to prove that the faith Somerville put in its students' ability to cope was not misguided, for the last two weeks of the Long Vac we both worked a ten-hour day, barricaded against all comers by the two-volume Liddell and Scott Greek dictionary, the Classical Dictionary, diverse annotated texts of Herodotus' *History* and of Plato, and sheaves of lecture notes. At my home in North Wales these sheaves would have risen into the air like a flock of seagulls if the door was opened, because it was a household where there always seemed to be a through draught. We wrote a letter of excuse to Isobel Henderson, saying that Herodotus went down in the sinking of the *Star of Malta,* and asking for a postponement of beginning of term tests. We buried ourselves in our books, but it was not adequate. Would we be sent down?

Oxford – Autumn term

Beginning of term tests were postponed for us, to give us a chance to catch up on work missed. Looking back, I cannot understand why they treated us so leniently. I can see it was the policy of our principal, Janet Vaughan, to support initiative, whereas the other women's colleges at that time tended to be over protective, wary of anything that might endanger academic standards. Janet Vaughan was the first married woman to become a College Principal, a lifelong campaigner against social inequality and injustice, and in favour of equal rights for women.

In early December Sally and I put in a request for another travel grant, for the following summer. We outlined our plans for understanding how the ancient merchant ships of the eastern Mediterranean sailed. In spite of our naivety, Somerville College supported us again with a travel grant for the coming long vacation. Our plans for research were still unformed, a shapeless little embryo that would take on form and life as it was fed by what we met as we sailed. We had learnt that it was no good trying to tack in *Crab* on a passage, and that it was no good straining the engine by motoring into a head wind, so that for passage-making we must wait for a fair wind and a following swell before setting out. But by the time we had returned to Dover our intentions had become more ambitious than in the letter from Sally to her parents written when we first bought the boat. We hoped next summer to collect the boat from Malta and set off straight away via Sicily and the tip of Italy for Greece. Perhaps the shipwreck of the *Star of Malta,* which held us up for nearly three weeks, had been a boon, not a setback. The Malta shipwreck experience certainly taught us persistence.

Evaluation

Bit by bit we had learnt to get the best out of our boat. The first stage, while in Valletta waiting for our luggage, had been to learn to cope without an engine. This was vital, in view of the way the engine invariably failed us in a crisis. The second stage was eventually learning to try and stay dry. In the Comino Straights between Malta and Gozo we had had our first experience of being chilled through and through, though the sun was shining brightly. The third stage was learning the danger of an onshore wind, such as drove us in to Pozzallo. Both Sally and I had become completely hooked on this way of life.

Sally had been somewhat stand-offish about the engine - she and engines were not naturally soulmates, and when there were deficiencies for which I could be blamed, I found I lacked an ally. But in other ways she was a loyal friend - and the shipwreck of the *Star of Malta* threw us together. Sally was fiercely self-sufficient. The fact that at the young age of five she had been sent away because of the German air bombardment, could account for that. I too was self-sufficient - in my case because of the responsibilities as second-oldest in a large and Bohemian family. We seem to have worked together well as the long-term crew of *Crab* because we were such opposite personalities - both lunatics, but our lunacy different.

We had already decided to make Greece our goal - the boat's name, *Kabouni* (a misspelling of the Greek word for 'crab', *Kavouri*) was witness to that.

*

I seem to have been unaware that I had troubled my parents back home in North Wales by our setting off in unsettled September weather, against a head wind, thus flirting with shipwreck off the south coast of Sicily. It was only when I came to start writing this book that I found the following letter to my father from Warden Baker in Syracuse, in response to a now lost letter from him, written at about the time my parents got news we were safely back in Malta. It was clear that my father was worried enough to have taken the trouble to find the address of the vice-consul at Syracuse from the Foreign Office. The British vice-consul's letter cannot have proved reassuring:

Vice-Consolato Britannico
Syracusa Sicilia

28th September 1955

Dear Mr. Hughes,

Many thanks for your letter 24th September just received. I was wondering whether the Crab's owners, if they really want to get to Greece next summer, should not consider shipping the boat to Piraeus, and then from there go visiting the islands. A sea trip from Malta to Greece in the Crab should certainly not be considered. My own boat the Pijoto could do the trip and she is free until June next year, when we shall be starting again for July–August work in the Grand Harbour here.

Other craft available is a 5-tonner owned by Edward Shute of the British Embassy Rome. I understand that he wants to sell and get a larger boat, now that he is married. She is fully found.

The Italian authorities are considering prohibiting cruising from Italian ports for boats not considered suitable. This also applies to the qualifications of the declared Master, who must be able to navigate.

Yours sincerely,
Warden Baker

We had never thought of sailing direct to Greece – it was to be a slow coastal journey, hugging the shore, and picking our weather before embarking on a crossing. Warden Baker seemed to think the authorities would deem *Crab* unsuitable even for that, since his suggestion seemed to be that we should charter a proper yacht, buy a five-tonner of our own, or ship *Crab* to Piraeus. He also warned that we would have formidable problems with the Port authorities because of Sally's lack of experience and qualifications.

My father understood this. He too took stock. His solution was not to try and forbid further journeys, but to join us in Malta the next year as a member of the crew, so as to smooth our departure. This solved the bureaucratic impasse, but it was quite a leap of faith on his part to venture on so small a boat, with such minimal sleeping space.

HEELING OVER AFTER RUNNING AGROUND ON A REEF
NEAR GRAND HARBOUR, MALTA
THE *STAR OF MALTA*, FROM WHICH TWO WERE LOST

WEARING LIFE JACKETS, SURVIVORS FROM THE *STAR OF MALTA* CLAMBER TO SAFETY, HUNDREDS OF PEACHES, PART OF THE SHIPS' DECK CARGO, FLOAT AMONG THEM

Lateen rig fishing boat in Syracuse Harbour

Local fishing boat with two-masted yacht in background

Underwater archaeology in Syracuse Harbour – Boats servicing divers

The day's finds

Early morning, chilly start for Malta (Donald, Sally, Penny)

Sheltering in Casibile Creek (Donald on board)

Sally on her birthday (Photo taken by Richard Davy)

Crab with fair weather main and spinnaker off the coast of Calabria
(Photo taken by Richard Davy swimming ashore with camera)

Captain Sally planning the route, Maggs at the helm

Maggs untying a knot

The All-Purpose Benches

Dawn, Mesolongi – Benches for sleeping

Morning – For preparing a pot-roast

Afternoon – Relaxing

Evening – Cooking

2 Braving the Adriatic (1956)

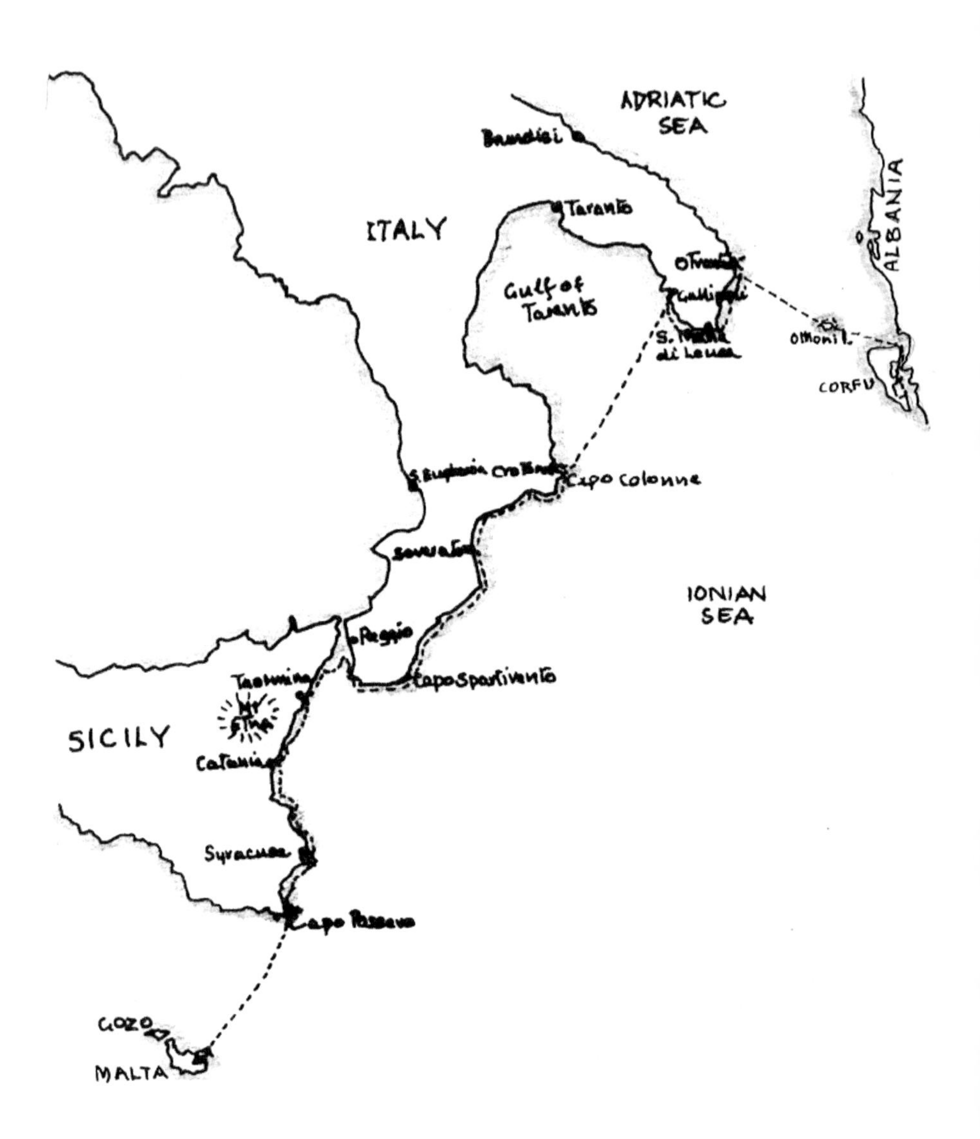
ADRIATIC
SEA
ITALY
Taranto
Gulf of
Taranto
ALBANIA
CORFU
Capo Colonne
IONIAN
SEA
Reggio
Capo Spartivento
Taormina
SICILY
Catania
Capo Passero
GOZO
MALTA

1. Big Friendly Giant on Board

We were gathering crew for our second summer. Once we had shown it was possible to cross the open sea in *Crab,* there was no shortage of new people asking to join the boat for two weeks of her journey. Skipper Sally was able, on the whole, to choose people with sailing experience for the open sea crossings. She warned them about the rigours of being out at sea in an open boat, fried from dawn till dusk by sun and wind, while proceeding towards our destination at half a knot for hours on end and being constantly doused with spray, but it did not deter them. Robin, the third co-owner, was back in UK. He had liked Africa but not Shell and was looking for another job; he could not join the boat. When Sally heard that my father, fourth co-owner, planned to join us for the first fortnight she was surprised, and also, I guess, apprehensive. It would not be easy to have a cabin boy with nearly forty years' experience in small boats, and in his own yacht. All his books had to do with the sea - *A High Wind in Jamaica* was set in the West Indies, on board a not-very-competent pirate vessel. *In Hazard* described how a large modern merchantman was caught up in a typhoon and carried along with it for five days, yet survived - a true story.

During the winter I had re-read Joshua Slocum's *Sailing Alone Around the World,* first published in 1900. I had first read it as a young teenager in 1948, when my father Diccon had reviewed the reprint with the introduction by Arthur Ransome. Slocum's voyage reminded me slightly of our previous summer on *Crab:* like him we were frequently given presents of second-hand sails and fresh fruit, and were a magnet for curious small children whenever we tied up. The other book reviewed by Diccon and formative for all my family was *The Ashley Book of Knots,* a tome heavy enough to use to knock a burglar senseless. Whenever Sally came to stay, she and my older brother spent happy hours learning short and long splices, back-splices, Turk's Head knots and other intricacies.

Diccon wanted to join us for the first fortnight's sailing. Sally and I would arrive in Malta in late June. He was to join us a week later, by which time we hoped to be fitted out and ready to get our papers stamped and set off.

*

We had left *Crab* bottom-up on the quay in Kalkara Creek at the end of September 1955 - something of a mistake. In the early spring a letter from my policeman friend had said: "Your boat has a hole from the wind and the dawn". Diccon at once knew that this meant that *Crab* had dried out and we would be able to see daylight between the planks.

Erroll Bruce had seen to *Crab's* registration at Lloyd's during the winter. She could not be registered under the name of "Crab" because apparently another sailing boat already had that name. So she became *S/Y Kabouni,* a slight mangling of *kavouri,* the Greek word for "crab". But for practical purposes we just went on calling her *Crab,* which had the suitable derogatory ring to it that all our parents wanted. And it suggested a certain perversity. A name like *Alert* would have given the wrong impression to those asking to join her as crew.

Our 1956 plan was to try to get as far as Corfu. The three stretches of open sea would be the main challenge. We already had experience of the Malta Channel in hostile mood. Crossing the Gulf of Tarentum from the toe to the heel of Italy would be a longer but easier journey than that from Gozo to Sicily. We reckoned that crossing the Adriatic Sea from the heel of Italy to Corfu, which would again involve a night at sea, would be the hardest. In the Adriatic it seemed almost impossible to find weather conditions that did not involve large seas and howling winds.

When we crossed the Gulf of Taranto, and then the Adriatic, we would be following in reverse the route taken by the thirty merchant ships and host of transport vessels which accompanied the vast Athenian armada that attacked Syracuse in 415 BC. Our destination, Corfu, was where the disparate fleet had assembled. We hoped to visit all the likely stopping-places along the route.

Ricasoli Point (June 27th to July 9th)

It was exciting to be back in Valletta. We had made many friends among ship chandlers, water police and others who lived or worked "downstairs". Erroll Bruce insisted that we bring *Crab* and come and stay in his family house at Ricasoli Point while we were refitting, instead of working on her in Kalkara Creek at Hay Wharf, across the harbour from *HMS Duquesne*. Some years later, one of the Bruce children, by then grown up, confided that the commander of *HMS Duquesne* had written to their father in desperation, requesting he find some tactful way of ridding his quiet harbour of the two girls in bathing suits and their little boat, because they were proving too much of a distraction for his ratings.

Sally wrote to her parents:

We live in great luxury with hot baths and beds and all our meals provided. They seemed very eager to have us and have lots of Maltese servants so I don't think we are a nuisance, except by asking for things for the boat, which we would probably be doing anyway. We have her hauled up on a slip at the officers' bathing beach here, so that strange young men wander up and ask to help us all the time, to find out who we are and what we are doing, though most of them seem to know, our fame seems to have spread pretty well ahead of us. It's a heavenly place to work – just wearing bathing costumes and swimming every now and then to cool down. Lots of expert help. Weather is heavenly...I hope our luck holds...

At the moment we spend a lot of time being charming to people who are going to register and measure the boat, and cultivating the friendship of various custom officials – I hope it will come in useful.

When we put *Crab* in the water she sank, as we expected. We kept her under water for forty-eight hours, and then beached her. She was hauled up on a slip to be painted and to have mastic forced into the worst of her crevices.

In Sally's next letter, written on July 5th, Diccon has arrived and she says that we hope to get loaded up on Friday night and leave for Sicily on Saturday. The Bruces extended their hospitality to him too. He was allocated the veranda, which in early summer in Malta was a great luxury. In the short time he was in their house they became such good friends that when the Bruces returned to a posting in England they stayed with my parents in North Wales more than once.

Friday July 6th

We launched *Crab* and found she was still leaking, and quite fast. We would have to submerge her, giving the planks more chance to swell. No chance of loading her on Friday night and leaving on Saturday.

We took the delay as an opportunity to explore Malta. Sally was impressed by the yellow limestone fortifications built by the Knights Hospitallers. Diccon was excited more by the very ancient temples, some of the oldest in the world. Bones of dwarf elephants, hippopotami and deer of a species that suggested that Malta was once linked by land to

Europe were found in the cave of Ghar Dalam. There were plenty of Neolithic remains, such as sling-stones, to suggest that the inhabitants of Malta hunted game and there was carbonised barley, wheat and lentils to show they grew crops. They used imported lava to make querns for grinding corn.

Only a mile inland, in the suburb Paolo, was a labyrinthine underground sanctuary discovered by accident in 1902 that dated back to 3,500 BC. The entrance was in Burials Street. Its relief carvings, especially the friezes of animals, were impressive. Diccon wrote to my mother: *Their carvings in the round were mostly of a very fat old woman (Graves' 'White Goddess?'), usually nude, but sometimes seated wearing a full skirt and looking rather like Queen Victoria.*

On Sunday we were able to load *Crab* and move on board. The pile of equipment alongside astonished Diccon - he could not believe it could possibly fit. I showed my father what was stowed where. In addition to the original small, heavy-duty, red storm-mainsail and jib, a total sail-area of only fifty-one square feet, *Crab* now had both a fair-weather mainsail, mounted on a separate yard, and a cut-down spinnaker (a present from someone in the Navy) plus an old spar to use as a spinnaker boom, plus an awning. Even stowing these sails, the awning and our stock of charts was problematic, and there was no room for improvements to our lifestyle, apart from two small steel ammunition boxes which were waterproof enough to be used for storing provisions.

When not in use, the outboard engine lay on the floor of the boat. Anyone moving about had to pick their way delicately between the outboard and the shin-barking solidity of the ammunition-boxes.

Crab's "galley" comprised a primus and three nesting billycans, their lids doubling as frying-pans. When in use, the primus stood on the central bench amidships, with an assistant to hold it in place if cooking at sea. As cook, I prided myself on being able to produce food under adverse circumstances and on using food bought locally, since there was so little storage space.

I think my father's heart may have sunk when I explained to him that at night, when on passage and watches had to be kept, people slept end-to-end along the eighteen-inch-wide bench on the lee side of the boat. How could he sleep on so narrow a bench? We would bundle up our day-clothes to make a pillow, pull on long trousers, shirts and sweaters for the night, and cover ourselves with one of the awnings against the dew. I said that although in busy harbours everyone had to sleep on board, more often the boat would be in some quiet bay where those with broad shoulders, like my father, could sleep on the sand or pebbly shore.

The Malta Channel (Monday July 9th)

Accompanied by Diccon, and armed with our registration at Lloyd's as a "seagoing vessel", Sally went to get port-clearance and the necessary Bill of Health. We set out at 10.00 am and headed straight for the coast of Sicily. Or, since *Crab* never "headed" anywhere, we proceeded roughly in the direction of Sicily. Conditions were far more settled that they had been the previous September. The wind blew steadily from the west and there was little shipping. Once, near the horizon, we sighted a naval vessel. She was heading to cross our path at some distance but she altered course and approached, so that she passed within two hundred metres of *Crab*. She was flying flag-signals, which Sally deciphered with the help of the key in the *Admiralty Pilot*: "Proceed with caution: submarines operating in the vicinity."

We all kept a sharp eye for periscopes, and after about twenty minutes thought we saw one.

By 5.00 pm we were still only eleven miles from Valletta. We had organised to each take two hour watches in turn, as we had done the previous year. After supper Diccon took the first watch, with Sally and I lying stretched out head-to-toe on the benches. It was a brilliant starlit night, the finest I had ever sailed in. I woke as light began to filter across the eastern horizon and realised that we had slept right through. Diccon had stayed at the helm all the hours of darkness and not woken us. He told me he had enjoyed it hugely - his capacity to stay awake all night had been acquired when he was in the Admiralty during the war, doing his stint of fire-watching on the roof of some big building or staying up through the night to produce some extra-urgent report. He was glad to be on watch because his shoulders were far too broad for the eighteen inch benches. He had little chance of real sleep, except when he could sleep ashore.

There were disadvantages as well as advantages in having Diccon on board. He was rather like Raoul Dahl's Big Friendly Giant - apart from Dahl's giant's delight in farting. Diccon was almost as strong as us two girls put together, but with his six-foot frame and middle-aged spread he was also nearly twice our weight, and a sudden movement on his part almost catapulted us overboard.

On the other hand, Diccon helped us realise the potential of our boat. He had the comfortable view that having stayed alive for fifty-six years, he was likely to stay alive a few more. He was of course a far more experienced navigator than either of us. Sally was usually right, but she lacked confidence. This little boat of ours was fit to keep the sea in almost any weather. She would go anywhere, come through any gale. The only danger was of her arriving empty because her crew had been washed overboard.

Capo Passero (Tuesday July 10th) – A quarrel

We sighted the high land of Sicily clear ahead at dawn. By noon we had reached Capo Passero, the south-eastern tip. The wind strengthened as it entered the funnel between Passero Island and the mainland. A quarrel flared between Diccon and Sally. He wanted to put on as much sail as the boat could stand and see how fast she could move but Sally's instinct was to shorten sail, in case the mast or the yard snapped. Sally won. We shortened sail till we were under storm jib alone but we still popped out of the straits like a cork out of a champagne bottle.

It continued to blow hard, so at 2.00 pm we found a sandy cove and beached for the night, hunting enough shade for a siesta.

Capo Passero to Syracuse (Wednesday July 11th)

We rose at dawn the next day and continued northwards up the coast, our destination Syracuse. Mid-morning we saw what seemed to be a deserted bay and decided to put in, anchor, and have a swim. To our surprise the bay wasn't empty.

As we rounded the headland we saw a row of Italian women wading into the water, wearing black petticoats, holding large black umbrellas over their heads. They saw a small open boat with clumsy red sails and three people on board: two dishevelled girls in bathing costumes and a distinguished but eccentric-looking gentleman, wearing bright blue trousers and a beard, elaborately curled moustaches and a floppy straw hat, of the same shape and dilapidation as those worn by Italian horses. The evident astonishment of the bathing-party would have been much greater, had they known that it was we two girls who owned, captained, and navigated the boat.

This is Sally's description – we did not in fact land, not to intrude on the bathing-party ("Odyssey Crabwise", 1956, an unpublished article).

Syracuse appeared in the distance, a gleam of white sprawling over the hillside. Seen from a distance by the crew of *Crab* it looked huge. Indeed, by the time Athens invaded in 415 BC, it had already become confident, though inexperienced in warfare. Sally and I were studying Thucydides, the contemporary historian, at the time and were fascinated to find how accurate his topography was. We read that at first many Syracusans did not believe the news that Athens, on the pretext of helping her ally Segesta, was preparing an armada in order to capture their city. Others in Syracuse reckoned that the Athenians intended to annex the whole island, which would be easy once they had conquered Syracuse. These people saw correctly, however, that Syracuse could win, even though outnumbered, because their enemies were far from home and their supply-lines were vulnerable.

At the time Thucydides wrote, writing about history was not an accepted literary mode. People knew about epic poetry, short lyrics and tragedy; they watched the dramatic contests in Athens that lasted for days on end. Some think Thucydides' history is shaped like a fifth-century tragedy. We have the unique good luck that the Great Athenian Expedition was written about by a contemporary, a man with a passion for accurate detail and strict impartiality.

In 415 BC the newly arrived Athenian generals, encamped a day's journey northwards, lured the inexperienced and overconfident Syracusan generals by false intelligence into an overland march to attack the Athenian ships, a day's journey northwards to Catania. As they marched north, the Athenian armada slipped away down the coast to land and position themselves for attacking the city. In the bloody battle, many Syracusans lost their lives. What finally saved the city itself was their cavalry, far superior to that of the Athenians, who were forced to withdraw.

We learnt that, over the following winter there was feverish activity in Syracuse. Potential landing places were made inhospitable by driving stakes into the shore and throwing up a wall round the city, encompassing such a wide area of suburbs it would be impossible to surround and starve it into submission.

The estuary on whose shores I and my family lived in North Wales was similarly staked against invasion 2,355 years later when there were fears the Germans might invade via Ireland. The posts and their interconnecting wires remained for years after the war.

We entered Grand Harbour and sailed past the place where the Anapo river flowed into the bay. The war between the two superpowers culminated in 413 BC in Athenian disgrace, and it was here that the fleeing Athenian army found their ford blocked by Syracusan troops. Those who did not die were rounded up and imprisoned in the quarries on the outskirts of the city.

Diccon said: "There were stories of prisoners who secured their own release because they were able to recite long passages from Euripides' tragedies for the cultured enjoyment of wealthy Syracusans. I've a rotten memory for quotations but I'm a dab hand at making up spoof ones which sound genuine. I think I would have been one of those survivors."

He was more interested in what happens to ordinary people in times of war than in questions of strategy or resources. He was beginning to write a novel, originally to be set in the Second World War, but quickly he had become more interested in the seeds of conflict in the preceding peace time and conflict's ability to spring up against all odds.

*

Crab arrived in Syracuse at 2.00 pm. We looked forward to meeting Richard Davy, Sally's Oxford friend who was now a journalist. He was to become the fourth member of the crew. Sally had instructed him to come to the waterfront and search for *Crab*. He said he had little difficulty picking us out.

"I saw a small open boat, quite low in the water. The loops of ropes along both sides made it obvious it was a ship's lifeboat. And in it a solitary man, with a bushy grey beard."

We began to get to know each other. Richard had already graduated and was in his mid-twenties. His previous sailing experience was unusual. During his National Service he found himself running an army education centre near Ismailia on Lake Timsah, one of the lakes through which the Suez Canal runs. Since the centre opened in the mornings and evenings, he was free to sail on the lake almost every afternoon. He entered races and said that he gradually learned to win them.

In the evening of Richard's first day we sat and watched the evening *passeggiata* of Syracuse's smart young things, girls in groups and young men in groups, to and fro by the Fountain of Arethusa, quite close to where we were moored.

A night in mosquito territory, then to the village of Priolo, (Thursday July 12th)

We woke to a fresh westerly wind and spent a long morning in the *Capitaneria,* registering *Crab's* entry into Italian waters, and our new crew member, Richard Davy. The wind stirred up a choppy swell within the Great Harbour, making cooking on board intolerable. A friendly bystander who spoke some English suggested we move and anchor the other side of the bay, in the mouth of the River Anapo. He assured us: "There are no mosquitoes there now – the police have chased them." At first we thought this was a joke but someone explained that the police had cleansed a malarial spot of mosquitoes with DDT spray. It was sobering to think of malaria so close to Syracuse, a big, modern European city. Again and again we were to find signs of the changes mosquitoes could make to an economic landscape.

The ship's giant, my father, was suffering from severely swollen ankles from too much sitting. He suggested that we three youngsters spend the night at the mouth of the River Anapo, while he went to a *pensione,* where he could stretch out full length in comfort.

We moved across the bay to the area where the Anapo flowed greenly into the waters of the harbour. It was a strangely deserted spot, so green and lush and empty, yet so near to the city. The place had a sinister feel. We spent the night at anchor near the shore, but moved out into the bay for breakfast and left the mosquitoes their kingdom. We had the feeling that the effects of the police DDT would not linger for long, and that the insects' retreat was temporary.

The boat was suffering in sympathy with my father. She was still leaking so much that I wondered if my toenails might begin to fall off from being wet all the time, although Sally assured me this only happened in fresh water, not in salt.

Syracuse was no place to find the sort of boatyard we needed and we also had to drop off Diccon and pick up a new member of crew. So we left the harbour of Syracuse and headed northwards a day's journey up the coast till we came to Priolo, a small fishing-harbour. Priolo was only a couple of hours in the local bus from the airport at Catania. If I travelled to the airport with Diccon, I could meet our next crew, John Warden, off his plane. When he and I returned to the boat, we would sail northwards up the coast to find somewhere small that built fishing boats, where we could overhaul our boat.

2. The Big Friendly Giant's Parting Gift

Priolo (July 13th to 14th)

Friday 13th seemed an inauspicious date for Diccon to have chosen to catch an airplane from a small boat. He had hoped we might have reached Taormina where he had friends, but there was no chance as we were still many miles to the south of Catania and the airport. By late afternoon we had reached Priolo, and the next morning I went with him by bus to the airport. He told me about the friends in Taormina he had hoped to call on. They were Polly and John Hope, a young couple of about my own age. He bought a post-card to send to them, and wrote down their names for me. He did not know their address - *poste restante* should suffice, he said.

Priolo to Augusta (July 14th)

After seeing Diccon onto his plane, I met our next crew member, John Warden. We spent that night at Priolo and the following night in Augusta, a harbour town halfway between Syracuse and Catania.

"I got on better with your father the last day or two," Sally said to me, "but it *is* nice to have no grown-ups again. I don't think he liked me being in charge - telling him to put his things away, for instance."

I was reluctant to listen to criticism of my father, especially from a good friend. It threatened my basic assumptions. In our lives my father was larger than life, a hero, a champion, and in our household criticism of him was taboo. My mother was fiercely proud of him and protective. Eight years after he died, my memoir *Richard Hughes, Author, Father*[3] was published, a book which still tended towards unquestioning hero-worship. My mother was very much still alive at that time and more protective than ever after his death. When I came to write the book, one of my best sources of information outside the family was the tapes made by a producer at the BBC who was putting together an hour's feature on Diccon as a writer. Time and again as I listened to the recordings they would be broken off. "Switch off, we mustn't offend Frances," Amabel Williams-Ellis, a family friend, would say in mid-flow, leaving me tantalised.

---

[3] Penelope Hughes, *Richard Hughes, Author, Father* (Allan Sutton Publishing, 1984).

There were plenty of disadvantages to having a big friendly giant on the boat, but there was one strong advantage. My father's war years as a civil servant in the Admiralty had taught him the importance of meticulous planning. I mentioned in a letter to my mother that it had been a boon to have him with us on the first lap of our journey. I contrasted our lifestyle the previous year, when getting supplies seemed to keep us at full stretch from when we arrived to the moment of departure because nothing had been planned in advance. Diccon got us to work out every move while we were still at sea, leaving us time for talking, exploring and sight-seeing. But I certainly agreed with Sally about it being nice to have no grown-ups. His strength and experience were beginning to sap our initiative and independence.

"What if I were to persuade Owain to come?" I began to muse. Owain was the youngest of us five children, currently only twelve years old. Owain picked up practical skills fast – he had been driving my parents' car, a Jeep, since the age of seven, and by the age of ten he could back the Jeep and trailer more competently than my father, even though his spelling was atrocious, and he seldom read a book. I reckoned we would have to wait a year or two before he would be resilient enough to come on *Crab*. But if we waited till he was two years older, was there any chance he would still obey the skipper? I felt I knew him better than the others, because he used to opt to come and stay with me in Oxford for his spring half-term. This spring he had particularly enjoyed himself. Port Meadow alongside the river had flooded and then frozen, and he found himself in demand to helm the sailing club's ice-yacht because the ice was too thin to take the weight of the yacht plus an adult.

Augusta to Catania and Giardini Naxos (Sunday July 15th)

We woke to a *sirocco*, that south wind straight from the African desert, hot and dry and dusty, that seemed to snuffle everywhere like an escaped pack of hounds, tugging at the awning which we had spread over us for the night, knocking over dustbins, and sending up swirls of dust and grit.

We set off from Augusta at first light. Our crew now consisted of Richard Davy, the lanky six-footer who had joined us at Syracuse, and my friend John Warden, who had not had previous experience on boats. Sally describes life on *Crab*, in a spidery letter to her parents headed *At sea, heading for Catania*:

Richard D., who was full of complaints about his health when he arrived, has cheered up a lot and is very useful on the boat and with the engine: John W. is still rather in the settling down stage and apt to complain at being told to put his things away all the time, but I think he will be quite nice to live with...There isn't much more news really. We are eating, drinking and sleeping well, and I am picking up quite a lot of Italian, also getting brown all over. It's a nice life.

As we travelled on up the coast, bowling along on the south wind, we caught our first glimpse of Mount Etna, at 10,000 ft by far the highest peak in the central Mediterranean. We were keen to climb it. One could catch a bus at 7 am from Catania's central square, and be back the same evening. Alas, we overslept - and besides, found that we needed to pump the boat out, although we had done it before going to bed. With hindsight we decided the priority was to get to a harbour where we could beach *Crab* and do something about her leaks.

Breakfast was uncomfortable because there was a stiff breeze blowing. The primus was hard to hold steady on the bench while the kettle boiled and our coffee kept spilling. I reckoned that Richard and John, who had only just joined the boat, must have wondered privately whether they might not jump ship.

We stocked up with provisions and petrol at a small place called Riposto and headed for Taormina. With a strong wind behind us, we surfed along at what we thought might be five knots. It was an easy lolloping movement, the waves overtaking us from behind instead of slamming into our bows. But our speed put a strain on the planks, twisting the boat so that water oozed in along a dozen seams, and we had to pump out almost continually. It was not good to have a boat in such a state.

At midday we were already approaching our destination. From the sea it seemed like a town built on three levels, one above the other. We anchored off the north end of the harbour, and discovered the harbour was a separate town from Taormina, known as Giardini Naxos.

Giardini Naxos, (July 16th)

The official at the harbour office put us in touch with a local boat-builder, who said he would be free to help us beach the boat in the evening, and we could put our stores in his shed. But he told us there was definitely not enough space for us to live alongside the boat on the beach, as we had hoped to do. With some hours to wait, we went in search of a *poste restante* to leave a message for Polly and John Hope, after which we would have to search for lodgings.

From the quayside we could see a road snaking up the steep hill above the harbour towards Taormina. Leaving the other two to guard the boat, Sally and I started up the road. Nearing the town we passed a sign that said *Tombe Byzantine* and another that pointed to the *Teatro Greco.*

We reached Taormina's main square and stood astonished. It lay at the edge of a five-hundred foot cliff that dropped almost sheer. All around us houses were enriched with ornamental Muslim designs made with black lava and white marble inlay. It seemed to be something unique to Taormina – its signature-tune, perhaps.

We found the post office in the main square and joined the queue for collecting *poste restante.* In and out of the queue ran a volatile, sociable little poodle. Ahead of me in the queue was his owner, a striking girl burnt dark brown with the sun, with a short corkscrew-curled mop of deep yellow hair, a person whose clothes had been put together as a painter puts together a jug full of flowers to paint.

I had no idea what Diccon's friend Polly Hope would look like, but I knew she was about my own age – as was she. I went up to her: "Are you Polly Hope by any chance? I'm Penny Hughes, by the way." She was!

Polly said she had just received a postcard from Diccon who had posted it at the airport and written: "So near, and yet so far." So she was at least half-expecting us but not really expecting that we would call in at Taormina as we went past, since Diccon was no longer with us. She asked where we were moored and what our plans were. We had not yet had time to think about where we and our newly arrived crew would eat and sleep until we could get the boat back in the water. We told her that we had come to the harbour below for some repairs. Could she advise us on lodgings?

Polly took over our arrangements in a trice. By evening all four of us had transported our small bags to the rooftop terrace of an elegant family villa high up on the hillside above the town, with a splendid view of Etna dominating the landscape. She and John were lodged in a roof annex. Everywhere there were unframed paintings, a riot of colour, and to be in among them was a 3-D wrap-around experience of light and warmth. We were to sleep on the terrace for as long as it took us to put the boat to rights.

Taormina (July 16th to 21st) – How not to say "thank you"

Polly was tall and ebullient, with a very short version of a Burne-Jones hairstyle. I well remember her confident stride. John was compact and small, deep-thinking. We liked the two of them greatly. Here were people of almost our own age who were actually living in the Mediterranean, on the shores of this wonderful sea. John said he had never lived in a place where he was so happy painting. On the shores of the Mediterranean there was a brilliant vibrancy of colour. So different to England, in those days of pea-soup fogs and light that was hazy at best, not crystal-clear as it was here. But currency laws made it difficult for British people to live in the Med. You had to emigrate to do so – as John and Polly had done. We shared the excitement at getting away from the ten-year drabness that was post-war Britain.

I asked John why the town seemed half dead. He explained that the summer was the dead season. People were attracted by the antiquity of Taormina and its medieval buildings, but the place was famed for its winter climate. Between January and April prices were sky-high and the town was thronged with tourists, the hotels thriving. It was definitely not the place to be, unless you wanted to be part of that brittle, migratory, fashionable world.

I couldn't make sense of the topography. The pre-classical colony of Naxos had been founded in the eighth century BC, a little colonial outpost planted by the citizens of the Cycladic island of that name. By classical times Naxos had a big harbour, enough for the Athenian armada to drop anchor and use the place as a base for their thrust at Syracuse. John Hope explained the site was some distance away from our boat builder's yard in Giardini Naxos and was inaccessible by public transport, at the end of the neighbouring peninsula, with nothing much to see when you got there.

John did offer to take us all to the Greek theatre, with its superb view of Etna. It was on a hillside well inside the modern town's limits. It turned out to have been modernised and vastly enlarged by the Romans. In Magna Graecia it was the biggest theatre after Syracuse. Its auditorium had the same spectacular backdrop of Etna, with its mountain gently smouldering, as we got from our rooftop-terrace lodging.

The site was deserted. Many of its seating slabs had been used for newer buildings. For me, the important thing was the air and light between where one stood and the farthest point one could see, and the sense of being wrapped round simply with emptiness and nothingness.

*

Polly and John later told me, "When we met your parents in Marbella, I suppose they told us their names, but we didn't catch what they said. Your mother talked as if everyone in the world had heard of Diccon, so we daren't let on that we had never heard of him, and when we asked Diccon himself what he did, he just said he was a professor of Rhetoric, so he was known to us as 'the Professor' for the first two weeks or so, until we discovered their names by a visit to the *poste restante* together. It wasn't long till we got to know them a bit. He's a real dare-devil, your Dad."

Every morning we worked on repainting the beached boat, amid constant criticism and teasing from the local fishermen. Our afternoons we spent lazing on the tourist beach at Isola Bella - it was too hot to work. A prosperous, blue eyed Sicilian known as "Il Padrone", who ruled the fishing beach, became our firm friend and protector. We often heard him repeating solemnly to the crowd our explanation that we were "not lunatics, only students". He even understood us enough not to ask - as nearly all Italians did - why we did not have a much larger engine and just motor, instead of bothering to sail.

Meanwhile Polly provided wonderful meals for everyone each night. The previous winter at Oxford, when I ought to have been focussing on my work, I had drooled over Elizabeth David's *Mediterranean Cooking*. That already dog-eared paperback was part of our galley equipment, because it helped us live off the dirt-cheap local vegetables we found in village shops. Polly's cooking, however, was in another class altogether from mine. To my chagrin I found she was only a year older than me.

We were in a gastronomic paradise. Sicily had abundant fresh vegetables and good wine and catered to the upper end of the tourist trade. Polly told us that on the other hand if you wanted a dentist, as she did, the only thing to do was to go to Malta - they were going there shortly. Sicily was as low on dentists as it was high on aubergines and courgettes.

"Why did you leave Marbella?"

"We are on our way to Istanbul."

I think it was at that moment that we conceived the plan of getting to Istanbul in *Crab.* But I wondered which of us would get there first, at our present rates of progress.

*

While in Taormina we had received an encouraging cable from the vice-consul in Corfu. We had written to him about the possibilities of laying up *Crab* there for the winter, since it was the first substantial island on our route after crossing the Adriatic from the heel of Italy. The cable began "Conditions normal here..." That phrase lingered in the back of my mind as we travelled towards Corfu – why did he need to say that?

At last *Crab*'s leaks were cured and she was back in the water and loaded again with our possessions. How were we to repay these generous Hopes for their kindness. They arranged for us to sleep on their terrace. They had fed us at the end of our work each day. We would have invited them to come to a restaurant, but when we did they said: "We never go to restaurants. That's how we manage to live off so little money and to be free, both of us, to paint."

We decided to host a grand dinner on board. John Warden, the crew who had joined us at Priolo, offered to stage a display of home-made fireworks – he had done it before, he said. He spent most of the morning in the pharmacist, assembling his ingredients, and I spent as long scouring the shops for choice items of *antipasto,* and the ingredients of a really tasty *paella,* with fresh shellfish, a rubbery little squid complete with ink sack, and gleaming black olives.

When evening came, Polly and John met us at the harbour jetty. *Crab* bobbed alongside. A brisk little wind from the Straits of Messina was stirring up choppy waves in the harbour.

"We hoped to moor off the beach, Polly, but it is so stony our anchor would drag. We're going to row out a bit to anchor."

Richard and I each took an oar. As we rowed away from the jetty the water became even choppier. We anchored and dispensed glasses of wine. But the boat then began swinging on her anchor first one way, then the other, like a pendulum, but with a sharp jolt before changing direction. Polly and John were gripping the gunwale with one hand, while trying with the other to hold plate, fork, and wineglass. They watched listlessly as I struggled to reheat the *paella,* while the primus-flame was being blown horizontal by the wind. I noticed that meanwhile the *antipasto* was going almost untasted. Both Polly and John were pale, with an air of fixed concentration, and conversation was flagging. If only the damn boat would stop bouncing! Suddenly I had that feeling in my mouth that I was going to be sick – "sick out loud" as my mother used to call it. With a mighty effort of will I suppressed the urge, but I noticed Richard was paper-white. Sally seemed to be the only one not seriously affected. On the jetty, John Warden continued with his firework display, to feebler and feebler applause.

At 9.00 pm our guests excused themselves, pleading tiredness. We rowed them back to the jetty. The *paella,* almost untouched and stone-cold, was stowed away. We decided to move and position ourselves among the fishing-boats, ready for the morning's dawn start. We needed to call at Reggio, on the Italian side of the straits between Sicily and Italy, so as to swap crew members for the journey onwards. Richard had to be dropped off and Mike Waller, another friend of Sally's, was due to meet us at Reggio railway-station. The fishermen told us that north winds caused strong south-flowing currents in the straights, but the stronger the main current, the faster the back-eddy that could be picked up if you had sufficiently shallow draught to be able to sail close inshore. You needed local knowledge, however, because there were underwater rocks. Better to accept the offer of a tow from a tunny-fishing boat that was going our way.

Sunday July 22nd

We left before it was fully light, towed north very fast by the tunny-fishing boat, which steered alarmingly close to the rocks in order to use the back-eddy. At 5.30 am the fishermen cast us off. And then we found that the engine refused to start. Ignominiously we rowed, sailed and drifted to a fishing village called San Alessio only a few miles north of Taormina and Richard took the carburettor to get it thoroughly cleaned at a garage. At 1.00 pm, still on the Sicilian side of the straits, we arrived and anchored north of Capo d'Ali, a good stopping-off point, the fishermen had told us, for the crossing to Reggio.

We were told again and again that the coastline of Calabria, which lay ahead of us, was dangerous. In Classical times the Calabrian coastline had been dotted with ports founded, like Naxos, by Greek colonists from the Cyclades. The most famous was perhaps Sybaris, known across the Mediterranean for sophistication and delicate living. We were looking forward to visiting these cities, which I somehow imagined to be even more prosperous now than in the ancient world. I must have had something of a misconception, because whenever Italians heard we were heading for Calabria they shook their heads. Everything we had on the boat would be stolen, they said. Undoubtedly we would be raped and then killed.

3. Coast of Calabria: Antiquities and Brigands

Straits of Messina (Monday July 23rd)

We set off for Reggio at sunrise the following morning. The wind was in our teeth, and we seemed likely to have ahead of us a long morning's motoring, even though Reggio was close enough for us to be able to make out one or two features, such as the railway line.

It was a chilly, misty early morning, and soon we began to meet violent gusts coming down between the mountains. These gusts raised a short bouncy sea in the straits. *Crab* butted into the waves, repeatedly brought to a halt. Reggio was not far away, but it never seemed to get any closer. And then a jabbing wave chanced to douse the Seagull outboard with spray: it coughed and fell silent. Very soon Reggio started to get further away, minute by minute.

Weary with cold, we abandoned our plan of going to Reggio for the foreseeable future. Instead, we hoisted our storm sails and ran south-eastwards, downwind. We reached San Gregorio bay, on the Messina-facing side of the toe of Italy, and at 10.00 am anchored among the fishing boats, cold and wet to the skin in spite of our oilskins, after five hours of drenching spray.

We were in Italy! Never mind missing our landfall at Reggio! The luxury of Mediterranean sailing, we reckoned, is that after a few gruelling hours of sailing like this you drop anchor in a sheltered, sandy bay, nothing in sight except a few bamboos or prickly-pear trees, a few fishing boats drawn up on the beach, and perhaps a herd of goats in the distance, and spend the rest of the day bathing, basking in the sun, and sleeping under a Robinson Crusoe makeshift awning.

In the early evening, well recovered, Sally and Richard set off for the port of Reggio by bus to register the boat's arrival in Italy. It was also necessary to get Richard's name crossed off the crew list, as he would soon be leaving us.

"But where is the boat?" the officials in the office of the Port Authority in Reggio kept asking. What sort of a boat was this that was incapable of moving against current and wind simply to get from Taormina to Reggio? The two towns were within sight of one another! Richard explained the boat's limitations, and that we had a boat with such limitations because we were just indigent students. At the end of a long assertion that he was much enjoying the trip, the officials of the Port Authority said in unison: "But you must be mad, the lot of you, all the same."

A change of plan (Tuesday July 24th)

We had already decided that the direct sea route was not for us. On the other hand, if we followed the Calabrian coastline, as we would have to do in *Crab,* it meant almost a week of hugging a largely deserted shore. We had been warned that centuries of exposure to pirate raids had denuded the coast of ports, and there would be few fishing villages.

The coast seemed to be so inhospitable that we now abandoned the plan of staying within easy reach of Reggio for the changeover of crew, and pushed on eastwards, a fateful decision. Richard could catch a train at a place called Soverato on the southern coast, instead of our going back to Reggio. We would think how to pick up Mike when the time came. Little did we foresee the problems that would ensue from changing the agreed meeting-plan.

On our first day we sailed past Riace. After passing Riace we soon rounded Cape Spartivento, the southernmost point with its stubby little octagonal lighthouse clinging halfway up the precipitous hillside. In 1956, when *Crab* sailed past Riace, little did we know that the Riace bronzes, which are considered some of the greatest art-works in the world, were lying on the seabed close to *Crab's* route: bronzes encrusted with barnacles that had lain underwater for more than two millennia.

Our first impression of Calabria was of a bafflingly bare coast. We saw nothing but mile after mile of pebbled shore, a single-track railway line and beyond that a dust road. The villages we saw were all perched like eagles' nests on the top of pinnacles of rock, several miles inland. The chart did show one coastal village however, Bove Marina, a straggly village clustered around a river mouth under some sheltering cliffs. The actual town of Bova was in the mountains nearly 3,000 feet above sea level.

We left Bova Marina again at nightfall, trusting there would be an offshore breeze during the night. We had to reach Soverato, where there was a railway station within walking distance, for Richard. We got the offshore breeze we hoped for, and sailed through the night, keeping two-hour watches.

Calabrian coast (July 24th to 25th)

Next morning we sailed along the Calabrian coast almost straight into the eye of the sun, under a pale metallic sky. As the morning wore on, we saw what we took to be recently established smallholdings, precisely placed two kilometres apart, which was puzzling. We began to worry that nowhere on this coast would we be likely to find fresh water.

By evening we were not far from Soverato, bowling along with a following wind and the spinnaker set, the sail's long shadow racing ahead of us. We tied up in the harbour at 6:30 pm and Richard was able to catch his train. He was the most skilled helmsman we had had on the boat, and with his dry humour had been a good companion – I was sad to see him go.

Sally's letter home, written for posting at Soverato, said that she was missing the amazingly vivid colours of Sicily: black lava rock, blue-green seas, vividly green lemon groves and inky-dark cypresses. Writing to my parents too, I had looked back on the five days which we had spent repairing the boat in Taormina, enjoying hospitality and exploring a new friendship: *Taormina was lovely – and staying with the Hopes put* Crab's *standards up… It was so nice being with the Hopes for conversation too – one gets a craving for life in houses and general conversation, not about practical matters.*

Soverato to Torre Crocchio (Thursday July 26th)

We spent the night in Soverato harbour. Early next morning I woke to the sound of an octopus being smacked against a wall somewhere on the waterfront. While the other two were refilling the water-tank, I went in search of that octopus and bought it and a few vegetables. I did not take into account that when we stopped for the night in that barren landscape we might not be able to find any wood for a fire on which we could stew our supper.

*

Fifty-five years later I was back in Soverato, working my way along the coast by car, in company with a younger sister, in order to retrace *Crab's* journey. We had visited the Riace bronze statues in the national museum in Reggio, and our route had taken us along the shore of Squillace Bay in search of the ruins of a big monastery. Founded and headed by the scholar Cassiodorus, there had been workshops with up to one hundred monks copying classical Greek and early Christian manuscripts. We even found the remains of the *vivarium,* a sea-cave fish-tank where the abbot kept a good supply of live fish as sustenance for his team of scribes - and as an attraction to visitors.

Back in 1956, in *Crab,* we sailed parallel to the deserted shore of Squillace Bay. I had so little idea then of the rich past of this barren coastline. Our stopping-place for the night was Torre Crocchio, another deserted bay. We failed to beach the boat, lacking Richard who had been our strongest crew member, and had to anchor offshore with two ropes tied to rocks on the beach. I wanted to light a fire to stew my octopus - this was going to be a feat of culinary perfection. But though there was brushwood, there was nothing to hand to keep a fire going long-term. Our crew member John Warden had shown his skill at fireworks in Taormina, but fireworks were not going to cook an octopus. Sally suggested we try dried cow-dung, which was present in abundance. The octopus was eaten by starlight, after some two hours of stewing.

Sally and I felt that the whole coast had something of the sinister emptiness we had sniffed at the River Anapo, so close to the city of Syracuse and yet so lifeless. Much later, studying Thomas Hodgkin's *Italy and her Invaders*[4], I got a vivid picture of the incursions of Ostrogoths, Lombards, Franks and Spaniards. Towards the end of the nineteenth century, he said: *Instead of the white-robed Hellenes, wild-looking peasants clad in goatskins with their guns in their hands slouch along through the cactus-bordered ways. The Saracen, the Spaniard and the Bourbon have laid their heavy hands on this lovely region and brutalised its inhabitants.* Not having read Hodgkin at the time, I was still expecting white-robed Hellenes - or at the least a seamless continuity between classical and modern-day prosperity. In the classical world the cities of Sybaris and Croton had been bywords for luxury - for "sybaritic" life-styles.

Torre Crocchio – Overland expeditions (Friday July 27th)

Richard's successor as crew, Mike Waller, was due to arrive by train in Reggio Calabria from Naples to join us. But we had wildly overshot our schedule and were already 100 miles beyond Reggio. An alternative plan was now hatched. The Naples-to-Reggio railway line, by which he would come to join us, ran south-west along the coast, almost parallel to our route running north-east along the southern coast of Calabria. Sally decided she would cross the landmass at a convenient place and

[4] Thomas Hodgkin, *Italy and her Invaders* (8 vols., Oxford, 1880–1899).

intercept him on the train. She calculated that, on the day he was due in Reggio, we would have reached a place where there was a break in the Aspromonte mountain range and it would be easy to go west by bus across the isthmus to a station called Santa Eufemia, where she should be able to extract Mike from the train to Reggio.

Sally had arranged for a message to be given out for him over the loudspeaker at the previous point where he changed trains, telling him to get off the Reggio train at Santa Eufemia instead of going on to Reggio.

It was agreed that she should go to Santa Eufemia alone, while I went on ahead by the coast railway to Crotone to collect our mail and John stayed on board *Crab* to guard the boat.

Because of the timing of the bus, Sally would have a long wait at Santa Eufemia.

"Will you be OK alone, Sally?"

"I'll take a book. After all, I'll be with Mike for the return journey."

I was the first of us two to get back to *Crab*. No Sally – I began to get very anxious. Sally arrived quite late that evening, but there was no Mike. She had failed to find him on the train. This was a steep learning-curve. And in addition she had had a narrow escape. While she was waiting around till the train was due, she said, she got tired of people asking her questions: "So I reckoned I'd just go off into a secluded bit of countryside and bury myself in my book till the train was due – as one would in England. How could I be so naïve? A man came by with a frisky young mule, and showed clear signs of wanting to rape me."

"What happened?"

"Nothing clever on my part. He found he couldn't catch hold of me, and at the same time keep hold of his mule, and in the end decided he'd better keep hold of the mule."

Sally had been in very real danger. This was a second steep learning-curve.

To Crotone by train, and to a country estate (Saturday July 28th)

The three of us set off early the next morning, but there was no wind and, after two hours of using the outboard, the petrol began to run very low. We anchored in a cove. Sally and I went ashore with the petrol can and a string bag for vegetables. It was an hour's walk, mainly uphill, to the nearest village. No petrol. There was telephone connection in the village between nine and twelve and from three until six, and there was a railway station, and even a train. We were advised to go by train to Crotone to buy more petrol. In Crotone we would also use the telephone to leave messages for Mike everywhere we could think of, both in Crotone, and in the office of the British Consul in Reggio. There might even be a message from him at *poste restante* in Crotone. We also wanted to get there because our much-loved Greats tutor, Isobel Henderson, had said she was holidaying in Calabria and would be at the Grand Albergo in Crotone.

Crotone, the provincial capital, has not just one castle but two. The larger one was built by Emperor Charles V of Spain as a bastion against the Turks. Its massive walls protected the harbour - the only secure harbour between Taranto and Reggio. Sally and I emerged from the spacious railway station, carrying the petrol can and the string bag which we hoped to fill with vegetables. We made our way to the Gran Albergo Hotel. There they spoke French, in which Sally at least was fluent. Alas, we learned that Isobel Henderson had altered her booking and would not be there for another fortnight. We made our way also to the Central Post Office, in the hope there would be a message from Mike Waller in the *poste restante*, but there was nothing.

There was no convenient train running the other way, so we completed our purchases and set out on foot along the road back to our cove. Two young foreign girls on foot, carrying a can of petrol and a string bag full of vegetables, were not perhaps a common sight on the open road. A car approached from behind, and stopped. Two young men of our own age offered us a lift. We admired the car - such vehicles were a rarity, and they said it was their own. They invited us to come to their house and meet their parents. And so it came about that four hours after leaving Crotone on foot we were quite unexpectedly enjoying the cool depths of an Italian country house near the coast, being shown antiquities by the Marchese Lucifero - these ones inherited, this one turned up by the plough, this one brought in by someone on the Lucifero estate. It was an afternoon of delight.

Afterwards the Marchese's two sons drove us right to the water's edge, curious to see our tiny boat.

4. Crotone, and a Crossing with No Engine Backup

Barce Vercillo to Crotone (Sunday July 29th)

The following evening, the seventh after leaving Taormina, *Crab* arrived in Crotone harbour, our starting point for crossing the Gulf of Taranto from the toe to the heel of Italy. We had anchored in the Porto Nuovo, the New Harbour. We were suddenly conscious that we were dirty and tired, and that our hair was so stiff with dried salt spray that it stood on end. Fresh water had been in such short supply on the Calabrian coast that we could not afford to waste it on washing ourselves. We were grateful to have a quay to tie up alongside at last, and the prospect of buying lots of provisions.

The waterfront was just coming to life again, people walking, meeting, relaxing in the cool of the evening. Our stubby little *Crab* with its twelve-foot mast attracted a lot of curiosity and, as soon as I went ashore to search for provisions, I found myself flanked on either side by a young man, fortunately speaking some English, who told me it was essential that I had an escort. In a place like Crotone young girls didn't walk about unaccompanied, they said. There was some altercation between the two of them and the younger of them yielded to the older and left him in sole charge. He said he had a hair-dressing shop. He couldn't bear to see a person going around with a head of hair like mine, all standing on end. He was determined to get me into his shop and improve my appearance. To change the subject I asked him why there were no coastal villages.

He explained that Calabria had been depopulated for many centuries because of malaria. It had been almost empty of people. But since the war some United Nations organisation had disposed of the mosquitoes and the Italian government had been able to re-populate the area with families from the overcrowded slums of Naples, placing them in the small-holdings we had seen along the coast at a good distance from each other. "The present people living in the countryside of Calabria are brigands, they don't have anything much to do with each other, like people of a village do," he said, "At each other's throats, so that the countryside is not a safe place for anyone now. I'm surprised you weren't robbed when you stopped at night – robbed even of the clothes you stood up in."

When we parted I agreed to come to his shop about 9.00 pm, just after closing time, and have my hair beautified. The cost of this was a decorous kiss.

Porto Nuovo, Crotone (Monday July 30th)

In the harbour area there seemed to be almost no shops. Exploring together, Sally and I came on a shop that sold local hardware – panniers for donkeys, tin mugs and plates, and decorative hand-made whips, whips with a reach of more than six feet. I could not resist buying one, because the decorative leatherwork on the handle was so fine. It cost me 250 lire, a little less than the cost of one camera-film.

What do you want that for?" the shopkeeper asked.

"E por il marito" (It's for my husband), I joked, with "women's lib" in mind.

The shopkeeper laughed, and shouted to a friend. Clearly he mistook my joking reference to women's lib – such a concept had not penetrated this far. Echoing away up the street from mouth to mouth, amid gusts of laughter, went *e por il marito.*

Sally and I found the *poste restante*, but there was no message from Mike. We phoned in all directions, leaving another message at the British Consulate in Reggio.

In the afternoon, while everything was shut for *siesta,* Sally and I went to explore Crotone, especially Charles V's enormous castle and moat that dominated the waterfront, which now houses the town museum. Crotone was famous in antiquity for the skill of its Greek doctors and then for the philosophy school of Pythagoras. Much later it had become a central Mediterranean strongpoint in the bitter sixteenth century conflicts between the pope, Venice and the Ottoman Turks. This culminated in the Siege of Malta in 1565 and Don John of Austria's victory over the Ottoman fleet at Lepanto in 1671.

We came back to the *Crab* to find that Mike had unexpectedly arrived. We had almost given up all hope of finding him. He told us that the reason why Sally could not find him on the train when it stopped at Santa Eufemia was that he had decided to come on an earlier train, to see something of Reggio. He had returned to the station at the appointed time, but could not see us. In Reggio he searched the harbour for us, and enquired with the harbour police. He had been found, on the third day, by a man who worked at the British Consulate, who was going home by motorcycle and noticed a disconsolate-looking foreigner sitting dangling his heels on the harbour front. He asked whether he was searching for a boat called *Crab*. Mike had been taken up to the Consulate on the back of the man's motorcycle and had got our message to come to Crotone.

To celebrate being united with our lost crew we went out to supper with my *perruquier*. We had decided to move early next morning to a more secluded anchorage at Capo Colonne, a couple of miles south-eastwards down the coast.

Capo Colonne (July 31st to August 1st)

Setting off at 6.00 am, we moved as planned to Capo Colonne, anchoring in a rocky harbour where the bottom seemed to be clay. John and Mike spent the last free day of our stay in Crotone on an excursion boat, fishing for sharks.

The final day was spent stocking up for crossing from the sole to the heel of the "boot" of Italy, a journey of some seventy miles. Letters were stamped and posted, water tanks refilled to the brim, our stock of food replenished. Mike and John took the engine to a garage to get it cleaned and serviced, and bought petrol.

Capo Colonne to Gallipoli (August 2nd to 3rd)

7.30 am. Goodbye to Calabria! We had a favourable wind, although it was not very strong. We proceeded under sail north-east all day till evening, with an average speed of about two knots. Towards sunset we became becalmed. But when we tried the engine we found that it would not start – it must have been reassembled wrongly after being taken apart for cleaning in Crotone. This was the first time on a crossing that there had been no engine as back-up. We would simply have to wait till some wind sprang up.

Crab rocked gently in the swell, her sails listless. As the sun set, in the brightness of the western horizon we could still just see the land behind us, but now at last there was the faint outline of mountainous land ahead too. We worked out this must be the mountains of Albania, on the other side of the Adriatic. I wondered if we would get a glimpse of the Greek mountains also, the Pindus range.

The darkness gathered. There was not much chance of sleep, because the lack of wind meant that the boat was heaving and rolling unpredictably in the confused swell, rolling us off the narrow benches on which we were dozing. And then at last, about an hour after midnight, we got a little wind from the west, and were soon crunching eastwards through the darkness. At 5.30 am, as the dawn began to spread across the sky, we were able to make out the lie of the land ahead, Isola Andrea. We were almost precisely where Sally intended to be. We anchored in the lee of a cape, Punta Pizza, and all four stretched out along the benches and slept till 4.00 pm - ten-and-a-half hours!

While we slept the wind steadily strengthened. When we set off, *Crab* was under storm mainsail alone. We had a fine spanking wind from the south - a wind that brought on board sheets of spray.

We were sailing towards a part of Italy that had once been a cultural Mecca. Beyond the hills, near Otranto, there had been the famous monastery of St Nicholas, with a substantial library of classical texts and a team of monks trained as copyists, just as there had been in Calabria.

At 5.30 pm we reached Italy's Gallipoli, with the Old City crowded together on its rock, connected by a bridge to the mainland, and with a clean and pleasant harbour. We were soaked and exhausted, but proud to have done the journey unaided by an engine.

5. Rounding the Heel of Italy

Gallipoli (August 3rd – 7th)

I sent my father a terse postcard which bore a grandiose picture of the Piazza Tellini, Gallipoli with the sea as a backdrop:

You were wrong when you said we didn't need oilskins. We arrived with trousers so stiff with salt they could stand alone. Crab *very wet to windward in seas, particularly at night, when hard to see waves coming. Population here is 12,000. In the evening they all come on their motor-bikes to watch us, and wherever we go now, we are known. Very friendly, but too public.*

Clearly we were longing to get to Greek soil and hopefully to anonymity again…

Sally commented that to come from the rugged mountains of Calabria to the white, Moorish-style houses and narrow streets of Gallipoli was almost like entering a different country. She wrote to her parents from Gallipoli:

Crossing over – rather wet – but very fast – 70 miles in 28 hours. I seem to have managed to get tummy trouble again, but will probably be OK by tomorrow. Michael is very useful on board and knows more about sailing than I expected. John leaves tomorrow morning early. This is a very nice place, built on a rocky island joined to the mainland by a bridge – touristy, but very clean and attractive. We shall be here a few days, probably, before going on to Otranto...So far your letters have been keeping up with me very well – one you wrote on 21st July was forwarded on to Crotone before we left – and I presume there wouldn't be any since. Did Richard ring you up? I asked him to, but he might be too shy.

At Gallipoli John Warden left - he had been with us for almost four weeks, and had become a good helmsman. For the next two days we were confined to the harbour, the winds too strong for us to venture out. At last, on 7th August, we reckoned we could leave. It was only about fifteen miles to our next harbour, Santa Maria di Leuca, but the journey took eleven hours. We anchored in the harbour off the sumptuous yacht club.

Santa Maria di Leuca (August 8th – 11th)

Sally wrote:

We are stuck here because of adverse winds but it is a nice place to be stuck in. Tourist resort (Italians mostly), with a grand Yacht Club outside which we are anchored, with lavatories and baths and a bar, and very smart Stars and a nice friendly caretaker who complains all the time about the "capitalists" who frequent the place but fortunately does not class us as among them but instead invited us to 's'accomodare sense ceremonia' which we have! The town is full of large villas in very comic architectural extravagances of style – a bright pink French chateau, and another house painted red white and blue, like a madder sort of St Margaret's Bay near Dover – with lovely gardens full of pine trees and oleanders in flower. Tremendous change from Calabria which was so very grim and poverty-stricken, especially Crotone which was full of gangsters, or so everyone assured me, including one rather dim lot of would-be thieves who came and sat on the quay above our heads and wondered in quite comprehensible Italian when we would leave the boat unguarded and go off to our hotel.

Gallipoli was lovely – very white houses of rather Moorish type – built round courtyards with balconies, and with archways over the street, and with very nice churches. We stayed there about three days – having lots of time at present because the next crews don't come till the 12th and we can't go without them. Also we are only 3 because John ran out of money and left us at Gallipoli…probably we will go to Otranto some time anyway as it is a much better place for starting the crossing.

It was on the strength of Sally's mention of the Royal Corinthian Club that we were invited to moor off the smart yacht club. *Mad architecture,* Sally writes in the log, adding, *Colony of orphans.* Sally's letter to her parents from Leuca vividly describes the yacht club caretaker, whose hatred of the "capitalists" who employed him was counterbalanced by phenomenal generosity and kindness to us indigent students – we even received presents of whole fish. We had struck lucky, since Leuca had very few shops, despite the film stars who frequented it, and there was nowhere to do something so plebeian as to change a traveller's cheque. The villas were crazily ostentatious and garish. Leuca at that time must have been a prototype of what Hollywood has become.

Sally's parents may have suggested we go to Otranto because of its rich history. The obvious starting point for Greece in modern times for good-sized boats has always been Brindisi with its massive harbour, but for something with *Crab's* limitations, Otranto, small and on the easternmost tip of Italy, was much better.

Santa Maria di Leuca to Otranto (August 11th)

Strong winds from the north kept us penned up in Leuca day after day. We finally left Leuca at 4.15 am, when it was still dark, so as to try and make headway towards Otranto before the north wind blew up, as it usually did at about 8.00 am. It blew up as expected, and duly headed us. Chugging along under engine (it was working at last), making no more than between one and two knots, we were offered a tow by a fishing boat.

While under tow there was nothing to do except bale the boat at intervals. With leisure for a change, I strained my eyes to try and see the mountains of Greece on the eastern horizon. Somewhere in those hills was the oracle of Dodona, much used by pilgrims who, like us, had come from the Greek cities along the coast of Calabria. I fumbled in the luggage for Robin's *Guide Bleu* to try and find out more about it, beginning to dream of a visit.

I read that the route to Dodona from the coast ran up the valley of the river Oropus, off the road to Ioannina, among steep mountains. Dodona's vast theatre seated slightly more even than the theatre at Epidauros. Would we get the chance to visit it? I have read somewhere an account of some of the questions asked of the oracle. What had stuck in my mind was that the questioners came from Tarentum, Heraclea - cities strung along the south coast of Italy. We hoped to get up into the hills and visit Dodona on our way south from Corfu. More recently I've had the chance to visit Jannina. In the archaeological museum I copied some of the questions asked of the oracle by people from southern Italy:

God, Good Fortune, is it better for myself, my wife and my children to settle in Croton? (400–390BC)

Exachon asks Zeus and Dione whether it is good for him to settle on the Pharos. [A small island in the Adriatic]

Should I take another wife? (400–390 BC)

Has Lyson cast a spell on my children, my wife, and myself? (400–350 BC)

And there were persistent questions from the Corfiots, asking Zeus and Dione what god they should sacrifice to... *so that they can have a rich and good crop.* (350–300 BC)

Having a tow was a mixed blessing. We were moving through the water at more than *Crab's* usual speed, and as a result were being constantly drenched with spray. We were being towed into the eye of the wind, and the constant thudding as we met waves head-on reminded me of when I was learning to ride at a trot, being bumped up and down on the pommel of the saddle. But after a couple of hours the north wind shifted into an easterly direction, and we were able to cast off the towline and hoist our sails. There were still heavy seas, but they were infinitely easier under sail.

Ahead of us we could just make out Otranto. As we approached the harbour entrance, we could see that its little ancient cathedral was too near the water to be visible against the sky, a small city with streets too narrow for cars, dominated by a huge fortress, quite out of proportion to the simple fishing harbour. We rounded the long harbour mole and tied up to the quay among the fishing boats at about midday. Having set off at 4.15 am, we felt we had accomplished a good day's work. Sally and I collapsed and slept, Mike went off to check the time of his train. At 4.30 pm we said our goodbyes. We were expecting his successor David Witt, a fellow-classicist, that same day, but not till 9.30 pm. Sally had complete confidence that in that small port he would find us in spite of the darkness - and he did. The other man who was joining us, Peter, was not due at the railway station till 4.30 pm the following day.

Otranto (August 12th to 15th)

In Otranto harbour we woke to a *sirocco* - warm, humid air, a cloudy sky, and a strong south wind that seemed to blow in every direction. We had not had a *sirocco* since Sicily. It brought with it mosquitoes. Sally and I felt lethargic, David still more so, exhausted as he was by his journey. We contrived a little shade alongside *Crab* and collapsed for a siesta, and it was there that Peter Thring, our fourth crewmember, found us. Looking back, he wrote:

I had had very limited foreign travel previously and just getting to Otranto was an adventure in itself: three nights and two days, eight trains (I think) and a ferry. I remember walking down to the harbour at Otranto on a boiling hot afternoon, wondering how to find you, and then coming across this tiny craft, with two bronzed semi-naked beauties lying beside it. I hope you never realised how naïve I was in 1957 (or was it 1956?). The whole trip was a huge experience to me.

The four of us went out onto the breakwater that evening at sunset. The sky was grey, the sea confused, a mass of restless white horses. A long swell from the north was competing with the seas raised by the *sirocco*.

Fast-moving cloud was coming in from the north and dispersing. It was plain to us all that it would take time to settle, and there was no possibility of leaving the next day. Sally talked to the fishermen in neighbouring boats, and they said that when there was a *tramontana* sea running it was a sure sign that a strong north wind was on its way, and would be with us tomorrow.

Next morning Peter, David and I went off to explore - Sally said she'd prefer to stay with the boat, and take any chances that came up to talk to people and get advice. Ahead of us lay the hardest crossing of the whole journey so far.

We returned from our exploring bursting with a mixture of impressions.

The best thing by far which we had seen, we told her, was a splendid mosaic floor in the cathedral. It showed the Tree of Life, with a few biblical scenes thrown in for good measure. We told her we had found a giraffe on the tree of life, and a galloping ostrich. There were elephants, and classical heroes such as Atlas with the world on his shoulders, and Alexander the Great, rubbing shoulders with Noah, Jonah, and Adam and Eve. And near the top, hidden among the Tree of Life's twigs, we found our own King Arthur.

We had discovered there was also a crypt - another church below the current one. The other two described how we went down the winding staircase to this crypt. Its ceiling was supported by a network of pillars. I had found it a startling experience - too startling to feel like chatting about it yet. As I had moved towards the altar I had suddenly become aware I was being stared at - by the huge sightless eyes of countless skulls, neatly ranged in rows inside glass-fronted cupboards behind the altar. I had lowered my eyes, and had felt myself backing away. Then curiosity had become stronger than fear. A plaque on the wall told me that these were the skulls of those who were martyred when, in the summer of 1480, a Turkish armada had appeared on the horizon, amongst the armada fifty of the hated galleys - hated for their unstoppable speed, and for their stink of human excrement. Otranto capitulated, and the 800 male survivors of the siege were ordered to renounce their Christian faith or face death. They refused, and were led out to the Hill Minerva and executed, together with their executioner, who was so impressed by their unwavering faith he declared himself also a Christian. Their bodies were left to rot on the hillside, since there was no one left to bury them. The skeletons lay there, scattered on the hillside, until the following year, when Alphonzo recaptured it from the Turks, and gave them decent burial.

The following day, Tuesday, would be a big fiesta, we were told, and they would carry the skulls of the martyrs round the city in procession. There would be fireworks both tomorrow and Wednesday. Sally was keen to get away.

"You can't go yet. The sea is far too rough still," the fishermen told her. "You see that motor yacht over there, which came in just this evening. Go and talk to them about what the sea is like out there!"

The motor yacht had left Corfu some two days before, but had had to take shelter on Othoni, a little island on the route, because the sea was too rough. The crew advised us to wait at least a day, and to make for Othoni, and not try to do the whole journey to Corfu in one. Here at the southern end of the Adriatic the seas had had many miles to build up strength.

Wednesday evening was taken up with the procession of the bones of the martyrs. Everyone in the town seemed to have turned out. Sally described it:

...celebrated with the inevitable fireworks, street illuminations, sweet stalls, and galaxy of brass bands: less common features were a procession of church and civil dignitaries in their robes and cocked hats, escorting a casket of bones around the walls, a water-ski gymkhana, and a procession of lighted boats. When they had rowed to shore, and the singing and fireworks had died away, we hoisted our sails and set out – it was a perfect moonlit night – for Corfu. ("Odyssey Crabwise")

6. Island of Widows

Otranto to Othoni (August 15th to 16th)

Neither of our crew had much idea what to expect - almost their only experience had been in sailing-dinghies. And even for young adults, we were extraordinarily naïve about the sensitivity of the border area between Albania, part of the Soviet bloc at the time, and Corfu, very much part of Western Europe. The Soviet bloc could have been on Mars, as regards our ignorance of what happened in it. Several people in Otranto had warned us that we must keep well away from the Albanian coast. If we were in difficulties, with the wind turning westerly, we could take shelter on the little island of Othoni, and should not risk being carried onto the coast of Albania. This was a little more than forty miles from Otranto, and only eleven miles from the north-west tip of Corfu. The harbour to make for was Ammos, at the eastern end.

Before we left, the skipper of the motor yacht had given us useful tips, among them that on the whole Greek winds only blow strongly between twelve midday and eight in the evening. Leaving at 8.30 pm, we were able to leave under our fair-weather mainsail and, once clear of the shore, we hoisted our spinnaker also. At 9.00 pm we set the watches, David and Sally were to be first, while Peter and I were to grab some sleep if we could. Instead we sat up watching the sky behind us lit up by firework after firework - fireworks that had probably started life as naval flares but had been "liberated" when WWII ended. They were very splendid - falling stars, exploding in a burst of magenta-coloured sparks.

We two came on watch at 11.00 pm. Till I tried to move about I had not realised quite how big and lumpy those Adriatic waves were, even though the wind was light. We had to move more or less on all fours to avoid losing our balance. There was a good-sized moon, which was a help.

A steamer passed close astern of us, which I found scary, given our lack of manoeuvrability. I got Peter to shine a torch on the mainsail, and another on the bellying spinnaker. We had no way of knowing whether we had been picked up on his radar. At ten minutes past midnight the moon set. This meant it was much easier to see the lighthouse signals. I identified St Maria di Leuca's light and took a bearing on it. When Sally came on watch at 1.00 am the wind was already freshening, and the seas beginning to get bigger. Peter had been kept busy baling during the latter part of his watch. Sally furled the spinnaker and set a course for the northern side of Othoni. She identified Capo di Otranto's light dead astern, which meant we were on course, in spite of coastal currents. Forty-five minutes later the light had dropped below the horizon.

A few years ago, I came across an account[5] in French of a voyage in the summer of 1925, led by young woman of twenty-five, Hermine de Saussure, who owned and skippered *Bonita*, an eleven-metre fifty-year-old Brittany-built yawl, without an engine, on a voyage from Marseilles to Piraeus. Her crew were slightly older than we were, their average age was twenty-three, but a lot more experienced: the first mate, Ella Maillart from Geneva and daughter of a naval officer, had already taken part in the Paris Olympics; Marthe Oulié at twenty-three was completing a doctorate in Classical Archaeology; and the fourth member of crew was to be Hermine's older sister Yvonne de Saussure. The size of their yawl dictated a different itinerary. Their yacht was too large for the Giardini Naxos harbour, and they took the direct route from the Straits of Messina to Corfu. This meant that they could not pick their weather for crossing the Adriatic. It was extremely rough, and they lost their gaff, which meant they could not use their mainsail. They limped into Argostoli on Cephalonia, where the British fleet was at anchor. Like us, they had an immense amount of generous help from British naval officers. I was intrigued by their account of negotiating the Corinth Canal without an engine.

Sally put in an extra hour before waking us, so Peter and I were the ones on watch when dawn broke at 4.40 am. As the light strengthened, still an hour or so before sunrise, we were able to pick out impressive mountains on the port bow, with two distinct peaks. It was an exciting moment. Othoni lay ahead of us, still below the horizon.

By 10.00 am, Othoni could be clearly seen and we headed for the port; we had only two hours left before the wind would start to blow in earnest.

With a strong current carrying us, we swept along the north coast of the island and rounded the north-eastern tip. The Mediterranean Pilot told

---

[5] Marthe Oulié *Cinq filles en Méditerannée 1925*. (Republished in 2004 by Edilarge S.A. – Editions Ouest-France, Rennes.)

us there was a "fishing harbour" - but this was too shallow even for *Crab*. We anchored in a bay south-west of Aulaki Point - feeling rather as if we had just slid downstairs on a tea tray, faster than we intended.

The first sound that greeted us was the long, drawn-out wail of a donkey, one of the most melancholy sounds I know, a kind of primeval cry of protest. Othoni was our first taste of Greece. It was a strange island which seemed to be inhabited only by old women in black.

The sea in the bay was flat calm, even though there were squalls swooping down on us from the mountains behind. Little houses fringed the water's edge, and there were two churches clinging on the hillside above the town.

The villagers were very friendly, and to our relief spoke Italian as well as Greek.

As we were talking with the women, there was a stir. An elderly Greek American arrived, bearing a bunch of flowers from his garden for us, the only man on the island as far as we could see. We sat and had coffee together on the harbour front. He told us that he had come back to his birthplace to end his days. He said that all the men had emigrated in search of work, so that it seemed like an island of widows.

Back on board, David and Peter asked us what our plans were once we had reached Corfu.

"Extremely vague," Sally said.

"This is because for once I am insisting on contributing to them," I explained, "instead of Sally being completely autocratic, because I am completely ignorant."

We had no plans of going beyond Corfu, I said. Our intention was to lay up *Crab* there for the coming winter. Sally put in that we were fairly confident that the yacht agent in Corfu, who doubled as British vice-consul, would be able to fix us up.

"Penny has friends of friends in Corfu, and if we have time we could seek them out also..."

"So you've been to Greece before?" Peter asked.

"I have, but Sally not," I said. "I came for six months during my gap year, as an *au pair*." Suddenly I felt awkward. What a household of royalists I had found myself in! The King of the Hellenes, though supported by

Britain, was not a popular figure in Greece. Together with his family he had escaped to Cairo as the Germans began to advance through Greece in 1941. After the civil war a plebiscite was held in Greece, and he was invited to return, but the voting was widely reported as rigged.

"Who was your contact, the friend of these friends you want to find?"

"I can't remember," I said lamely, my memory in a funk because I felt so embarrassed about the grandeur of the household where I had worked. It was so out of place, in a country utterly impoverished by the German occupation.

Storm-bound on Othoni (August 17th to 18th)

As I was falling asleep that night I suddenly remembered who it was who had given me the introductions. It was January of 1953, and it was my one and only visit to my father's London club. Ladies were only allowed in certain parts of it, at certain times of day. My Dad had arranged a meeting with a writer-friend's friend, a person who knew Greece well. We waited in hippopotamus-sized armchairs in the sitting room for his guest – like us not a Londoner, in fact seldom in England at all. He turned out to be so good-looking and with such charm that I was bowled over. Diccon outlined the problem. In order to go to Greece during my gap year, I had found myself a job as an *au pair*, but this was in the house of the Grand Marshall of the Greek court – and I didn't know how I was going to cope, leftie as I was. I would be a lady-companion to his wife, teaching her English.

When this good-looking man heard the name of my host, an initial wry smile turned to a mischievous twinkle. He talked for a bit, and then wrote out for me some names and phone-numbers. What he did was to give me a list of people to contact, people who would move in completely different circles to my host family, in fact would cause an explosion if I so much as mentioned some of them. They were young Greek writers. He had worked in Corfu, lecturing for the British Council, and he gave me some names of friends in Corfu for good measure.

At breakfast on *Crab* next morning I said, "I've remembered the name. It was something like Paddy Leigh Fermor."

Peter chided me, "Penny, haven't you read *Ill Met by Moonlight*? Really! They're shooting a film, with Dirk Bogarde as Paddy. Never heard of Paddy Leigh Fermor! He was in German-occupied Crete during the war and helped hatch a plot to kidnap a German general."

Sally commented, "I've read somewhere that the trouble was that the reprisals on the Cretans by the German army were fearful, and he felt implicated."

David told me he had read that Leigh Fermor was now working on a book on the Mani, a wild promontory in the southern Peloponnese.

We returned to the discussion about what we planned to do once we arrived. "One of my introductions is to a person in Corfu, the Greek widow of an English admiral, by the name of Vaughan-Hughes. She's from an old landed Corfiot family. She lives at Kouloura, on the narrow straights at the north end of the Corfu channel, a bay we'll pass on our way to the town of Corfu. I've kept her phone number safe. I want to see if we can visit her. She may help us."

I was glad Peter and David had not quizzed me as to the household where I had been working. What I vividly remember at that brief meeting in London with this man Leigh Fermor was the mischievous twinkle that had come into his eye when he heard that I would be working in the household of the Grand Marshal of the Greek Court, and him doodling on the list of names and telephone-numbers, drawing an exploding bomb alongside one or two of the names.

All the next day it blew too strongly for us to leave Othoni, but Sally and I climbed the three-thousand-foot hill, from which we had a magnificent view of the mainland and all the surrounding islands. Two tiny Byzantine chapels clung to the hillside at the top. The Greek American, like everyone else, advised us to keep well clear of the Albanian coastguards, who would shoot if we came within range.

Othoni to Corfu Town (August 18th)

Two days after our arrival we set off at 5.30 am, and at that time of day the sea was calm. We sighted five minesweepers we thought might be Albanian – and shortly afterwards a sudden fog enveloped us. We slowed down the engine, keeping just enough speed to have steerage-way. Then as the fog cleared, we continued south-eastwards. In the log Sally wrote, *13.13. Under fire (but Peter says it is a minesweeper signal).*

In the event, the general vote was that we should go straight on and get to the harbour in Corfu, without trying to stop. After that gunshot from the direction of the Albanian coast, we were nervous. Perhaps it was just a signal between the minesweepers, but we would be wise to take no chances.

So we went straight on, towards the city of Corfu, through the straits between the north end of Corfu Island, and the Albanian mainland. We cut across the bay, making for the city we saw gleaming in the distance.

It was evening when we arrived at the harbour. Sally and I took our papers to the Port Authorities, feeling quite pleased with ourselves. But it was clear at once that we were in big trouble. Because of my six months in Greece before going up to Oxford, I was fairly fluent in modern Greek, and I was the spokesman, so I took the rap. They told me roundly that the straits between the island of Corfu and the Albanian coast were forbidden to all shipping, and we ought to have known that. Shipping was expected to go right round the island of Corfu and approach the port from the south. Kouloura was in a military area, and we would even need a special permit to visit Paddy Leigh Fermor's Greek friend, Mrs Vaughan-Hughes.

7. A Barn for Laying Up the *Crab*

Corfu To Kouloura (Sunday August 19th)

The following morning, we had a long trek from one office to another in order to acquire the necessary permit to go to Kouloura. We were not able to get through on the phone to the lady at Kouloura. It was not till 4.30 pm that we set off from Corfu Harbour north-westwards up the coast, to visit Mrs Vaughan-Hughes at Kouloura, so it was not surprising that we were overtaken by nightfall. In the dark we put in to a bay which we reckoned must be Kouloura. We lit a small fire and started to cook our supper. Someone materialised out of the darkness - a gendarme of some sort. What were we doing here? We showed him our permit.

"But Kouloura is not this bay, it is the next one."

"Can't we stay here the night and move early tomorrow morning, when it is light?"

The policeman was adamant that we must move. Apparently Kouloura Bay was a different district, and we would no longer be his responsibility.

"Go quietly," he said, "The Albanians BOOM BOOM!! if they hear you."

We rowed quietly round the headland, and in the darkness almost bumped into a fishing boat moored at the entrance to the next bay. A figure rose up, and splashed off ashore. When we went ashore with our mooring-line in the darkness ourselves, we were met by a very grumpy policeman, who had been pulled out of his house by the figure from the fishing boat shouting "the Albanians have invaded and where is our policeman? Fast asleep!"

When the policeman saw our permit, however, his mood changed abruptly. It seemed that the lady we had come to visit, Mrs Vaughan-Hughes, owned the whole bay, including the land on which his police station was built.

Kouloura to Corfu (August 20th)

Early next morning we called on Mrs Vaughan-Hughes, who lived in a splendid, old, Venetian-style castle on the edge of the water, from which she had a commanding view of the straits. Many years before, she told us, not so long after her admiral husband's death, some naval ships had passed through the straits and she'd hoisted his white ensign on the flagpole in salutation. This apparently was a serious breach of naval etiquette - the white ensign was only to be hoisted on board ship, and only when an admiral was on board. She told the story with relish.

Mrs Vaughan-Hughes was generously open and welcoming. When we arrived she was supervising a complicated task: there was a visiting seamstress at work, re-covering down-filled pillows with new pillow-ticking, while two other women were putting all the mattresses out in the sun, and beating mats hanging on a line. She explained to us that these were lean times, and she tried her utmost to find jobs that could be done in-house so as to give people from the village the occasional chance to earn money.

On her advice, we aimed to move back down the coast a few miles to the bay of Dassia. For a very modest sum, she said, we would be able to anchor close to a good supply of fresh water and scrub out the boat and our belongings. She pressed us to keep in touch and visit her again before we left Corfu.

As we sailed back towards Corfu City, we sighted the fluttering flag of the recently arrived Club Mediterranée holiday resort - early warning of the tourist swarm that was to overrun island Greece in the coming years. Just one Tahiti-style straw hut could be glimpsed under the trees, behind a high wire fence. Noise pollution in the form of loud, non-stop music reached us across the water - but Greeks love noise; we were the odd ones out.

At midday we arrived back in Corfu, and mid-afternoon decided to move to the Old Harbour, where there would be less disturbance from the wash of big ships. There we met Umberto Cutajar, the British vice-consul from whom we had received that cable in Syracuse, assuring us "Conditions here normal". The dressing-down we had received in the office of the Harbour Master had given us to understand what "conditions here normal" meant, in the context. Cutajar told us he had expected a seventy foot boat, not a boat of seventeen feet in length. We must have been a source of deep disappointment, but he continued to treat us with courtesy. He showed us a commodious place where we could leave a seventy foot boat for the winter. The price was well out of reach for us. We would have to try our other contacts, and look for a place out of town, we told him.

Crab's voyage around Corfu

Corfu Old Harbour (August 21st)

Some days are like a game of Snakes and Ladders. David and Peter set off for a day's sight-seeing at Palaiokastritza, at the northern tip of the island. But they missed the only bus of the day. Sally and I, on the other hand, managed to get through on the phone to my other contact in Corfu, a member of the Aspiotis family, and he was very welcoming. He suggested the possibility of his cousin Mme Theotaki looking after *Crab* for us for the winter. She was widowed, managing an estate at Krevatsoula on the water's edge, not more than about five miles from Corfu. With her, we would be closer to town - and we would not be in a military area. He offered to phone her on our behalf. We began to realise how different the culture was from in Italy, here in Greece. Here wandering seafarers seemed to be made welcome, instead of being regarded as deluded, if not totally mad.

Corfu to Dassia (August 22nd)

This was a day of paying calls. First we headed for Krevatsoula and dropped anchor. We waded ashore and met Mme Theotakis and her companion Mme Moucha. Mme Theotakis said that, provided we could acquire the necessary permits, there would be no problem about laying up the boat, and showed us a barn on the water's edge where it would be under cover for the winter. We couldn't believe our luck. Her advice was to move down the coast to Dassia, where there was a good supply of fresh water, and once all was clean and snug for the winter, we would bring her to Krevatsoula for beaching.

By bus to Corfu (August 23rd)

It was decided next morning that I - as the only Greek speaker - should go back by bus to Corfu for supplies and still more permits, leaving the other three to rinse salt out of the sails, and scrub and de-rust and grease or repaint, ready to lay the boat up for the winter.

The bus left very early, and I arrived in Corfu as children were going to school. There was rain in the offing by the smell of the air, but it was a beautiful early morning. I was alone, and I relished it.

My way led past the Orthodox Cathedral, where a queue had formed stretching out of the door. On a sudden impulse I joined the end of it. After a bit of silent shuffling forward I fell into conversation with the people around me in the queue. I learnt that we were queuing to touch the mummified body of Saint Spyridhon, to pay the saint our respects. He was a very ancient saint, I was told, who had lived at that point in history when Constantine gave the church official recognition. Bishop Spyridhon had attended the very first Council, at Nicaea, in 325 AD. He was such a holy man, my neighbour said, that when he died at the age of eighty, his body, instead of decomposing, had remained intact. And it was still intact, to this day.

"He is a good friend to us Corfiots - and you don't even have to be Christian, he answers the prayers of Jews too," said my neighbour. "He is a miracle-worker. He saved us from a plague. And he saved us when the Turks invaded our island. He was a very simple man, even though he was a bishop. Throughout his life he lived as a shepherd, it was work he had done since childhood."

In the queue there were schoolchildren, calling in on their way to school. My neighbour even told me that the day before the local football team had come, dressed for the game, before setting off for an away match. Most of the others in the queue seemed to be peasants from the countryside. Others, well-to-do elderly ladies, looked as if they were visitors to Corfu. I surrendered to the mood of respect and quiet expectation, taking my lead from the children. Moving forward, I suddenly found myself close to the bier. It was an extraordinary feeling, to follow behind the woman in front of me and kiss the stony-hard brow of someone who had lived seventeen centuries earlier. Afterwards I sat briefly on a bench in the quietness of the cathedral. As I got up to go I felt a touch on my elbow. One of my neighbours in the queue had sought me out to give me a pamphlet about Saint Spyridhon, in French and English as well as in Greek. I would read it later, I said.

But when I emerged into the street huge dark blobs were appearing in the dust - it was about to pour with rain. So I dived back into the Cathedral for shelter, and to find out more about the saint. With relish I listened to the drum-beat of rain on the Cathedral roof. How wonderful to be under a solid roof just now, not crouching under a piece of canvas! I learned that Spyridhon had been bishop of Tremithus in Cyprus. Many centuries later that town was razed to the ground by our Richard Coeur de Lion. The saint's relics survived that invasion, and were then moved to Constantinople. In the mid-fifteenth century, his followers had brought his body here to Corfu to keep it safe from the Muslim invaders.

According to the leaflet, quoting from the *Great Synaxaristes of the Orthodox Church* (the Greek *Lives of the Saints*), the first Council was on what we now call the Arian heresy, and the eloquence and learning of those who advocated the doctrine seemed to be swaying the assembly. They argued that Jesus was not co-eternal with the Father, but a creature made by God, through whom God created the world. It was impossible that the same being could be both God and a man. Finally Spyridhon, the uneducated bishop of Tremithus, rose from his seat, asking to be heard. Holding a simple clay tile aloft in his hand, he began to speak.

Just as it is impossible to put the breadth of the oceans into a small vase, likewise it is impossible for the human, finite mind to contain the infinite breadth of the incomprehensible Divinity. Therefore, so that you might believe this truth, look carefully at this small, humble object… I want to prove the truth to you before your very eyes, from this common tile which is composed of three elements, and yet is one in substance and nature.

So saying, St Spyridhon made the sign of the cross with his right hand, and holding the tile in his left said, "In the name of the Father". At that moment the flame with which the tile had been baked rose up out of the clay, to everyone's astonishment. The saint continued, "And of the Son," and before the eyes of the assembly the water which had been mixed with the clay came streaming out of it, "And of the Holy Spirit", and opening his hand the saint showed that in his palm was only the dry earth from which the tile had been moulded. The result in the Council was consternation, the leaflet said, and the impressive rhetoric of Eulogius did not win the day.[6]

It seemed to me that perhaps the saint's greatest miracle was to have made the people of Corfu still so devout and devoted to him, sixteen hundred years after his death.

I completed the permits for laying the boat up at Krevatsoula, and did the needful shopping. As I sat on the jolting bus that was taking me back to Dassia I thought about the Orthodox concept of God as Trinity, God as companion and partner, three-in-one, rather than God as boss. I became aware I would need to get my northern and Protestant head into a different mind-set.

I climbed down off the bus near Dassia at 2.00 pm. The other three had been scrubbing, de-rusting with emery-paper, and repainting. But for the rest of the day it rained. In the evening we made a trip to Krevatsoula to deposit the clean dry sails and some bundles of rope, and then had a long-drawn out meal at the Nausikaa Taverna on the shore, where there was shelter. Nausikaa - who was the proprietor - was insistent that two of us at least must stay the night because of the downpour: the rules of hospitality were paramount. So we drew straws, and David and I were the unlucky ones, who were to sleep on the boat under the awning, while Sally and Peter slept at Nausikaa's cafe, with Sally in Nausikaa's bed, and Peter on the floor at her feet, while Nausikaa made do in the kitchen.

Krevatsoula (August 24th to 25th)

We set off at crack of dawn from our anchorage at Dassia, and by 7.45 am were unloading the boat, ready for pulling her up the beach. Mme Theotakis sent someone to Dassia to fetch an additional helper. It took nine people to pull *Crab* on rollers up a steep part of the beach. Once she was high and dry there was yet more scrubbing and painting to be done. Mme Theotakis had coffee brought to us, and a bunch of wonderful grapes picked from the vine against her house.

The following day, a Saturday, we finished painting *Crab*. At lunchtime, with the help of every able-bodied person who worked on the Theotakis estate, we tilted her on her side, eased her through the entrance into the

[6] Quoted from *Life of Saint Spiridon,* in *The Great Collection of the Lives of Saints* by Saint Dimitri of Rostov. Translated from Russian. Chrystosom Press. In progress.

barn, covered her with an awning and sewed her in – the best we could do, since there was no room to roll her bottom-upwards.

Then Mme Theotakis invited us up to her house. It had been the family home for generations, she said. Half-buried by its garden, the house was crammed with ageing treasures, including Wedgwood willow-pattern plates on the walls which the family had acquired a century before. It was powerfully evocative of home to recognise the familiar willow-pattern.

There are moments in one's life which transcend time and stay vivid – reaching the front of the queue to greet physically St Spyridhon by touching the stone-hard knees was one such; it is a moment still vivid to me now. Another was encountering those willow-pattern plates hanging on the wall of a Greek family house half submerged in old vines on the shore of the Ionian Sea.

On Sunday August 26th the four of us left with great regret for the overnight journey to Brindisi on the ferry boat. Plans were already taking shape for next year's sailing among the Greek islands, in preparation for an eventual journey to Istanbul.

*

Two months later, almost simultaneously with the Suez Crisis, the Hungarian Uprising exploded on the western world. Between October 23rd and November 10th, for a heady few days the frontiers were down, and some 200,000 Hungarians, mostly young people, escaped to Austria and thence to the west. Near London, families were asked to take in as many young people as they could house, until a more permanent place could be found for them. Robin's mother accepted two young men and a girl. Robin's older sister, by then working as a journalist, seems to have learnt Hungarian just as fast as they picked up English. She and Robin spent the whole of the Christmas holidays in their company.

But the event even had an impact in North Wales. Only eight miles away from my home, in the sleepy little town of Tremadoc, a house temporarily empty had been offered to house young Hungarian escapees. The Women's Institute rallied round with winter cardigans and blankets. Once their immediate needs were met, word went round that what they most wanted was people of their own age whom they could talk to. My brother Robert was fluent in German and French. We realised we could travel round the estuary by train to visit them; we did not need parental transport. So we spent many hours with them, and they coloured our political awareness. I began to read newspapers avidly, especially the feature articles, and become more aware there was another world behind the Iron Curtain, that frontier we had been so close to when we had reached Corfu.

3 The Ionian Isles, Mainland Greece and Beyond (1957)

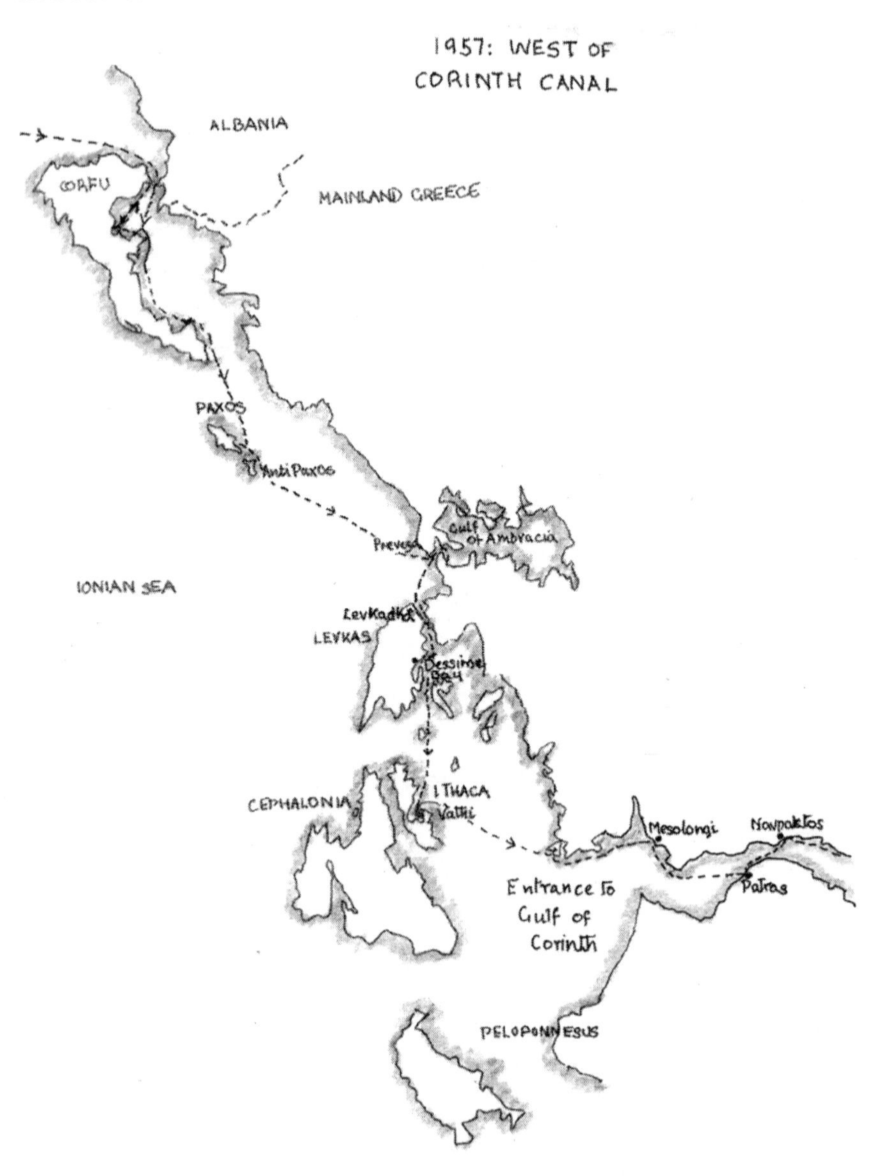
1957: WEST OF
CORINTH CANAL
ALBANIA
CORFU
MAINLAND GREECE
PAXOS
Anti Paxos
Preveza
Gulf
of Ambracia
IONIAN SEA
LEVKAS
Bessimse
Bay
ITHACA
Vathi
CEPHALONIA
Mesolongi
Nowpaktos
Patras
Entrance to
Gulf of
Corinth
PELOPONNESUS

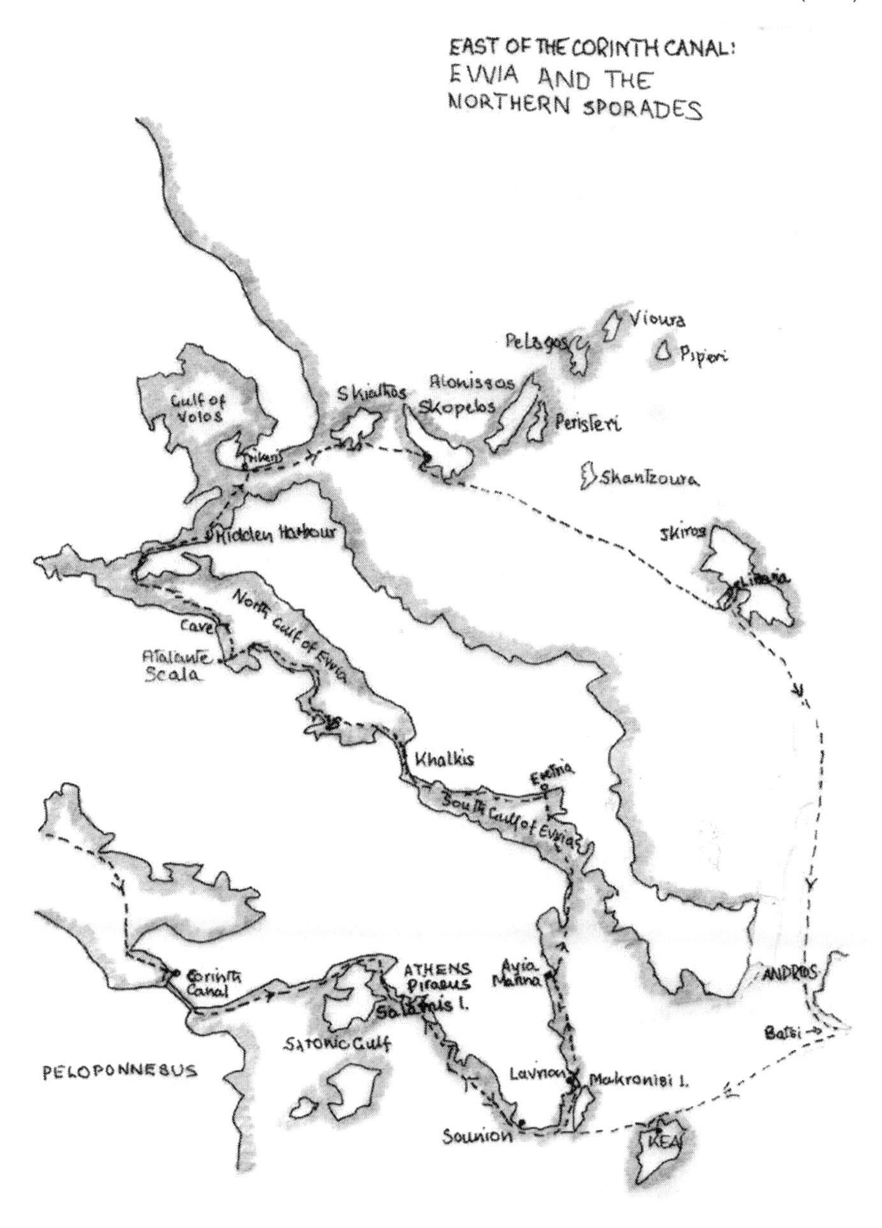
EAST OF THE CORINTH CANAL:
EVVIA AND THE
NORTHERN SPORADES
Vioura
Pelagos
Piperi
Alonissos
Skiathos
Skopelos
Peristeri
Gulf of Volos
Shantzoura
Hidden Harbour
Skiros
North Gulf of Evvia
Cave
Atalante
Scala
Khalkis
Eretria
South Gulf of Evvia
Corinth Canal
ATHENS
Piraeus
Salamis I.
Ayia Marina
ANDROS
Batsi
Saronic Gulf
PELOPONNESUS
Lavrion
Makronisi I.
Sounion
KEA

ITHAKA

Setting out on the voyage to Ithaka
You must pray that the way be long,
Full of adventures and experiences.
The Laistrygonians and the Kyklopes
Angry Poseidon – don't be afraid of them;
You will never find such things on your way
If only your thoughts be high, and a select
Emotion touch your spirit and your body.
The Laistrygonians, the Kyklopes,
Poseidon raging – you will never meet them,
Unless you carry them with you in your soul,
If your soul does not raise them up before you.

You must pray that the way be long;
Many be the summer mornings,
When with what pleasure, with what delight
You enter harbours never seen before;
At Phoenician trading stations you must stop,
And must acquire good merchandise,
Mother of pearl and coral, amber and ebony,
And sensuous perfumes of every kind;
As much as you can get of sensuous perfumes;
You must go to many cities of Egypt,
To learn and still to learn from those who know.

You must always have Ithaka in your mind,
Arrival there is your predestination.
But do not hurry the journey at all.
Better that it should last many years;
Be quite old when you anchor at the island,
Rich with all you have gained on the way,
Not expecting Ithaka to give you riches.
Ithaka has given you your lovely journey.
Without Ithaka you would not have set out.
Ithaka has no more to give you now.

Poor though you find it, Ithaka has not cheated you,
Wise as you have become, with all your experience,
You will have understood the meaning of an Ithaka.

C. P. Cavafy[7]

---

[7] *The Poems of C. P. Cavafy*, translated by John Mavrogordato (Hogarth Press, 1951, pp. 47–8).

1. Corfu, Island of the Phaeacians

Corfu Town (July 22nd)

To reach Corfu, we travelled by train to Brindisi, then by ferry, deck class - myself, Sally and Maggs Whitehead, then a student at Bristol University, who had been my closest friend from the years before Oxford. Sally was going to spend the forthcoming year at the British School, and had brought with her a trunk full of clothes for the winter, and books and papers for her research. The trunk was also a useful place to pack all our charts. Her plan was to ask Mr Cutajar to help her get said trunk overland to Athens. This he agreed to oversee. But when she unlocked the trunk to extract the charts, she found they were not there - she had forgotten to pack them. A skipper without a single chart to refer to! There was no question of asking her parents to sift through her untidy stock of charts and select the ones she would need and post them out to her - even the prospect of parcelling and packing them would be daunting, let alone trying to select the right ones. The ever-encouraging Mr Cutajar said he could get the charts we would need and have them sent direct to Corfu.

We would be joined after five days by Robin, who would take responsibility for the engine. Robin was now working as a teacher in Hackney, in the East End of London, a job which gave him the long summer holidays free for sailing. We hoped that before he came we might succeed in meeting up with our tutor Isobel Henderson, whom we had so narrowly missed in Crotone the previous year.

Krevatsoula (July 22nd to 28th)

Here is my first letter home:

We found Crab in such an undisturbed state two families of mice were nesting in her. They had eaten away most of the bung, as happens to the villains in fairy-stories, but luckily no holes in the planks. Until two days before we came, the whole potato-harvest was heaped round her, they told us, but when we arrived the barn was beautifully clear. At the other end of the shed are two olive presses, one of which works by a donkey walking round and round, and the vats of waste from the pressing were still there. They smell rather foul till you get used to them. We have been living in great luxury, with a stream nearby for washing and for drinking water, and presents of plums, new-made bread, cheeses. For my kitchen table I use the window of the barn, which is huge, and the sea is straight outside, within throwing distance. Yesterday everyone on the estate, including some visitors who happened to have come, were collected for pulling Crab out of the barn (we painted her inside). They took one barn door off, and the other fell off, but she stuck firm between the doorposts, and had to be pulled back and tried a different way twice.

These people took immense trouble, hanging all the sails and ropes up so that the mice should not get them, and storing the boxes and engine in a dry loft, and then they brought it all down again just before we came... (Letter to my parents, July 1957)

The place was idyllic. Who expects to find themselves camping in a barn whose end wall was within sound of the sea, and which was so broad that the window sill, though uneven, could be used as a kitchen table?

*

It was our third evening at Krevatsoula. We finished putting away brushes and tins for the night and stood contemplating *Crab*, now afloat, an ink-black profile against the hazy mountains of the Albanian coast, which lay bathed in evening light – a moment of contentment.

Behind me I heard the sound of a distant car, and turned and looked back. The dry sand immediately behind us was marked by the deep line gouged by *Crab*'s keel, and by the jumble of footprints belonging to the men of the Theotakis estate who had helped drag her out of her winter quarters to the edge of the sea that morning. In the evening light we could see a blue Volkswagen Beetle winding its way down the track that linked the Theotakis estate at Krevatsoula with the coast road. This must be our supper guests – our tutor Isobel Henderson and her friend Honor Smith, a doctor. We hurried across the dry sand to greet them as they got out of their car.

"But you're FILTHY, the two of you!" exclaimed Isobel, "I've never seen two girls so absolutely filthy!"

Moment of dejection as I realised we both had a good coat of antifouling on ourselves, as well as on *Crab*. My friend Maggs was not quite so messy. How had Sally managed to get some of it even on her back? We explained that a boat has to be launched even before the antifouling has set hard, in a hot climate like Greece.

"No, it's not just the black stuff. I can read the whole history of what you have been doing! Three or four days of cleaning rust off all your metal objects, I would say, then applying anti-rust primer, and painting the topsides of the boat etc. And we had hoped to take you out to drinks across the bay to the bar at the Club Mediterranée! And now you are planning to cook us supper with hands like that! Where's the meths or turps or whatever - come on, we'll scrub all three of you."

This wasn't what I had expected. Two weeks earlier we two had received our Finals results - Sally a First, I a Two-One. Receiving them had marked the beginning of life as full adults: leaving the cocoon of Somerville College would surely put a subtle barrier between us and the denizens of that former life. As I submitted to having antifouling scrubbed off my back (apparently I had more even than Sally), I realised my Greats tutor had never been what I expected. I still remember being sent to her for being caught climbing into the college an hour after lock-up. Instead of lecturing us, she told us how she too had been caught climbing in. In her case she had been the Somerville Junior Fellow. Returning from a fancy-dress party, to which she had gone dressed as a lobster, she found she had to make use of the route through the bathroom window of the college dean, because the college gate was already locked. The dean came into the bathroom through the door as she came in through the small window. After that she decided to live out, not in college.

Skin tingling from the scrubbing, we walked with Isobel and Honor round the curve of the bay to the bar at Dassia, where the nucleus of a prospective Club Mediterranée was being rapidly expanded, its assembly-kit Hawaiian-type huts multiplying by the day.

"We've got the bar to ourselves," said Sally with satisfaction. "The serious drinkers are still probably having siestas in their huts. We wanted to come early so there would be time left for cooking before darkness fell completely."

Sally and I had planned the feast together. We wanted to say thank you to Isobel for more than two years as our tutor, and particularly for the stimulus of her fortnightly teaching sessions at her house out in Park Town. There was still more: she had helped Sally apply for an Archaeological grant that would give her a year at the British School at Athens, and she had even found a slice of the grant for me. This was to fund me the following year to work on a site in Crete for two weeks, and then to research into ancient merchant-shipping routes as Sally's second in command.

What we set before them was intended as quite a grand meal – the centre-piece was *filets de boeuf flambés, Avignonnaise.* It required a "small, thick fillet of beef for each person", a slender loin, and a slice of bread to slip under it. Alas, the "fillets" in the butcher in Corfu were thin and very sinewy, but I had determined this would be the evening's dish. "Put a little butter into a thick pan, make it very hot, and put in the fillets." Our frying pan was not thick, and I had difficulty in finding butter. But I did sizzle the meat until the fillets were very brown, and I did then add more butter, and as soon as that had melted I drenched the pan with brandy and set it alight. In the evening light, with a backdrop of Albanian mountains, it certainly looked impressive. The meat turned out to be tough and gristly – it was probably goat, which I was too naïve to realise. We had supper under a big tree on the shore, watching the sun go down.

"The generosity of Mme Theotakis is amazing," we said. We told how they stored the metal boxes and the engine in a dry loft and brought them down just before we came, and of the little presents of home-grown food that arrived to encourage us.

Isobel and Honor had briefly glimpsed the Theotakis family house when they arrived, and remarked how impressively solid and ancient the house and its surroundings looked. The place seemed to have grown out of a Venetian coastal fort. It was clear that the terrace had been as it was a long time, with the vines huge and ancient and gnarled, the paths grown narrow.

"One thing is fairly clear," our visitors remarked. "The owners aren't from Athens, on a whistle-stop visit to their holiday home."

Far from it! The estate was a living community. Most people existed hand-to-mouth as Greece gradually recovered from four years of German occupation, followed by civil war. The town of Corfu – like the town of Zakinthos also – suffered from both German and Allied bombing, and rebuilding was a slow process.

I told them of a conversation with M. Mouchas, the husband of Mme Theotakis' companion. She had arranged for me a lift with her husband in the car to Corfu town. Cars were a rare luxury at that time. By way of small talk, I said to him that the Corfu countryside looked rich because it was so green. I said it in Greek accidentally, not in French, as I realised when he answered me in Greek. He gave me a fierce lecture on how the only rich soil in Greece was in Macedonia and Thessaly, and how in spite of its green appearance most of the land I saw was so poor it was only fit for making bricks.

"You know Lawrence Durrell's book, *Prospero's Cell*?"[8] asked Isobel. "He published it around the end of the war, 1945 or thereabouts, but it is based on his pre-war time living on this island. What a contrast! It's a simple life, people make a living by fishing mainly, but there's a reasonable amount of prosperity - a sense of contentment."

"These people here in the big house have been so friendly to us," Sally said. "They have even told us to take any fruit or vegetables we want from the garden! Mme Theotakis showed the three of us round the house last night, and it's lovely - very old. And some lovely old furniture, also some Wedgwood dishes with a bluish-grey design and some gilt on, marked Wedgwood with a triangle and a rosette and a D - apparently an heirloom which came into their hands originally when the English left the island."

"You are so lucky in this family here," Isobel replied, "Lucky as Odysseus when he got to Phaeacia. Corfiots claim this *was* Phaeacia, by the way."

"Local traditions of how to treat strangers seem to be still around."

"But they aren't escorting us to show us the way," I complained. "All we've got is the Admiralty Pilot, which is designed for big naval vessels. And we scarcely ever meet another yacht to share knowledge with."

"I should imagine that the other minus factor is that on *Crab* you get even less shelter from the wind and waves than you would have had in a Homeric ship," Isobel put in. "There you could at least crouch in the forepeak, or if it's a bigger ship, there's the hold."

"But the plus is that we get to sleep under the stars, night after night."

Honor Smith asked us our immediate plans.

"We plan to leave here on Sunday. Then we will probably spend one or two days in Corfu itself, stocking up, and meeting Robin, our ship's engineer, off the Monday ferryboat. After that we will sail south - Levkas - Ithaca - then Mesolongi."

---

[8] Prospero's Cell: A guide to the landscape and manners of the island of Corcyra [Corfu] (Faber & Faber, 1945).

"In Mesolongi look for the memorial to the Philhellenes - the foreigners who fought in the Greek War of Independence, alongside Byron."

"And your plans, Isobel?"

"One of the places we are going to is Ithaca. We'll tell them to look out for you, and be nice to you. I'll tell the draper, who is an important person there."

It was near midnight when we waved as the blue rental VW departed up the long track to the tarmac road.

*

Krevatsoula to Corfu (July 28th)

Next morning, Sunday, we ran into problems. Before we could set off for the big city, we would have to grease the gearbox. And on Sunday morning we found that the grease gun seemed to be broken. Sally and I loaded the engine on board, and rowed across the bay to the Club Mediterranée at Dassia in the midday heat, to find someone who could grease it for us. *Place is full of seductive wenches in bikinis,* wrote Sally in the logbook, in disgust that we never found an engineer to solve our problem for us.

When we got back we found the staff of the estate lined up for formal adieus, with much handshaking and wishing *kalo taxidhi.* I was very moved by the warm open-heartedness of the people of the Theotakis estate.

Meanwhile Sunday had more surprises in store. The Mouchas family had invited their distinguished neighbour Admiral Lepas for cocktails, and two American naval attaches and their wives had been invited to meet him - and, so it turned out, had we. For us it was not leisurely at all - without being given time to change out of shorts, we were dragged off to meet the guests. The American couples were excited to meet us, and produced a cine-camera, at that time a great rarity.

"The Captain wants the crew of Ulysses' boat in his picture. My girls will be just thrilled to see this."

Fortunately by afternoon a delightful south wind sprang up. Even though the engine was out of action, we were able to hoist sail while still at our moorings and leave in style. Corfu town was about five miles from Krevatsoula, a journey in *Crab* that day of two hours.

Corfu Harbour (Sunday July 28th – Tuesday July 30th)

We anchored in Chondra Fossa - Narrow Ditch. We found there was a *festa* under way, with bands parading on the waterfront, and a game of cricket. We knew they played cricket on Corfu, a relic of the days of British occupation, and I had somehow expected the formality of English cricketing attire. I was disappointed to find the teams were in vests or even had bare backs. Following the cricket there was a game of football, and a *dromos* - a race, with seemingly all the young men competing. Around us were ice-cream carts, peanut men, and stalls selling hot *tyropitta*. It was the first time any of us had tasted these cheese pastries, a mouth-watering Greek speciality made with feta cheese and filo pastry, the pastry turned over and cooked a second time to avoid the typical sogginess of English pastry.

We asked if we could see the church.

"The church is closed, because it is Sunday."

I spent some time exploring the old port, tucked in below the citadel. Not much room for anchoring. Yet Thucydides tells us that it was in Corfu, at about the same time of year as we were there, that the fleet assembled for the Athenian attack on Sicily. *Most of the allies, with the ships carrying corn, and the smaller craft, and the rest of the equipment, had received orders to assemble at Corcyra* (Corfu), *so as to cross the Ionian Sea in one body.*[9] It was easy to imagine that vast fleet anchored in the bay which we had just passed in *Crab*. There seems to have been a re-think, for Thucydides tells us that in the event the fleet was divided into three sections, which were to set sail separately, so that they did not experience difficulties with getting sufficient water, or a safe anchorage. The scale of the expedition was unprecedented. Here is Thucydides' vivid description of the Athenian fleet setting off from the Piraeus:

The Athenians themselves, and any of their allies who were in Athens at the time, went down to Piraeus at dawn on the day appointed, and manned the ships for putting out to sea. The rest of the people, in fact almost the entire population of Athens, citizens and foreigners, went down to Piraeus with them. Those who were natives of the country all had people to see off on their way, whether friends, or relatives, or sons, and they came full of hope and full of lamentation at the same time, thinking of the conquests that might be made, and thinking too of those they might never see again, considering the long voyage on which they

[9] Thucydides, *The Peloponnesian War,* translated by Rex Warner (Penguin Classics, 1954, p. 427).

were going from their own country. At that moment when they were really on the point of parting from each other, with all the risks ahead, the danger of the situation came more home to them than it had at the time when they voted for the expedition. Nevertheless they were heartened with the strength they had and with the sight of the quantities of every kind of armament displayed before their eyes. As for the foreigners and the rest of the crowd, they came merely to see the show and to admire the incredible ambition of the thing.

...The fleet was in a high state of efficiency and had cost a lot of money both to the captains and the State. Every sailor received a drachma a day from the Treasury, which also provided empty ships (sixty fighting ships and forty for the transport of hoplite-soldiers), all manned with the best crews available. The Captains too offered extra pay...and they went to great expense on figure-heads and general fittings, every one of them being anxious that his ship should stand out from the rest for its fine looks and for its speed. As for the land forces, every one of them had been chosen from the best men who were liable for calling-up, and there had been much rivalry and much pains spent by everyone on his armour and personal equipment.

...When the hymn had been sung and the libations finished they put out to sea, first sailing in column and then racing each other as far as Aegina. So they made good speed on their way to Corcyra, where the other forces were assembling.[10]

We spent Sunday night in harbour in Corfu. Mr. Cutajar hailed us with the news that the charts had arrived. Early on Monday morning we visited the harbour-master's office, but found no-one. At last, at 9.00 am, the proper official came. He gave us a travel pass permitting us to stop anywhere on our route from Corfu to Piraeus, instead of insisting we specify where we expected to stop each night. Mr Cutajar brought the charts to us on the boat.

At midday we collected Robin off the ferry boat, and in the evening we made a dinner party for Mr Cutajar, who was from Malta. He seemed to enjoy the evening, though he spent most of the time telling us how he had looked after Onassis when he came to Corfu, and saying "But why don't you buy a bigger boat?" That evening the wind was from the east, but there were clouds round the summit of Mount Pantocrator, which Mme Mouchas had told us meant that the wind would be from the north.

[10] Thucydides, *The Peloponnesian War.* Trans. Rex Warner. London: Penguin, n.d. Book VI, Section 31, pp. 427–9.

Corfu Town to Leucimme (July 30th)

Next morning it was not till 11.00 am that we set off. We rowed and pushed *Crab* through the shallow south entrance of the moat, where there was scarcely eighteen inches depth, but with many willing Greek helpers. Was it that they were intrigued that anyone should go to sea in a boat of quite such shallow draft? Or was it Greek hospitality and generosity? With the ship's engineer at last on board, we headed under engine for Cape Kanoni. At about 11.00 am the wind came, and we hoisted sail and set off southwards, heading for Paxos.

It was two years since Robin had sailed on *Crab*. Coming straight from a summer term spent teaching in a school in Hackney, he had had no time to get acclimatised and sunburnt before we set off. Sally wrote to her parents:

...It is lovely to be on the move again. At the moment we are all rather at the stage of having to cover ourselves up to prevent sunburn, especially Robin who has wound himself up in the jib till he looks like a corpse ready for burial overboard, but in a day or so we shall all be happily chocolate-coloured, I expect.

2. Advice Ignored

How a four-horse team
whipped into a run on a straight way
consumes the road, surging and surging over it!
So ran that craft, and showed her heels to the swell,
her bow-wave riding after, and her wake
on the purple night-sea foaming.
Hour by hour
she held her pace; not even a falcon wheeling
downwind, swiftest bird, could stay abreast of her
in that most arrowy flight through open water.

Homer[11]

Corfu to Paxos (July 30th to 31st)

Our own journey was somewhat less idyllic than Odysseus' homecoming to the shores of Ithaca. We had our supper on the move, and, as dusk was falling, spent our first night at anchor off a small jetty near the salt-factory in Levkimmis Bay at the southern end of Corfu. Next morning we headed first for Sirota, a tiny rocky island covered in dark woods, then set our course for the twin Paxi islands. On the way we passed a *caique* with two masts, the main mast carrying a square sail, like an ancient merchant ship.

At five in the evening, with the wind freshening, we reached Porto Gaio on Paxos, a mouse hole of a harbour, with houses like tight-packed white sugar-knobs. Inside the harbour the water was still and serene, the houses reflected in the water. All of us except Sally were very seasick from those first two days at sea, and took some time to recover - it was as much the effects of exposure to sun and wind and spray, hour after hour, as the boat's motion. A friendly woman took us to her house and helped us wash the salt out of our clothes - the openness and kindness of Greek women never ceased to take us by surprise.

The curiosity and persistence of small Greek boys also never failed to surprise us. Throughout the evening the small boys on the quay plied us

---

[11] *The Odyssey*, translated by Robert Fitzgerald, (Book XIII, ll. 100–109, Everyman Library, 1992 p. 232).

with endless questions. Finally, for some peace and quiet, we rowed away from the quay and anchored for the night off the little island of Aghios Ioannis in the middle of the harbour.

Paxos to Preveza (August 1st)

By 7.00 am next morning we were under way. Our next stop would be on the mainland. We were planning to go inland by bus from Preveza, a harbour town at the mouth of the Ambracian Gulf, close to the stretch of water where the famous sea battle off Actium took place.

Actium was one of the strangest sea-battles in history. Strange that Romans were fighting against Romans: Octavian, later the Emperor Augustus, was fighting Mark Anthony, Cleopatra's lover; and that it was at sea, which was not the Roman metier. Strange because of the presence of Cleopatra in person, along with her fleet. Strangest of all was that near the beginning of the battle, Cleopatra suddenly hoisted sail and sped away southwards, although Mark Anthony at that stage had the odds on his side. He felt he had no alternative but to follow her, as vivdly described by Shakespeare in the play *Antony and Cleopatra*.

The new city of Nicopolis which Augustus Caesar founded to celebrate his victory at sea over Anthony and Cleopatra lay northwards from Preveza. Sally mentioned that Mark Anthony had had a daughter called Antonia by his wife Octavia, sister of Augustus, and that she and her son Germanicus, with a flotilla of six triremes, had anchored at Preveza, where we were heading. This Antonia never saw her father, of course, since he was already dead months before she was born. She was in her fifties when she accompanied her son Germanicus on this tour, bound for Trebizond on the Black Sea. For Germanicus, who was immensely popular and a charismatic general, tipped to be the Emperor Augustus' successor, it was an official state visit. I wondered what his mother Antonia would have felt privately, visiting this bleak site where her father's fate had been sealed. The formal focus of Antonia's visit would have been the state reception in Nicopolis. It must have been bittersweet to her, to be wined and dined by the dignitaries of a city founded to celebrate the final defeat and disgrace of her illustrious father. But, even though disgraced, Antonia inherited her father's Egyptian estates.

Although the flotilla of triremes reached Trebizond as planned, Antonia had returned to Rome alone. Her golden son Germanicus had died inland under suspicious circumstances after a banquet. In Rome, Antonia used all her resources and high connections to pursue the matter in the courts, but got no redress. The Emperor Augustus was succeeded by the unpopular Tiberius.

Hustled along by a fresh north-west wind, we reached Preveza as the light faded, and found a place where we could tie up to the quay. Preveza stands at the mouth of the Ambracian Gulf. East of us, the pale blue waters of the Gulf stretch away into the distance, a seemingly endless land-locked expanse. We were mesmerised by the mist-clad mountain range towering above the shore of the Gulf to the east of us. We knew that Preveza was on a bus route and we would surely be able to catch a bus up into the mountains, if not to visit Dodona, at least to reach the lakeside city of Ioannina. Two members of *Crab's* crew went ashore to glean information.

We learnt that at 7.00 am a bus would leave for Arta, the junction for the road to Ioannina. Maggs and Sally elected to go. Someone had to stay and guard the boat, as always. Robin and I agreed to stay.

Sally, Robin and I were classicists, but Maggs' passion was history. The Peloponnese had been Turkish for more than three hundred and fifty years, she told me, and some of the rest of what is now Greece remained under Turkish control as late as the twentieth century. But Ioannina was famous for its prosperity and as the seat of the fiercely independent pasha, Ali of Tepelen. Byron was his guest once, and his impressions of the pasha were vivid:

His highness is sixty years old, very fat and not tall, but with a fine face, light blue eyes and a white beard. His manner is very kind, and at the same time possesses that dignity which I find universal among the Turks – he has the appearance of anything but his real character, for he is a remorseless tyrant, guilty of the most horrible cruelties. Very brave, and so good a general that they call him the Mahometan Buonaparte… He has been a mighty warrior, but is as barbarous as he is successful, roasting rebels etc etc.[12]

The night at Preveza was restless – it appeared that the place where we had anchored was the rightful property of a mosquito and his wife and extended family, and they made clear their feelings towards us with persistence throughout the hours of darkness. We woke very early as a consequence, and Maggs and Sally left in good time for their 7.00 am bus.

---

[12] Letter to his mother from Preveza, dated November 1809, quoted in *The Flame of Freedom*, by David Brewer, John Murray, London, 2001, p. 36.

The north-west wind still blew briskly. Robin and I spent the whole morning spring-cleaning the boat, which was much easier when there were fewer people on board. Robin had come out for nearly five weeks. It was good to have someone with a longer-term interest in the boat.

In the heat of the day we relaxed with Robin's *Guide Bleu* to find out about Ioannina, and in particular about Ali Pasha. It was hard to take in what we were reading because we were so steeped in the classical period. So far as we knew, at the end of the classical period the Greek nation had disappeared underground into a tunnel from which it had only recently emerged. But now we learnt that there was very colourful history in between, particularly at the outset of the nineteenth century. We learnt that the brigand chieftain was already forty-nine when he became Pasha of Ioannina in 1788. It was a huge town for those days - 21,000 inhabitants, almost entirely Greeks, but with 2,000 Jews. It was a centre of learning, where literary Greek, Latin and French were taught at an advanced level. Ali Pasha was an international figure, famed throughout western Europe. France, England and Germany all had consulates in Ioannina.

We read about the commercial wealth, about the power of Ali Pasha rivalling even the *pashalik* of Egypt, and about how the Turkish sultan became worried by his defiant independence, and in 1820 tried to relieve him of his post. Ali Pasha resisted, offering his Greek subjects the bait of an independent state if they came to his side. He held out against the sultan's army of 10,000 besieging him until February 1822. We read about the drama of the death of this fierce old man. Penned up in a monastery on an island in the lake, he locked himself into an upstairs room. He was shot from below, through the floor. Meanwhile, all over Greece the local population rose in revolt against their Turkish rulers - including in Mesolonghi, where we were heading - and in Patras. Robin and I were fired with longing to come back one day and visit Ioannina.

*

At evening the other two rejoined us. To get to Ioannina and back would take more than a day. They were very disappointed. We realised how inadequate the infrastructure still was in the country, how fragile the economy, with people still on the edge of starvation - certainly with no money to spare for riding far on buses. In Western Europe we had already had almost twelve years of peace and reconstruction since the end of World War II... Here in Greece the German Occupation had been followed by a civil war.

The north-westerly was still blowing, kicking up a wild area of white horses in Preveza Strait. The advice from the fishing boats moored round us at Preveza was that we should wait till the wind dropped before setting off, which would probably be two days at least. Instead we decided to move inside the Gulf and spend the night somewhere more sheltered, and perhaps leave early, before the wind had had time to get strong. The Ambracian Gulf is sheltered from the sea by the promontory of Actium. We opted for the inner shore of Actium promontory (where Mark Anthony had had his fleet), and found a sandy cliff close under which we could anchor. This promontory was where Mark Antony had encamped his troops before the battle on September 2nd, 31 BC, a vast area sheltered from winds from the west, where his fleet could safely lie at anchor alongside the troops. It was a good, sheltered anchorage. The disadvantage was that we were alone, with no fishing boats to consult as to the weather forecast before setting off.

Preveza to Levkas Bridge (August 3rd)

Early next morning the decision whether to set off that day or not seemed such a minor one. Yes, there had been a lot of wind in the night, but now - dawn - it was amazingly quiet, though it was cloudy, which was unusual. Yes, the fishermen at Preveza had told us yesterday evening that we should wait a day at least. But we would be quite close to land; it was not like setting off to cross the Gulf of Taranto, or worse still the Adriatic Sea. Ten miles or so to the south of us lay the island of Levkas, barely separated from the mainland. In the channel between island and mainland there would be sure to be shelter.

There was so little wind at 6.15 am when we set off that we left under engine. But once past the protection of the promontory of Actium, we found a lively north-west wind was blowing. At the middle pair of buoys in Preveza Strait we hoisted our storm sails - sails made of canvas designed to withstand an Atlantic gale. Wind and seas were constantly increasing, and at the outer pair of buoys we decided we must haul the engine on board for safety, tying it down amidships.

After we had changed to storm sails, Sally put me at the helm. In this situation, running downwind, the helm was generally given to me. I had grown up on the edge of an estuary where the spring tides ran at up to four knots, and if tide was running against wind, short steep seas would be pulled up in a matter of minutes. The waves were now of a considerable size. It was exhilarating to be at the helm in this weather. It was not just a matter of co-ordinating hand and eye, and the feel of the wind on my cheek. I sat perched up on the gunwale so as to be able to swivel round and see what was coming up behind, being constantly drenched with cold spray. My oilskin jacket had a hood of course, but I could not use it because I needed to have all-round vision.

"I wish I had the eyesight of a woodcock – they can see directly behind them!" I muttered to Robin, who was close to me.

"Really?"

"They can, Robin! They feed in mud, and predators would be able to get them while their bills are immersed. So Evolution has produced a bird with eyes in the back of its head! Wow! That was a big one! This is fun!" I exclaimed, trying to convince myself that I wasn't at all frightened.

The wind was impressive now. It tugged at the small sail, visibly lifting the boat as the gusts came. The helm was hard to control. This was unlike any conditions I had met. In the estuary if a sudden gale blew up one could anchor and ride out the gale till the tide dropped and one could wade home.

In a wind like this I had never actually been at the helm. Here there was no alternative but to push on. These waves started somewhere in the northern end of the Adriatic, and had rolled their way southwards, gaining momentum. They were as big as elephants, and I was scared.

My chief difficulty was that the wind was on our quarter, which meant our course lay diagonal to those waves. Whenever a particularly steep wave rose up behind us I would have to swing to meet it fair and square, the pointed stern directly cutting it. If I should turn the boat too late, and catch a big wave on her quarter, she would be swung round sideways by the wave's impact. The technical word for this is "broaching-to". If we were to broach-to in this way, and the boat were to lie sideways to wind and wave, the full force of the wind would suddenly hit the mainsail, at a moment when we were already tilted by the overtaking wave. We would turn over – everybody and everything getting tipped overboard as if dumped by a dumper truck. With one hand on the tiller, in my free hand I grasped the rope that controlled the foot of the storm mainsail. And in order to keep swivelling round every few minutes to see what was coming up behind us, I still sat perched up on the gunwale, with no hand free to hold on with. I remember like yesterday the utter drowsiness induced by being constantly drenched with cold water, till I was chilled to the marrow. Once I almost went overboard – I must have momentarily fallen asleep. What was worse, I had the tiller firmly grasped in my hand as I began to fall – the crew would have lost their tiller as well as their helmsman. Sally raised a strong arm and grabbed the tiller; either Robin or Maggs must have grabbed me.

We intended to aim for the harbour of Levkas, but the entrance to Levkas Sound was impossible to make out, the island lying so close to the mainland. Ahead there was no other vessel which might have indicated the route to us. Visibility was poor – the air laden with fine spray. Robin moved close to me, singing a seemingly endless repertoire of Irish folk tunes in a soft voice, to keep my spirits up.

Maggs drew my attention to a *caique* which had become visible behind us, under shortened sail, but overhauling us. It was enormously comforting to see another boat in the distance. All of a sudden Maggs, who was baling, shouted that it was gone. She had seen it keel over and disappear. None of us three saw what happened, all we knew was that it had been close enough behind us for us to hazard a guess – from what we could see – that there was only one man on board, and then suddenly it had disappeared from view. We knew we ought to go back and try and rescue that man we had seen at the helm, but we also knew we would never make headway against that sea under sail with *Crab,* and that lifting the engine and lowering it overboard to mount it onto its brackets, would have been out of the question in such rough water. No one said anything. Words couldn't help in this situation.

I don't think Sally realised how serious our own situation was – or else she was too dazed with cold to realise anything till we got quite close to the shore of Levkas and still could not make out the harbour entrance. We were now rapidly approaching to a shore which consisted of a harbour-wall built of boulders and concrete, but we still could not make out the actual entrance, and the sea was as rough as ever. I shouted to her that we needed her, and it was her sharp eyesight that first made out the entrance to the Sound. She guided me towards it, and then, quite suddenly, we had rounded the harbour-wall and were in quiet water. We were safe!

We were safe, but we were still travelling at five or six knots. I was stiff with cold and exhaustion I suppose, because before I could turn *Crab*'s head to the wind we hit the quayside head-on with our prow. I still recall that resounding thump, and my cringing embarrassment.

Alerted I suppose by the loud thump, people emerged from a little café on the Levkas quayside. I remember their bemused faces, and them helping us ashore, stiff and dizzy with exhaustion, and the owner of the café insisting on giving us glasses of *ouzo* to revive us.

We sat recuperating at a table in the little *kapheneion*. We must have been there at least for an hour. In our dazed state, we saw a woman come in with some news that was causing a stir.

"What are they saying?" I asked the café owner.

"A fisherman capsized just this morning and his boat sunk. But he swam and the wind blew him to shore."

The good news was a huge relief, especially to Maggs who had actually seen the boat suddenly capsize and sink. We struggled to our feet to thank the woman who kept the café. "Photograph!" she said. Robin offered to go back to the boat and fetch his camera. We lined her up with us, soignée in her green jacket and neat headscarf, whereas we had not even had the energy to peel off our oilskin jackets, let alone try and run a comb through salt-caked hair.

The good news gave us the energy to get on our feet and go back on board. The wind was still buffeting, but the sun had come out. When we stepped down into *Crab* we found that salt had dried and crystallised on the benches, so that everything one touched felt gritty. We hoisted the storm sails and, timing our approach so as not to collide with the chain ferry, sailed close under the walls of the Venetian fort of Santa Maura, with its elegant aqueduct, and continued our journey, following the narrow channel that separates Levkas from the mainland. Here there was less wind than outside, and the water was smooth. We longed to find somewhere with a supply of fresh water, so that we could wash. Our faces were rimed with salt. Robin's hair was so stiff with salt it stood on end, Mohican-style.

"I love you when you're totally focussed at the helm," Robin said to me quietly. "I've not met anyone else with that power to be so focussed."

"You mean – even when I hit the wharf? I did it on purpose of course – to tell people we had arrived!"

3. More Ionian Islands

Levkas Town to Dessime Bay (August 3rd)

Forty-five minutes later we reached Levkas port, and moored off the quay, right next to a gleaming yacht named *Aegean*. It was the first yacht we had encountered in Greek waters. Only mythically rich people like Onassis owned yachts in Greece, we had concluded. We spoke with the crew. The *Aegean* had come from Athens. The owner (who was absent) was an American, the crew consisted of a Spaniard and two Greeks, and there were some French passengers. The skipper (also absent, on a shopping trip) was someone Sally was to meet again in Athens - he was currently head of the Classical Association in Greece. His wife was Greek, and had previously been married to a Greek poet.

Sally had been on two family holidays to Spain and spoke some Spanish, and got on famously with the Spanish member of crew, who was from Majorca. They had a conversation in a mixture of Spanish, French, English, Italian and Greek. In the absence of his skipper he invited us on board for *ouzo* and showed us all round the boat, which was most luxurious, with a brass dolphin figurehead.

After talking with them Maggs and I went ashore in search of provisions. I had quite forgotten that Levkas had been flattened by an earthquake in 1948, and then shaken again in August 1953 by the earthquake that flattened all Kephallonia's beautiful Venetian buildings.

The 1953 earthquake had occurred shortly before I left Greece after my first six month stay. I was fluent enough in Greek then to be able to listen to the news as it unfolded. I was also able to get a first-hand account of it from a writer friend, Kay Cecillis, eight years older than me, who worked for Athens Radio - another of the contacts from Paddy Leigh Fermor. When the earthquake occurred she was in her home town on Kephallonia, which lies alongside the small island of Ithaca. Later she turned her experience into the novel *Death of a City.*[13]

People were rebuilding their own houses. A local style had developed - corners were defined by a solid pine pillar, squared off and topped by a

[13] Kay Cecillis, *Death of a City*. First published in English in 1953.

carved capital, and all the upper walls were of corrugated zinc, white or colour-washed. We saw whole families at work. The streets were narrow, presumably just as they had been before the earthquake, so that no vehicle bigger than a laden donkey or a motorcycle could negotiate them. First-floor balconies jutted out above the street, and washing was draped from balcony to balcony. The town had an idiosyncratic, indigenous feel. Years later that I learnt that the reason for the local style was a government regulation, which said that upper storeys must not be built of masonry. Apart from that, people had a free hand.

Oh, to be able to rinse the salt from our clothes and dry them and ourselves in the sun! We talked to the captain of a *caique* moored near us, who reckoned the storm would continue for two days. After lunch we left, hoisting the storm mainsail and scudding southwards down Levkas Sound with a fresh following wind.

The Levkas channel opened out, but it was still relatively sheltered. We were determined to reach Roudha Bay on the southern tip of Levkas before night, a good stepping-off point for Port Polis on Ithaca. But two miles short of it we found ourselves becalmed. So much for the three-day storm! We rowed back to a deserted bay called Dessime we had passed earlier. Not a house in sight. One of the most beautiful anchorages I have known.

We dropped the anchor over the stern, and let the boat drift towards the shore. We would take a line as`hore and wrap it round a boulder, so that we could land and have a walk, and then pull in on the anchor rope so as to be further away from the shore for the night. Stepping ashore, we found ourselves quietly greeted by a family of Greek peasants who were already there. We apologised for intruding. They protested they were glad to welcome us; it was seldom they saw anyone. They offered us a drink of cool water, by way of hospitality, and delicious home-dried raisins, showing us a few vines which they had planted nearby, and their orchard. They said their winter house was near to the *kapheneion*, at the head of the bay, but they also owned this small patch of land on the water's edge.

For their summer home they had made themselves a platform in a tree on the water's edge. A cheese in muslin hung from one corner of this platform, so they must have goats. And a fishing boat was moored a little way away, along the shore. There was a well, and they invited us to take as much water as we liked the next day, and wash the salt out of our hair and clothes.

We sat in the cool of the evening talking with them for some time. The fisherman did not tell us we ought to have a bigger, faster boat, as the Italians always did. Instead he told us how, during the German occupation, in a boat no larger than ours, and moving only during the hours of darkness, he had travelled regularly to Methone on the southern tip of the Peloponnese and to villages on Corfu, in search of provisions.

We shook hands and said goodnight, and the roughness of the mother's palms took me by surprise. Clearly their life was incredibly hard, compared with anything I had experienced, and yet as a family they seemed utterly content, rooted in their own place. When I thanked them, the mother said it had been a pleasure to make us welcome; "Zeus protects the stranger," she said, by way of explanation. The first time I had heard those words.

The family had told us they had plenty of water. We cleaned our teeth, changed into warm clothes for the night, and stretched out on the benches to sleep, relaxing into the welcome of the smooth horizontal surface, hard though it was. I was deeply moved by the evening's encounter. These people seemed to be giants of endurance, of skills and strength. When I later looked at the photos taken by Robin I realised how, like Gulliver, Sally and I towered over them.

I thought over the day, and the kindness of the people in the little *kapheneion* near Santa Maura fortress, where we had staggered in, exhausted, after we had so nearly drowned ourselves. And I realised also that from now on things were different between me and Robin. The sound of his quiet singing of Irish folksongs, close by, had seen me through what had been the scariest hours of my life.

I reckoned I was quite adept at resisting the easy charm of good-looking undergraduates, but I could not resist the lure of a good voice quietly singing. It had melted my heart and there was no undoing of that.

Dessime Bay to Vathy on Ithaca (August 4th to 6th)

We spent an idyllic Sunday morning washing our clothes and drying them spread out on the sun-baked rocks. At midday we set off, intending to reach the place on Ithaca we had set our hearts on reaching, the small harbour of Port Polis on the western side of the island.

For visitors to Ithaca, the obvious place to anchor is Vathy, the port at the head of a long bay where the ferries call, an easy half hour from the southern tip of Levkas. But our plan had been to spend the night on the western side of the island. Fifteen minutes walk uphill from Port Polis was the village of Stavros, and excavations in the thirties had established that a settlement flourished on nearby Pelicata from 2200 to about 1200 BC. The village stood on a site on which in all likelihood once stood the town that nestled below Odysseus' palace.

We had left under engine because there was no wind, but wind there soon was, and from the wrong direction. By 1.30 pm we found ourselves butting into a choppy swell from the south-south-east. We were off Cape Ducata on the south-western tip of Levkas, Port Polis in view, but it was clear we were making no progress towards it. So we hoisted the storm mainsail and ran back eastwards to a deserted island that lies in the straits, Arkhoudi. We fetched up under the north-eastern side, and rowed into a bay below a ruined house. Two fishing boats were already sheltering there. They gave us bait and told us how to fish. Their friendliness and unquestioning kindness was overwhelming.

Sally wrote to her parents from Arkhoudi, where we lay at anchor waiting for the wind to moderate:

It is sad we have been held up, as it means we will have less time for exploring Ithaca and the other Ionian islands, but they are very lovely just to sail past – great high mountains, and white cliffs with pine woods on top, and lovely deep blue sea. Lots and lots of little islands as well as the four main ones, which I hadn't realised before. (August 4th 1957)

We would have to lower our sights, and be content with putting in at Port Vathy, the ferry-terminal for the island of Ithaca. This was not the Ithaca we dreamt of. We tied up against the harbour quay at midday. Vathy had been an attractive little harbour town, with a diminutive Venetian arcade leading to the waterfront. The earthquake of 1953 had destroyed it. This arcade was re-built clumsily in concrete. It is hard to conceive anything uglier than the chunky, grey, elephant-legs of that once elegant little arcade. Maggs even now remembers the surprise and disbelief she felt as we came towards the quay, and found most of the town in ruins. She still remembers that sense of shock, and empathy with the people who had to somehow cope, their town obliterated, and their houses unsafe to enter.

We stayed overnight, but reluctantly. We would have preferred to be in some deserted bay and dream of Homeric voyages. But Isobel Henderson, true to her word, had spoken of us to the draper. His nephew (who was called Adonis) insisted on giving us coffee and grapes when we went to the café in the evening, and they all had tremendous respect for the name of Oxford.

Moreover, I discovered that next morning would be a feast-day of a patron saint. This was to be celebrated in the chapel on the little wooded island in the middle of the bay. The island had been used by the occupying imperial powers in previous centuries first as a prison, then as a *lazaretto* (a quarantine station). Robin and I got up while the others were still sleeping and joined the families crowding onto a *caique* to troop across to it.

The chapel was already full to overflowing by the time we got there at 7.00 am. Overcrowding did not matter, since everybody stood, and people could gather four deep around the open door. I joined the women, most of them in black, and Robin went to stand with the men. I looked at the weathered faces of the women, now deep in prayer. We left again halfway through the first part of the service to rejoin the boat - by 8.30 am we were under way.

One of my favourite poems in my final year at university was Cavafy's Ithaka, which I have quoted at the beginning of this section. For New Year 1954 Donald had given me a copy of the collected poems, translated into English by John Mavrogordato. I thought about the poem as the island receded behind us. I suspected that it was too soon to visit Ithaca, too early in my life.

A restless night on Oxeia (August 6th to 7th)

Our destination was Mesolongi, but we knew it was more than a day's journey for *Crab*. A long steep island lay directly in our path - Oxeia, an island so barren as to be almost uninhabited, close up against the mainland, notable mainly for the powerful lighthouse at its southern extremity. A huge hillside towered up to the north of us, dark and veiled with a scarf of mist on its summit - it reminded Sally of that Gothic novel *The Mysteries of Udolpho*. We anchored in the anchorage marked on the chart on the south-eastern side, but it was steeply shelving, and poor holding-ground. At one in the morning Sally and I were woken by the sound of swell on the shore and the rocking of the boat. The wind had shifted round to the south-east, and at any minute we would start to drag anchor and be washed onto the shore. Rousing Robin to get the engine started, we raised the anchor and motored off cautiously northwards for forty minutes to the Limen Petalas, through the darkness. As soon as we were in shallow enough water we dropped hook again, sat up for half an hour to see whether the anchor was dragging, and then went back to bed. And so passed our last night among the Ionian Isles. Tomorrow we would be at Mesolongi.

4. Mesolongi –First Taste of the Greek Mainland

Oxeia to Mesolongi (August 7th)

Ahead towered the Pindus Mountains, an impenetrable range separating western and eastern Roumeli. It was an impressive sight, to look up at that wall of mountains ahead from a small boat with only eighteen inches of freeboard.

By land, armies invading from the north had to come either to west or to east of that landmass, and the route was wild and rocky. Mesolongi stood on the western side, and it was the first harbour. It was a town in the middle of a waste land, its sole source of wealth fishing for grey mullet and harvesting the highly-prized roe.

Looking at the chart, we could see that ahead was an inhospitable shore. There was no harbour before Mesolongi. The Admiralty Pilot was not encouraging, warning that the coastal strip up to a mile offshore was or might be a military area. Nevertheless, for a boat like *Crab,* Mesolongi was an obvious place to stop - provided we could find it, lurking hidden among mudflats and shallows.

When Byron crossed from Cephalonia to Mesolongi in midwinter of 1823/1824, during the War of Independence, this town was under siege by the Turks. Byron died only three months after landing. Worn down by frustration and endless mediating, he died of a fever which flared when he was caught in a heavy downpour while out on horseback drilling his Souliot troops. But his death achieved far more than his living presence at Mesolongi could have achieved.

*

Slowly, so slowly, we crept towards Mesolongi in *Crab*. We knew the harbour would be hard to identify. The wind was light and changeable, and at 2.00 pm we had only reached Cape Scrofa, the first piece of low-lying Greek mainland. We ambled slowly along eastwards, under full fair-weather canvas. The advantage of this was that it provided some shade; the disadvantage that, with our big spinnaker, our view was severely restricted. It billowed out ahead of us, swaying as the wind shifted. But as the heat of the afternoon wore on, gradually the wind picked up, and off Tholi Island we lowered our spinnaker. Suddenly we had an unrestricted view. Quite close ahead of us was a flat little island we identified as Tourlis because of the causeway we glimpsed behind it. Tourlis was, in Byron's day, the Fort of Vassiladhi, an important Turkish gun emplacement. It was here that the landing-pier for ships visiting Mesolongi was located, and the Customs and Health offices. We were still about two and a half miles away from the town.

There were formalities with passports, but the people in the harbourmaster's office were very welcoming. From where we were moored against the quay, on our left we could see a string of buoys receding northwards, and decided to follow them, but cautiously. To starboard was the causeway, with a very occasional vehicle. The port bank was marshland, lined in a random way by fishermen's houses on stilts. There was no sign of power or telephone lines. Each little house had room perhaps for a smallholding, each a flat-bottomed boat moored to a very makeshift jetty. The occasional bleat of a goat, or the voice of a cockerel asserting his territory, floated to us across the water. We glided slowly up channel, passing one buoy after another, and finally fetched up in a harbour basin used by *caique*s.

In harbour at Mesolongi (August 8th)

Next morning Robin, Maggs and I set off to visit antiquities, while Sally, who was not feeling well, stayed with the boat. She wrote to her parents:

I have got a touch of tummy-trouble, very slight, and am looking after the boat…I am having a luxurious and very funny time, as we were moored off the harbour-master's office and when he heard I was ill he carried out a bed and put it in the shade, so here I have been lying, writing letters and being questioned and being given cigarettes and advice on how to treat my "estomacho" by everyone who passes. It is now siesta-time so there are odd sailors and people spread out on mattresses all round me.

If you were going to be ill, Mesolongi was the place for it! Greece had taken Lord Byron to its heart, and we vagrant travellers were reaping the benefits of what he had given – his fortune, his time and his life.

Mesolongi was truly "in the midst of wasteland". The place seemed to be neither land nor water, and everything seemed to be covered in a fine grey dust. The town was built on a spit of land projecting into a lagoon most of which was only two or three feet deep. It was stiflingly hot, a humid heat not typical of Greece. We others had an abortive morning of taking the wrong bus and getting lost, but in the end we found a barren Garden of Heroes, the memorial to Lord Byron, and a museum, as Isobel Henderson had told us.

In the museum we found out what happened in Mesolongi after Byron's death. The Turks brought up huge reinforcements and subjected the town to two years of siege. Provisions ran out, the people were starving, so they decided collectively to make a break for it, an exodus. But the very old and the women who had small children could not leave, so they blew up their arsenal to prevent the Turks getting it, blowing themselves up with it. It was a heroic final gesture of defiance. The able-bodied tried to slip away during the night, but they were betrayed and ambushed. For some time their bones lay strewn on the hillsides, there being no one left to bury them.

Death on such a scale leaves its mark on the place; there was an ugliness and a lifelessness about the town. And besides, there seemed to be nothing left of the old Mesolongi. Even the house where Byron had died had been deliberately destroyed by the Germans during the Second World War.

On our way back to the boat at lunchtime, a fisherman outside his house called out to us. He was sitting on the ground, slitting grey mullet and taking out the roe, and he offered us some of the gutted fish. We accepted with pleasure. He explained he was taking the roe for *avgotaracho*, a kind of red caviar, which would be packed and hermetically sealed in beeswax. We talked with him for some time. His boat was one of the traditional flat-bottomed punts known as *monoxyla*. He said he was also expert at catching frogs. The whole town lived by exporting pickled frogs, and by catching grey mullet merely to use the sac of eggs within the females, but these luxury exports were a poor source of livelihood – he told us that people were desperately poor.

Immediately after we had eaten we left under engine, because there was not a breath of wind. The town was so low it had somehow disappeared from view before we had even reached the end of the causeway. As we headed out across the straights I looked back at the small island of Tourlis at the end of the causeway, little more than a currant bun. Fortified by the Turks when they were besieging the town of Mesolongi, and armed with three large cannons, this was the legendary Vassiladhi, which had been an impregnable fort. In 1827 Lord Cochrane, with a fleet of twenty-three ships, had failed to capture it. It was almost impossible, because the water surrounding it was so shallow.

But the island fort *was* once captured during that war, as I later learnt. It shows how Greek naval strategy was much more inventive and risk-taking than military strategy, much more open to cutting-edge technology. In the 1820s among the industrial nations a new force was beginning to need to be reckoned with - the power of steam. An English naval officer, Frank Hastings, had come to Greece to offer his services to the cause of Greek Independence, and successfully advocated that £10,000 from the Greek loan raised in London should be set aside to purchase one of these new-fangled steamships, so far used only as pleasure boats to convey day trippers. The Greeks were the first to use a steamship in war.

The year we visited, I957, was the 130th anniversary of the arrival off Mesolongi of an extraordinary-looking ship. Long and low, like a slug, without the customary snail-like aftercastle. It had four masts, in pairs. And between the two pairs was a tall black funnel as high as the masts. Most ships of the time - even those built for the peaceful purposes of trade - had an array of gun ports along the side. But this vessel's sides were cumbered by a huge pair of paddlewheels. This was one of the earliest steamships, named the *Karteria.* She had to burn either coal or charcoal - wood could not generate sufficient heat. She had been built on the Thames, under the supervision of her captain, Frank Abney Hastings, and her engines had been made by the firm of Galloway. Because there was almost no room for guns, the four she carried were very powerful, with twice the range of the guns on HMS Victory, where Hastings had served as a midshipman from the age of ten to the age of fourteen. She had sailed out to the Mediterranean through the Bay of Biscay. Like the rest of the Greek fleet, however, she was unable to get close to the fort on Tourlis because of the mudflats.

Captain Hastings well knew how shallow the lagoon was. He knew he had to be content with firing from a distance of a mile and a quarter if he wanted to avoid the risk of his ship getting stuck in the mud. But he had picked a day of flat calm, and his long guns could fire shells at an elevation of up to twenty-three degrees. The third shell, with the elevation calculated and the gun pointed by Hastings himself, landed plumb in the arsenal of the fort, which blew up. Hastings gave orders to man the ship's boats and capture the fort. Rowing the intervening mile and a quarter, they found a scene of utter bewilderment: a thunderbolt had come inexplicably out of the blue sky, the Turkish soldiers shouted, and had exploded the arsenal. The boat crew found the dead bodies of twelve men, and took prisoner the other bemused thirty-nine in the fort.

The sequel to this feat of marksmanship is wryly told by Finlay in his *History of the Greek Revolution*:

These prisoners were then taken on board the Karteria, but Hastings, who had been feeding his crew at his own expense for some time, resolved to put them on shore as soon as possible. He therefore informed the commandant of Vassiladhi that a 'monoxylon' (canoe of the lagoon) would convey him to Mesolongi, to enable him to make arrangements for sending off flat-bottomed boats to land the prisoners without loss of time. The Mussalman, remembering the manner in which both Turks and Greeks disposed of their captives, considered this to be a sentence to an honourable death. He supposed that he was to be taken to the nearest shore where he could receive burial after being shot, and he thanked Hastings like a brave man, saying he was ready to meet death in any way Hastings might order. The conversation passed through an interpreter, and Hastings being the last man on the quarter-deck to perceive that it was supposed to be his intention to murder his prisoner, the scene began to assume a comic aspect. The Turk was conducted to the gangway, where, seeing only a monoxylon, and one of his own men to receive him, he became conscious of his misunderstanding. He then turned back to Hastings, and uttered a few expressions of gratitude in the most dignified and graceful manner. The rest of the prisoners were landed the following morning, and an interchange of presents took place, the Turk sending some fresh provisions on board the Karteria, and Hastings sending back some coffee and sugar.[14]

*

We chugged away from Mesolongi on just such a day of flat calm as Frank Hastings had had, and looked back at Tourlis - Vassilhadi as was. Our next stop was Patras, the city that lies on the southern side at the mouth of the Gulf of Corinth. We wanted to be there before nightfall. Normally we avoided big ports, but this time we had no option, since we had arranged to drop off Maggs here for the boat to Brindisi, and to pick up a new member of crew, Ken Pitchford, a bearded American whom Sally had enrolled.

---

[14] George Finlay, *History of the Greek Revolution* (Part 2, p. 23, Zeno Press, 1971. First published 1877).

5. Nero's Silver Shovel

Patras (August 8th to 11th)

We had wanted to be safely berthed in the harbour at Patras before nightfall. But the sun set over the Ionian islands on the western skyline when we were still in the middle of the straits two miles from our destination. As soon as dusk fell we were able to pick out the Patras lighthouse signal. Once past it, we were supposed to follow a trail of leading lights that would take us to Aghios Nicolaos pier. But we were dazzled by the street signs along the harbour front, by the headlights of cars, and by the lights in the cafés that lined the waterfront. Eventually we found a pier, and guessed we must be in the right place because we recognised the outline of the very same yacht we had moored alongside in Levkas Sound, the *Aegean*.

With a sense of relief we tied up alongside. Luckily we found a place where there was a ladder built into the wall of the quay. The *Aegean* was the only yacht we had come across so far in Greek waters, and it was an excitement to find ourselves alongside it once again. It was also an excitement for their crew. The Spanish crewmember, Matthew Creux, treated us generously to drinks on board. Back at the boat, by the harsh and scanty light from the quayside, we cooked and ate the grey mullet we had been given that morning, and crawled into bed.

Next day turned out to be full of problems. At midday we went to dispatch Maggs on her ferry at 1.00 pm - only to find that it had left at 1.00 am the previous night. The next ferry onto which she could be booked was not till 8.00 pm on Saturday the 10th, so we would have to stay in Patras till then. Patras was not a place where we wanted to be stuck. The largest town in the Peloponnese, it had little to recommend it. How would we while away the time until we could be out on open water again?

Second problem - Sally had arranged to leave a message for the Bearded American at the office of American Express, but we could not find this office. Some instinct prompted me to go up to a large man and ask him where the office was. "I *am* the American Express." He told me proudly. But if the American Express was not an office but a large Greek who was walking about, how would our Bearded American find our message?

We were still carrying all Maggs' luggage with us. We decided to go back to the boat and deposit it with Robin, who was on guard-duty, and then go and find the market.

It was incredible to us young Brits to see market stalls piled high with deep glossy aubergines, brilliant peppers the colours of a Mondrian painting, tomatoes, grapes, still more to see live shellfish, and the shimmer of red mullet alongside the rosy pink of a cooked lobster. On the islands most people grew what they needed or went without, and there was little fresh food for sale at that time, so it was only when we came to a big city that we could indulge in the sensuous pleasures of an open-air food market.

*

Our second evening in Patras, with our boat full of fresh food and goodies, we gave Matthew Creux supper. As I cooked I noticed that a crowd had gathered on the quayside above us. In the cool of the evening, the entire population of Patras seemed to be strolling along the kilometre of waterfront. I heard people say,

"Now she's putting in paprika."
"No, it's turmeric!"
"Rigani would be better!"

I paused in my cooking and counted the onlookers. There were one hundred and forty-three. This was probably the biggest crowd we had collected, even taking into account the waterfront at Valletta, where we were shipwreck-celebrities.

After we had given supper to Matthew, he and Maggs and Sally went to the cinema together, as Sally described to her parents:

It was heaven as it turned out to be a Danny Kaye film called 'A Song is Born' with lots of Jazz and Louis Armstrong playing and singing. The Spaniard was very pleased with himself and treated us magnificently, ending up with a huge plateful of sticky cakes which he insisted on taking back to the boat for Penny and Robin (who were asleep, it being about 12.15), and which we all had to struggle through, feeling sicker and sicker and dropping pieces over the side whenever he wasn't looking. They still aren't finished! I think he liked us so much because he hardly meets anyone who can understand what he says (we only can in parts as it's largely Spanish and most of his teeth are missing) as he doesn't talk Greek, and anyway Greek girls are very prim and not allowed to go out with men. The other sailor on the yacht is Greek and seems to have relations everywhere so he has an unfair advantage.

As a result of all this feasting and staying up late we all have hangovers and have spent the last two hours or so flat out in the shade behind the café at the end of our pier, which has completely taken us under its wing, and allows us to sit, or sleep, or eat our lunch and use its lavatory – anything – and also supplemented the lunch today with a magnificent plateful of watermelon and ice.

While we were waiting to see Maggs on her way on the ferryboat, we made good use of the time. We varnished the spars, washed and mended our clothes, and mended the mainsail, which meant we had the painstaking job of unlacing it from the yard, and lacing it back again.

We also visited some antiquities. Patras is not an attractive ancient city, because when the Revolution flared up in the spring of 1821 the retreating Turks burnt the old city to a shell, so there are no pre-nineteenth century buildings. Sally and I went off to see the Venetian *kastro*, which had little of interest but a fine view of the Gulf of Corinth, and also the huge church of Aghios Andreas, which was situated right on the waterfront, on the site of an ancient Temple of Demeter. The building of this cathedral had begun in the 1920s, and it was not dedicated till 1974, nearly twenty years after our visit. It was shaping as a confection of red and yellow brick, with too much marble. It holds remnants of the cross on which the Apostle Andrew was crucified. The Orthodox tradition is that St Andrew had visited Greece and been martyred in Patras in 67 AD. Before that, chosen by lot to go as apostle to the city of Byzantium and to Thrace, Andrew had consecrated the first Bishop of Byzantium, and taught in the Danube Delta and around the Black Sea. Some traditions have it that he even travelled as far as Novgorod. Eusebius tells us he was chosen to go to the Scythians. And I learnt from a Scotsman that after visiting Russia he had crossed to Scotland. After surviving all those years among those savages, how ironic to meet his end in the so-called "civilised" Graeco-Roman city of Patras.

I was sad to see Maggs go. As I wrote to my mother, *When she's here conversation is about Byzantine history, or poets, or sharks – instead of just about practical things.*

There was still no sign of the Bearded American, and Sally decided we should stop waiting for him.

*

Gulf of Corinth: Patras to Itea (August 11th to 13th)

We had learnt from Robin's *Guide Bleu* that the idea of excavating a canal to link the Aegean with the Ionian seas had been around since classical times. According to Suetonius, the Emperor Nero had found detailed plans prepared by Caligula, and had attempted to cut through the isthmus: *Having made a speech to encourage his Praetorian Guard to set about the work, on a signal given by the sound of a trumpet, he first broke ground with a silver shovel, and then carried off a basketful of earth upon his shoulders.*[15] Caligula had sent him a workforce of 6,000 Jewish prisoners, but the distance was six kilometres, and the task proved too great. Work was abandoned, and not resumed until the 1890s, when for the first time the technology available was adequate.

Sally and I feared that we might not be allowed to go through the canal under our own power, and would have to be towed. The prospect of the canal alarmed me. Quite apart from the fact that the authorities might object to the fact that the skipper was a girl, with no formal qualification, would the boat ordered to tow us insist on towing us too fast, setting up stresses and strains that would mean the boat would begin to leak?

Robin's concerns were much simpler. He was determined that he would not pass Corinth without going to see the place where St Paul had preached, and without climbing Acro-Corinth, the Acropolis. He lodged his request with the skipper, who refused to make any commitment. He gritted his teeth.

We set out from Patras on Sunday morning, and crossed back to the north shore of the gulf. In the evening we reached the fort of Navpaktos, which guarded the entrance on the northern side, the fort which Byron had dreamed of taking by surprise in midwinter, capturing it from the Turks. It was off Navpaktos that the Battle of Lepanto had taken place, when the Turkish navy was decisively defeated by Don John of Austria. We climbed the hill so as to look down on the small harbour, with its massive bastions. The view was spectacular.

We worked our way eastwards along the Corinthian Gulf for the next few days. Mount Parnassus was always there in the distance, to north of us, head and shoulders above the other hills, its head veiled in grey swirls of cloud. Delphi lay there somewhere, nestling on the southern slopes of the mountain, out of sight from the sea. The plain between

[15] Suetonius, Lives of the Caesars: Nero.

Delphi and the gulf was famous still for its olive groves. We would not have time to go inland from its port of Itea and visit it. No tourists nowadays went up to Delphi from Itea, though it had once been a normal route for pilgrims from the western end of the gulf and beyond.

The Gulf of Corinth was too often windless, and the journey was slow. What was our reading-matter on board? The Bible which we girls shared was Elizabeth David's *A Book of Mediterranean Food.*[16] She agreed with the French chef Marcel Boulestin, who from 1906 made his home in London and also wrote cookery books, that peace and happiness begin, geographically, where garlic is used in cooking. On long days at sea Maggs or I would be reading devoutly one of the four gospels - Substantial Dishes, Poultry and Game, Vegetables, or Fish Shellfish and Octopus - and learning about how to tell an unsound from a sound aubergine, and how to stuff peppers. Elizabeth David commented that the Greeks more than any other people she knew had a culinary use for everything - anyone who had been in Greece for any length of time would be familiar with the eerie whistle coming from pigs' lungs in a frying pan, she said. I remember still the sound of an octopus being beaten against the quayside in the early dawn, and the warm smell of mountain herbs wafted across the water towards us from a sunny hillside as we approached our evening anchorage.

In Corfu we had acquired a big earthenware cooking pot for making *bourride*, which is a way of cooking fish such as grey mullet by poaching them, to be served up with *aioli*. In it we could also pot-roast the evening meal, using the charcoal from a small wood fire alongside, during the long midday break in some deserted bay. Some of Elizabeth David's recipes were for *klephti*-cooking - this meant actually wrapping the meat or vegetables in a casing of mountain herb sprigs, and burying it underground in hot ash. Cooking was done in this way so that the light of the fire or the whiff of wood-smoke could not be picked up by enemy soldiers - a way of cooking that came back into use during the years of Resistance to the occupying German forces.

Besides Elizabeth David, the Holy Bible was also read in the bows in the early morning quite a lot - Robin had a pocket Greek New Testament (which he still reads, sixty years later) and I a copy of the King James Bible, the pages so worn and huddled together by the stickiness of salt air and salty fingers turning the pages that it became harder and harder to

[16] John Lehmann, London, 1950.

use. Both of us had a pattern of trying to read regularly at night or else in the early morning, before the other two began to stir. Sally was of different stuff, and felt odd one out as regards reading-matter, as she had written to her parents in a letter posted from Paxos:

We are an astonishingly religious boatload, with Penny and Robin reading the Bible every night, and everyone rushing off to church from time to time (except me) which is rather extraordinary – as I am also the only smoker I feel very much the black sheep! (30.7.57)

For my part, a childhood of tagging along with my parents to church was followed by teenage rebellion and unwillingness, a period when I knew I didn't believe in God but still wrestled from time to time with what kind of a God it was I didn't believe in. But during the Long Vac the previous year I had come across an adult Anglican faith I welcomed - something very different from the moralistic faith presented at school. And for my final year I was to be lucky enough to be a lodger with Austin Farrer and his wife, in Trinity College. Austin, a New Testament scholar, and a brilliantly vivid preacher and writer, had been my brother Robert's inspiration when he was at Oxford, and had become a friend of our father Diccon.

As I visited Greek churches I was struck particularly by the way small children conducted themselves, very seriously lighting a candle and crossing themselves at the ikon of the patron saint of the church, and silently praying. In the Orthodox part of Christendom children are regarded as full citizens of the Kingdom, and receive the sacrament of communion even as small babies - more frequently then, in fact. This was most unlike the faith I was brought up in, which demanded that children should come to the age of logical understanding before being counted as full members of the church. This was a faith that seemed to be much less cerebral. The other difference was that the Eucharist was a drama that unfolded all around, instead of something performed two-dimensionally, up at the other end of the church. I found Orthodox services profoundly moving. Timothy Ware (now Metropolitan Kallistos of Diokleia), with whom I overlapped at Oxford, also reading Classics, was already intensely interested in the Orthodox part of Christendom, and I heard him speak once.[17]

---

[17] Timothy Ware, The Orthodox Church: An Introduction to Eastern Christianity (Pelican Books, 1963).

As the Gulf of Corinth gradually narrowed and the landmass to north and south closed in on us, we felt the atmosphere more and more airless and oppressive. Winds were light and capricious. Most of our progress was under engine, and places where we could buy petrol and two-stroke oil were hard to find. It was only the need to buy petrol that took us to Itea, where there was a surprise in store for us – this time a case of being found rather than of finding. We called there to restock with engine fuel – Itea seemed to consist of nothing except a godforsaken, barren quayside used commercially for the export of the olive crop. We bought petrol and two-stroke oil, changed money, and obtained some stores, and were about to set sail when a policeman called us back in a peremptory way. He told Sally that a member of our crew closely matched the description they had of an escaped criminal. Robin was ordered to step ashore, and was arrested and led away. Sally and I sat helpless. I wondered if one of us should try to go with him, but I did not volunteer.

I suppose it was only about an hour before Robin was back again, as cheerful as usual, but it seemed like much longer. He said that when they realised that in spite of his dark brown skin he wasn't Greek-speaking, interest dropped – the escaped criminal was Greek.

Itea to the Corinth Canal (August 13th to 14th)

Wednesday was the hottest day in a very hot week. There was not a breath of wind, and we were obliged to use the outboard engine hour after hour. We would have to stop yet again to buy petrol, going out of our way to Kiato, which would mean we would be late arriving at the head of the gulf. We knew from the *Mediterranean Pilot* that at the western end of the Corinth Canal there was hardly a harbour – you were expected to arrive during the hours of daylight, with several hours in hand before sunset.

In Kiato even the people who lived there complained of the heat wave. We felt oppressed and languid. We ate lunch in the water, on the shady side of the boat, eating watermelon with one hand, holding the boat's grab-rope with the other. But it hardly felt as if we were in the water, the heat was so oppressive. And it was not till 8 pm that we finally reached the head of the gulf.

It was dark. We could see a certain amount by the lights on the quays, but they dazzled us, so that we could not find the entrance to the harbour. We opted to anchor alongside a *caique*, and to our surprise bumped twice as we approached it. But as we got nearer we could see that it was up on legs on the shore! Eventually, creeping very slowly and taking frequent soundings, we found a berth and were able to settle down for the night. Fortunately there was no onshore wind.

Next morning our neighbours told us there was a fiesta, so we decided to delay for a day. This would give Robin a chance of a day's sightseeing in Corinth. For Sally and me, most of the time that day seems to have been spent on cleaning the boat thoroughly and washing our clothes.

The girls on the *Bonita* back in 1925 had made this same passage through the Corinth Canal in their fifty-foot yawl, without an engine. They were told they must be towed through the canal, but by seizing the chance to go at night when the canal was not in use, they actually managed to row their way through:

I am on watch with Hermine (the skipper). The nice little bed on deck, where I have not been to sleep, is piteously rolled up into a bundle. A faint, faint breeze takes us to the entrance of the canal. From the 'Instructions to Boats' we are aware that little sailing boats like ours do not have the right to pass without being towed by a steamboat, in order not to obstruct the entrance to the canal. We must wait till day, and a tow.

The cabin belonging to the canal supervisors is close at hand. We decide to ask them when we can pass...Who knows? Perhaps they will officially give us permission to sneak in; to get through by our own means, by rowing, before the main traffic of the day starts up. We should avoid showing these people, undoubtedly strict and surly, that our crew of five consists of two who are not yet adults, with a captain who is a young girl. With cap pulled down over her nose, wearing a heavy jacket, and speaking decisively, the 'captain' goes off in the dinghy to broach negotiations. We hear their conversation…this poor captain! Doubtless they take her for the cabin-boy!

They asked me how many men we have on board...I replied 'Five!' Laughter hastily muffled. The captain had given us orders to wear heavy jackets, so as not to blow the gaff, and with our hands in our pockets we wait.

We are all gathered on the bridge. At about four a.m. they shout to us to get ready. A steamboat from the eastern end is purring past us. Hermine is at the helm, Ella and I at the oars – Bonita's huge oars – now rowing, now backing-water. Ben [Hermine's teenage younger brother] helps us by towing with the dinghy, but as soon as there is a tow-path accessible, he jumps up onto it and tows Bonita with an improvised towline. Dawn begins feebly to lighten the sky at the exit of the canal. The silhouette of the great iron bridge spanning the canal becomes clearer. The current is helping us. We are already halfway through the six kilometre canal…

We begin to get the feeling that instead of pushing the oars, it is they which are pulling our arms, brutally. Ben, on the grey towpath, with the coil of rope on his shoulder, seems like an insubstantial little genie. The walls are so steep one cannot imagine how they do not cave inwards. And now the surface of the water and the sky ahead are all bathed in rosy light, though the sides of the canal are still in shadow...

Mariel relieves us each for a few minutes, time to draw breath, and return to work. We are getting near to the exit, but despite our efforts with the oars, a force seems to be holding the boat back – the current has begun to turn and flow the other way. Suddenly the tow-path comes to an end. Ben must get back on board. Hanging onto the halyard, he jumps and lets himself fall onto the foredeck, shattered with fatigue. This arm clamped to the oar no longer seems to belong to me, I am simply moving like a machine. At last! Here we are, bathed in sunlight, and again in open water…here are little white buildings, and caiques. We anchor near them, and go in the dinghy to pay our canal dues. Then, without setting things in proper order, we each crash out in our own corner, stiff with exhaustion and unconscious to the world.[18]

Through the canal (August 11th)

On Friday morning we approached the entrance to the canal - and were told to wait till it was the turn of the eastbound traffic. They warned us that there was a one knot adverse current, but made no objection to our going through using the Seagull outboard.

Our passage through was a vivid experience. It was 10.30 am when we were given the signal to go. As we entered the canal, the banks rose rapidly higher. Our speed was between four and five knots, which was *Crab*'s maximum. I had not expected the walls to be so steep. The sky receded - just a small section of sky straight above us. We felt so minute, dwarfed by those banks on both sides.

The narrowness of the canal meant we had blessed shade most of the way through. Alongside us there seemed to be the remains of a towpath. Oleanders had planted themselves in the sheer sides of the canal, and there were even pine trees, dwarf in size on account of the barrenness of the soil, but their roots strong and gnarled, groping for sustenance. There were plenty of varieties of grasses, including some pampas grass. We

[18] *Cinq filles en Méditerranée,* p. 150 (Author's translation).

glimpsed rock pigeons, but not much other wildlife - probably we were going too fast to be able to spot much. The canal is 81 feet wide, and 3.2 miles in length, and the limestone walls rise to the height of 250 feet in the central section. A narrow road bridge spans it near the eastern end - from our viewpoint the bridge looked absurdly small and frail.

Arriving in Isthmia at the other end of the canal, there was a long delay while the duty-officers worked out what dues they should charge us. They cannot often have had such a small craft wanting to use the canal. It cost us £5, which for us was a lot of money - perhaps £100, at today's rates. But it also cost us our wind. By the time we got under way, the north-west wind had dropped, and it was replaced by a wind from the north-east, which was in our teeth. We tacked slowly north-east up the coast, making about one mile per hour against the land. As I read the log, sixty years later, and see that we persevered with this tacking for six solid hours, I detect that we were all three of us longing to reach Piraeus.

6. Piraeus

Pasalimani (August 17th to 19th)

We were approaching Piraeus. Seen from the sea, what stood out as we approached was not the Acropolis Hill but the almost phallic Mount Lycavettus. Gradually we were getting nearer to the port. I had mixed feelings about arriving in Piraeus. I was absurdly proud to be co-owner of a seagoing boat, and was longing to show her off to the sailing friends I had made when I was in Greece in my gap year, and to introduce Sally. But it did occur to me that baths would be a good thing first, before meeting friends. And Piraeus was such a noisy, dusty, concreted environment - where on earth would we find baths? Perhaps we could use Sally's approaching residency at the British School of Archaeology, in leafy Odhos Suedhiou, as a pretext to go there, for baths?

Suddenly the shipping lane of the commercial port of Piraeus was upon us, and we had to pick our way between the cargo boats and huge passenger ships coming and going. We started the engine, but threading our way through the stream of ships from both directions seemed as hard as navigating Piccadilly Circus in a donkey cart. At last we were past the entrance to the Commercial Port. We chugged our way eastwards, following the skirts of the fortified hill that dominated the entrance, a hill which Themistocles had persuaded the Athenians to fortify, twenty-six centuries ago:

Themistocles liked the position of the place, with its three natural harbours, and he considered that if the Athenians became a seafaring people they would have every advantage in adding to their power... In breadth the wall was built according to his specifications, just as one can see it today around Piraeus. There was room for two wagons to pass each other with their stones for the building, and the space in between the outer surfaces were not filled in with rubble or clay; instead large blocks of stone were cut and fitted together, with clamps of iron and lead on the outside. The height of the finished wall was about half of what he planned.[19]

It was not hard to imagine those urgent months, as we chugged along looking up at the fortifications from our small boat.

---

[19]Thucydides, *The Peloponnesian War*, I.93.

We continued along the coast, looking for the entrance to Pasalimani, the section of Piraeus reserved for *caique*s and fishing boats, to which we had been recommended by the crew of the *Aegean.* Suddenly it opened up, and we chugged gently in. Both this little harbour and the still smaller Turkolimano were originally laid out in 493 BC, again by Themistocles. Pasalimani had the advantage of being central. On the other hand the harbour had a distinct odour of sewage.

We were awaiting the arrival of a new crew member, David Edwards, a close friend of Sally's. He was older than any of us three, already starting to work as a barrister, and had built his own boat, sold it, and subsequently owned two others, which he used for ocean racing. I wondered how he would cope with living on a boat as small as *Crab,* more still how he would cope with taking orders from a skipper younger and less experienced than he was.

We tied up to the quay, next to a *caique*. The men on board this *caique,* which turned out to be a Greek salvage vessel, invited us to sleep on board that night, since they would be ashore. For immediate use they gave us deckchairs and cigarettes, together with a tirade on the corruptness of the Greek economy. "One man pays out thousands of gold pounds on buying a motorboat to take out young ladies, while the rest of us go hungry."

They told us that there were plans for the harbour at Pasalimani to be dredged, and a breakwater to be built outside the entrance which would make it big enough to hold 320 yachts, and for it to be renamed by its ancient name of Zea – but they did not think the changes would include revamping the town sewage system. They advised us we could lay up at Vouliagmeni, further down the coast – or here in Piraeus, though that might prove expensive.

When night fell they left, and we moved onto their *caique,* immensely grateful to have a cabin roof between us and the street-lighting and the noise on the harbour front. Tomorrow we would start phoning the people we knew in Athens, mainly my sailing friends. We still had nearly four weeks left in Greece. We needed advice as to where would be best to go, and also as to somewhere to lay up the boat for the coming winter.

Sally's letter to her parents relates our going to the British School for baths, finding that her big trunk was safe, and meeting a group whom we knew and inviting them to supper on the boat. She then describes wryly the first visit by a sailing friend of mine to the boat:

We have just been giving drinks to a very grand friend of Penny's called Sir Lesley Kemp, who took her sailing when she was in Athens before. He arrived in smart car complete with liveried chauffeur, wearing a white suit and sunhat, and looked rather amazed when I scrambled up the wall of the quay to greet him. We took him on board via the next-door caique, which was rather embarrassing as we had made great friends with the crew last night and been treated to an oration about the wickedness of the system whereby the country is run by a few millionaires and the rest of the people are starving. Lesley Kemp invited us out to the theatre this evening but we could not go, having invited all the British School people to supper, which is very sad.

The caique is still being very kind to us and we can go and sit under their awning whenever we want shade, so we are very well off here. We are in a small yacht harbour outside Piraeus proper, recommended to us by the American yacht. It is pretty dirty but fairly quiet except for the US navy who seem to be here on a cruise and buzz in and out in small motorboats all the time, upsetting everything on board… (18.08.1957)

My own letter to my parents says that Lesley admitted to me as he was leaving that at first when I made contact he had no recollection whatsoever who I was, but had come to the rendezvous at Pasalimani all the same, curious to find out. During the course of conversation he had suddenly recalled that I had spent a weekend on his yacht *Daffodil,* invited at the last minute, at his friend Kosta's suggestion, to fill the place of the British ambassador's wife, who was unable to come.

Kosta had first met me at a British Embassy function, where I was trying to be on my best behaviour. Finding I had a passion for sailing, he invited me to come sailing on a keeled day-racer owned by his friend Lesley Kemp - the beginning of a friendship with him which was deeply disapproved of by my hosts, the Levidises. I suspect their disapproval made it all the more fun. I had not been able to contact Kosta as we approached Piraeus, however, so I had made contact with Lesley Kemp instead.

At midday David Edwards arrived at the boat. His arrival almost coincided with the arrival of Kosta Tsallis, who had come in his white almost-new TR2, to mark this as a special occasion. "Bring your boat out of here," he said decisively, "You'll be better in Turkolimano in sight of the yacht club, where our people can keep an eye on her for you. Then come and have lunch at the yacht club." Noticing that David Edwards was still in comparatively clean shore clothes, and had luggage, he offered to take him in his open-topped car, while we followed more slowly in *Crab.* David confided later to Sally that Kosta's driving had scared him rigid - a powerful sports car with a long bonnet was not the ideal vehicle for the narrow busy streets of the Piraeus.

As a young *au pair* I had fallen deeply in love with Kosta. I refused to admit this to myself, since he was almost as old as my father. He was such a useful person to know, I told myself. We told him now of our plan to sail to Istanbul and then to Rhodes. He was very interested to learn that Sally would be in Greece at the British School of Archaeology.

Turkolimano (August 19th to 20th)

Over a long, leisurely lunch Kosta began diverting us with modest tales of past sailing adventures, including arriving in Malta in January, blown there by a Force 10 gale. Between stories he attempted to educate Sally about the behaviour of Greek winds. We were in the season of the *meltemi,* a north wind which began with the rising of the Dog Star and would continue well into September. This much we knew - and that it was caused by the rapid rising of the hot air above the land masses of Cyprus and the coast of North Africa at this season, so was unpredictable, blowing up out of a clear sky and with almost no warning from the barometer. He warned us that in the Aegean the wind could suddenly increase at midday, reaching Force 7 by the afternoon. Sometimes it died away at night, sometimes it continued all night long full strength. This wind blew with greatest strength in the middle of the Aegean - the hub of our journey. He also warned us not to expect to find shelter by seeking out the lee side of islands - the wind was actually often more violent under a mountainous coast than a few miles offshore. We had three or four weeks left of our holiday, and we asked him where we should go. Advice was that we should round Sunion and head north, hugging the coast, via the channel between the island of Evia and the mainland of Attica. He told us of many interesting places to go and visit on the way, among them the remains of a Byzantine church which dated back to the fifth century.

"Kosta, can't you join us for that bit and show us?" I interrupted impetuously. He gave me a long searching look, saying nothing.

Kosta also warned us that before the season of *meltemi* there was a season of thunderstorms, when no sensible yachtsman was out and about. Zeus wielded his thunderbolts just as threateningly as he had in classical times, and needed to be respected. For people like us, with an open boat, June was no time to put to sea.

Uniquely, the journal written by David day-by-day on this trip has survived. Neither Sally nor I kept a journal recording our private feelings. David has died, but his widow came across his journal of the trip with us just recently. His description of the first day of his Greek holiday shows the frustration of being in Athens for the first time, itching to go sightseeing, but having to be on good behaviour, as a newcomer to the boat:

Aboard Crab was a character called Tsallis who was a friend of Penny's and took us to RHYC for lunch. The Yacht Club looks right across Phaleron Bay and stands on a lump of rock at the Piraeus corner. It must have the finest site of any Y.C. in the world. Built 1936 and most excellently designed and kept…

After lunch (i.e. at 5pm) returned to Athens…To the Acropolis 20 minutes before it shut. The first thing that appears to a person who has only seen photos is the astonishing variety of the colour of the marble. The NIKE APTEROS very cool and elegant, is almost white. PARTHENON more ponderously pious, in a marvellous pinky marble which differently reflected the light at all hours.

Back to Turkomalini to a delicious meal on board. So to bed on the side thwarts – and very comfortable after the train.

David had no other chances of sightseeing in Athens.

7. David's Black Sunday

Up until this last four days in Piraeus, I only knew of the coasts we were about to explore because of events there five centuries before Christ, when they were the scene of naval battles between the Greeks and the invading Persians. But the hours we spent talking with the people in Pasalimani, with the boat-hands at the yacht-club, and then with Kosta Tsallis, had stirred our appetite for exploring everything we could. They saw these waters not as the scenes for ancient sea-battles, but as criss-crossed with paths of long usage, seaways that had been set by the pattern of winds and currents.

Kosta said, for instance, that when we reached the Gulf of Volos we would find a quite different sort of climate. Pine forests, and as well as cypresses and poplars there would be holm-oaks. He told us that all the traffic was by sea, because there was so much timber available for boat-building that the town of Trikeri on the mainland, for example, standing high on a cliff-top at the entrance to the Gulf of Volos, had no connection with the outside world except via the harbour at the foot of the cliff.

Kosta strongly recommended we should visit Trikeri, and also the Sporades islands, that were so lush and green, because their springs were linked to underground supplies of water on Mount Pelion, and never dried up. We would find cool and shady forest tracks, even now in mid-August. He told us to visit the boat-yards where they built the *caiques,* and use our eyes, observing what tools were being used.

He advised us to take the inward passage, between Attica and Evia, on our way northwards, to avoid the force of the *meltemi.* He warned us that when we came to Khalkis, the narrowest point of this Euripus Chanel, we would find a strong current running - at spring tides it could run at eight knots. We would also find our way blocked by a swing-bridge. This tide changed not twice a day, as in most places, but as often as seven times.

"There's a Venetian fortress there, for collecting toll off passing ships, so have your money ready!"

Before we left Kosta lent us detailed charts of the Sporades islands, and also a Greek edition of the *Admiralty Pilot,* which contained harbour-plans.

We travelled south-westwards towards Cape Sounion with a following wind. But this soon changed and we began to get a southerly wind. We anchored in a small harbour for the night, and sat up talking with him till after midnight – *Bad for the Boy Scout life,* I commented in a letter home. *He is very nice – usually I don't much care for Sally's boyfriends (presumably jealousy!) but this one is very amiable and also interesting.* David had a glorious repertoire of stories from the law courts already.

Piraeus to Lavrion (August 20th to 22nd)

David's diary describes his first day at sea:

Early up. Much provisioning etc., and left at 10.30. After a day of light airs and some motoring, we put in at about 5pm in a small bay behind Akra Kavouri, only about 10 miles from Turkomalini.

Not unpleasantly hot but shade necessary and swim marvellous when we tied up. The temperature of the water is perfection, and it is salt enough for fat people to be able to splash about in comfort.

One of Penny's delicious dinners, lots of wine, and bed at half midnight. Going to sleep in the open under this sky is wonderful, marred only by the hardness of the boards, which I suppose I will get used to.

In a letter home I describe how, as soon as we were under sail, he had begun eyeing the mainsail restlessly, tut-tutting about how it was bellying. I can see that to him a good flat mainsail was as important as a good flat tummy was to a fashion model. He saw there was room to tighten the outhaul, and tried also other adjustments. I wrote that I sensed it was going to be sometimes an edgy situation, having someone far more experienced, older – and indeed richer – in the position of cabin boy.

His journal was beginning to record how uncomfortable life on board *Crab* tended to be, but he has a good description of Cape Sounion:

Found the boards rather hard and was not sorry to get up at 06:15. Motored out of the bay. I found the sun unpleasantly hot and spent most of the morning trying to find shade…

By teatime, again with following wind, we are off Sunium, the S.E. point of the mainland which we pass before turning north inside Euboea. The temple on the headland looks marvellous – again the same gorgeous clean golden-coloured marble as on the Acropolis. The temple consists now of one line of columns facing the sea, half of the back line of columns and a little of one end. Its position, about 700 feet up, is superb, and it stands out wonderfully both from the biscuit-

coloured rock on which it stands and against the background of the grey mountain behind…

The ship's company, except me, are extraordinarily active. Penny is always cooking, preparing, writing, mending. I suppose I shall improve as I get used to the boat. But I doubt it….

A typical instance of Greek helpfulness. I go ashore at about 3.30 pm with a meths bottle. A Greek sees the bottle, asks what I want, and sends his daughter with me to buy it.

We rounded Cape Sounion just before 5.00 pm that day. What made the white pillars all the more impressive was that behind them, as Sally commented in the ship's log, small black nimbus clouds were coming up in a line from the west.

Was rain on the way? There was dampness in the air. Then the wind changed to west, shifting northerly, and we decided we must be sure of good shelter for the night. We fetched up in the port of Lavrion. In classical times it was famous for its silver mines, but it had come down in the world – it was now the centre of red oxide production.

Lavrion was a dirty, dusty port, but people were hospitable. A man from a neighbouring fishing boat came and hailed us from the quay, offering us his boat to sleep on if it came on to rain during the night. Youngish lads in another fishing boat told us the wind's usual habit of starting west or north-west, and veering to north-east during the day. It was good to be among people as dependent on the wind's routine as we were.

At 2.00 am I woke to the sound of the rain pattering on the shared tarpaulin, as predicted – it was a drop right in my ear that woke me. Robin was awake also, and we decided to shift to the offered *caique* for the rest of the night, and leave the other two double shares of the tarpaulin.

Lavrion to Khalkis (August 22nd to 24th)

We left before 7.00 am under storm sails. By then the rain had eased off, and the fishermen said the wind would be strong but it would be alright for us to go. Sally barked at David about his gear not stowed. I was worried – was there going to be conflict?

"I'll get my man to see about that," he replied airily, not losing his equanimity. Sally looked momentarily baffled and annoyed. But as soon as she wasn't watching the job was done.

There was a good fresh breeze when we set off, and it continued to strengthen. All round us the sea was flecked with white horses, and the surface darkened as squalls swept across. At first we crept from headland to headland, working north-eastwards, but then struck out across open water, in order to cross over to the southern tip of Evia. Short, sharp seas slapped against our bow, douching us with spray. But in some ways *Crab* went at her best in this, her original suit of sails, stiff dark-red, heavy canvas. David approved of the way the loose-footed little storm-mainsail was sheeted aft to a shackle on the top of the rudder, which gave maximum outhaul. He and Robin were baling, nonstop. Even two metre waves looked large when seen from an open boat with only eighteen inches of freeboard.

There was a lot of traffic up and down the Evia channel, in spite of the rough weather. We spent the night in Aghia Marina, at that time a very small village of plaited huts, with a shop and a bar.

After covering about twenty five miles we sailed into a bay on the mainland side in the evening. At first sight it appeared to be uninhabited, but as we approached the NW corner we could see huts on the beach. We moored to a rock nearby. Behind our rock a small pig was tethered. After a swim we went ashore to hit town, Penny having discovered that the place boasted a bar. The bar was built of fir branches, with a drinking area outside marked off by planks, and containing a couple of tables. I sat down on the chair which had no seat and Robin sat on the one with broken legs.

With our wine we had fish and tomatoes. The Greeks love interesting blotting paper.

[Sally later explained to me that "blotting paper" referred to the light food served to mop up some of the effects of strong alcohol - in Britain we have the ubiquitous potato crisps.]

The following night was spent in Eretria on Evia, not far from Khalkis. Sally and I tended only to notice landmarks from which we could work out our position. It was good to have someone on board who noticed a lot more than we did:

The colour of the island is splendid, the surface consists largely of pieces of marble - pink, white and black. The hut is made entirely of whitish marble. Looking NW up the gulf into the wind, the water is very blue and dotted with breakers. The marble at the island's edge has turned black, giving the shore a hard outline. The lumps of marble scattered all over this end of the island lie upon reddish-brown earth. Oh! To be a painter!

Next morning, approaching Khalkis at 9.00 am, we found there was a fast tide carrying us towards the bridge. We lowered the sail. But we were moving faster against the land than we usually moved under sail! I insisted we had just time to lower our mast before reaching the bridge, and Sally concurred – when she saw how low the bridge actually was, she was glad, as she mentions in the ship's log. For once *Crab's* diminutive size was an advantage: we did not have to hang around and wait for the bridge to open, and pay the dues.

But Khalkis seemed a noisy, inhospitable sort of a harbour, with the railway station right alongside the quay. Sally and I bought stores, and she insisted we push off again as soon as we could, under protest from Robin and David that we should stay to give the town a more thorough exploration.

Khalkis to Atalante Scala (August 24th to 26th)

We intended to make a longish passage and reach Atalante Scala by nightfall. But the wind was fluky or non-existent – it just blew for long enough to trick us into turning off the outboard engine and heaving it on board. Then the sun beat down and there was no breeze to alleviate the heat. Normally I went barefoot on board, it gave one a better grip, but that day the horizontal surfaces were so hot they burnt the soles of my feet and I was forced to wear sandals. David unearthed from his knapsack a large and venerable straw hat.

And so dusk found us too far still from our destination. We anchored in the lee of Gaidarosnisos, an apparently uninhabited island then. What I vividly remember was the shrill din of thousands of cicadas coming across the water from the wooded hillside as we approached. It exploded inside one's head, so that it felt it would burst with the noise. The racket made by a pneumatic drill five yards away in the street was nothing in comparison with this. David commented:

A fine place to anchor. On the mainland a slab of a mountain about 2,500 ft high rising straight out of the sea. Our island was ½ mile away and we were in a sheltered bay which we shared with 2 or 3 small fishing boats. They are not allowed to fish until September 1 because the fish are too small. The island is uninhabited but boasts a small church maintained in use. We wined and dined as well as usual and were in bed at 8.30. We live as nearly by the sun as is possible. Too nearly for me.

It was not a good anchorage, there was swell, even though we were in the lee of the island, and the holding was poor, the sea bottom too rocky.

I was so absorbed in practicalities that I completely failed to notice how David's spirits were becoming lower and lower. It was not just that he was against getting up and going to bed with the sun:

August 25, Black Sunday.

Morale very low. Started early, and motored a few miles to Larimna where we arrived about 10.30. This is an inlet with to starboard a smart new (German?) iron-ore plant, and to port a rather scruffy village in flat country. Reasons for disaffection

Anti Douglas Dixon methods and current atmosphere. Crew do not share in direction at all

Tired of motoring. Hardly ever sail.

Spend no time investigating shore.

Went ashore for petrol feeling bloody-minded. Seriously contemplating leaving at Atalanta(sic) where we are bound.

Presumably the Douglas Dixon he refers to is the retired naval officer who had taught Sally to sail. Barked-out orders would have been the method, and a chain-of-command approach, judging by the methods of my retired naval officer step-grandfather. David's central complaint was that every detail of the journey had been pre-planned by the skipper, there was no sharing of responsibility and initiative, no spontaneity. But I guess he must have found opportunity to share with Sally the reasons for his discontent as well as confiding them to his journal, because the very next day there was an unexpected expedition ashore which was full of surprises.

The time that Sally and I waited at the quayside in Larimna for Robin and David to return with petrol seemed interminable, because we found the inhabitants inquisitive, as if they had never seen a foreigner. They were not very friendly, and we were glad to push off again. We spent the next night at Atalante Scala - a very small place indeed - too small even for us to buy a loaf of bread, let alone petrol. When David asked where Atalante itself lay, they pointed to a winding dust road that disappeared into low hills inland. There was no sign of any vehicles on it. So David did not desert at Atalante Scala, as contemplated. His journal describes a restless night:

We moored bow-on to a quay from which operate night fishing boats (lamparis). They and the caiques which tow them are painted fine bright colours, the most common being red lead, which they manage to make look splendid. Ashore nothing but a bog, café and a few sheds. Sleep much disturbed by somebody drowning kittens. The Greeks are apparently so fond of cats that they can't bring themselves to weight the bag, with the result that the animals die very slowly, and with long forlorn cries.

The men from one of the fine red caiques moored at the quay get much amusement from watching Sally snoring hard at about 5.45 am.

Sunday night, lying awake listening to the forlorn cries of those kittens, was interminable. Fortunately the following day brought completely unexpected and delightful discoveries.

Looking back, I see this day as pivotal, in that from now onwards there was a whole variety of interesting trips ashore. Had he given the skipper a piece of his mind?

8. Investigating Ashore

Atalante Scala to Hidden Harbour [Krypholimani] (August 25th to 27th)

We left at 6.00 am. The wind was very light, and as we motored we pored over Robin's *Guide Bleu,* in which David while browsing had spotted a reference to the ruins of an early fifth century basilica not far from the shore, where in 1928 they had found fine mosaics. He suggested strongly that we go and look for it, since this must be the one Kosta Tsallis had spoken of. For once Sally agreed to spend a day investigating. This early fifth century basilica, called Aghios Konstandinos, lay somewhere between Arkistra and Livanateis.

David's journal describes setting off along the shore and slightly inland with Sally in search of Aghios Konstandinos. Meanwhile Robin and I had spotted what looked like a cave a few hundred meters away, almost on the water's edge. As soon as the other two had left we moved *Crab* closer. It looked as if it was in use by shepherds as a sheepfold. There was a timelessness about the place, and we were both reminded of the passage in the *Odyssey* describing how Odysseus' men came back and reported finding a cave used as a sheepfold, well stocked with provisions. The colour film was finished, so Robin took black and white photos.

August 26

Sally and I walked half a mile NW to a cypress grove which (according to her Guide Bleu) was a 5th century Byzantine church. Some thoughtful person had planted cypress all over the site.

On the way back from this place to the boat we encountered some Greeks who took us to the irrigation pump where they were working and gave us watermelon and much friendly chatter. The nicest one (called Costas!) went off and returned with a bucket of grapes and figs, and we returned to the ship with these and melons. She was moored in a cove with a huge cave about 20 ft. high, in which goats are now kept, but there once led into it the tunnel from the Byzantine church.

This whole episode greatly improved morale and put a stop to thoughts of desertion. We picked up a breeze and ran NW up the gulf to the NW corner of Euboea, which was our aim for the day. Still the same fine mountain background on each side. On the Euboea side we passed a mountain range, the peak of which was 4,000 ft.

We reached the corner of Euboea and sailed over to the mainland and anchored in a bay just E of a village. While Sally and I sat on the quay, drinking our wine, the lampari set off for the night's work. A good day, particularly because we covered quite a distance under sail for a change.[20]

*

We were under way again, feasting on melons as we went. We were beginning to long for the end of the Evia Channel, the chance of being again in the open sea, of visiting the Sporades Islands. Robin was due to leave us very soon, to be back in London in time for the start of the school term, and David was due to leave soon after him - we HAD to get to the Sporades before they both left us.

We were now approaching a stretch of coast that flanked the route of most of the great armies that had invaded Greece through the centuries. Not far to our left was Thermopylae, the narrow pass where in 593 BC, three hundred Spartans had held back the Persian host for several hours, giving the bulk of the Greek forces time to retreat in safety and re-group.. But we did not attempt to go and visit the site. We were heading for Trikeri, where we hoped to spend the night in the harbour at the foot of the cliff. We had heard of it from Kosta Tsallis - a town with no connection to the outside world, though in fact on the mainland: no road access, except by a steep mule track down to the village harbour, Trikeri Scala, on the shore.

Crab was shouldering her way through short sharp waves, heeled hard over, and seemingly not making any progress whatsoever against the land. It was clear that she was not a comfortable boat when both wind and tide were against her. There was nothing for it but to abandon our plans. We decided at 4.15 pm to put in to a cove on Evia called Krypholimani - Hidden Harbour, which David describes in his journal - his last entry:

We moored as usual, anchor astern, kedge on beach. The bay was surrounded by high rock, about 500–1,000 ft. high. A dried-up watercourse ran down the

---

[20] *Guide Bleu*, 1953, pp. 289–290: *Après avoir passé un col a 347 m. d'alt., la route descend sur le gros bourg d'Atalandi (4,818 hab.), puis continue vers la mer qu'elle atteint a Livanáteis (60 km de Levádia). Elle longe ensuite la coté. Entre Arkistra et Livanáteis on a trouvé en 1928 les restes d'une grande basilique (debut du V après J – C), belles mosaiques - (74 km. de Levádia) Aghios Konstantinos).*

central valley and there was a well on the beach, with only slightly brackish water.

The place was sheltered, with a steeply shelving shore and a well near the sea with slightly salty water. It was bliss to be in sheltered water after such a hard day's sail. But we had hoped to reach somewhere where we could replenish our stores. Robin and I offered to go and try and find the village, which was called Gialta, and bring back supplies.

We two had an enjoyable walk uphill, with the narrow Oreos Channel gleaming in the evening sunlight below us. But the terrain was wooded, so that it was difficult to have a clear sense of direction. By the time we had found the village and bought bread dusk was falling, the sky had clouded over, and there would be no stars to help us. Robin has a good sense of direction, but neither of us could recognise the way by which we had come. We struggled, often in circles, through dense scrub. It seemed to me to be as dark as a cellar. Sometimes the scrub was dwarf pines, which was manageable. At other times it was thorn-bushes. At one point I became totally entangled in a thorn bush, unable to go either forward or back. I felt like emitting a string of the choicest language I had learnt from sailing with my father.

"Will you marry me, Penny?" Robin asked.

Did he think this was a romantic setting, suitable for such a question? I certainly didn't!

I replied firmly that I didn't know yet.

It was 1.00 am when we finally got back to the boat. In the morning I found I was covered in scratches, but in unaccountably good spirits.

Hidden Harbour to Trikeri (August 27th)

When we left Krypholimani, Skiathos was already visible, a dark smudge on the horizon, and my spirits soared to see it there, long and low. Heading north east for the island of Skiathos, we could see the town of Trikeri gleaming on a distant mainland cliff top to north of us, at the entrance to the Gulf of Volos. Both wind and current were against us yet again that morning, and we were making so little progress that we decided to seek shelter in Trikeri Scala, even though it was only mid-morning.

The harbour-front was crowded with fishing boats. We managed to pick up a mooring buoy, and attach a stern line to it, and carefully edged our way forward under engine, so as to moor bows-to on the quay. Robin at once noticed a zigzag mule track up the cliff to the small town above, and persuaded David and me to go with him. He was a devil for following mule tracks up vertical cliffs, nothing suited him better. The mule track to the town on the cliff top on Santorini, the following year, was heaven on earth for him.

Sally stayed with the boat. Alone, she was soon talking to the people around her, and was invited into the house of a sponge fisherman, Yannis, whose wife gave her lunch. When we three came down from the upper town he invited us all into his house too, to siesta in his garden.

He already had other guests - relatives from London. They were twins, brother and sister, aged thirty-seven, from London, who spoke no Greek, though their father was Greek. They told us they were finding the visit weird - water had to be bought, they complained, and there were bedbugs, and soup was eaten from a communal dish in the middle of the table. It was a curious setup. But Yannis and his wife were delightful. There was a splendid scene when Yannis' wife tried on Sally's *Alien Glow* powder compact, and Yannis pranced round her smelling it with much enjoyment. It was the smell which counted - Max Factor's *Alien Glow* made no difference to her complexion, which had a glowing tan already.

In the cool of the evening Sally and I made our way along the footpath that threaded the village almost at sea level. Wooden balconies jutted out over the path at first-floor level. The shore was far too steep for any kind of waterfront or for much area for the evening *passeggiata*. But in a creek at the far end of the village we found a boatyard, with shipbuilding in progress - several *caique*s about fifty feet long were on the stocks. They had the traditional lines - square bilge, and clipper bow. We were to find even bigger *caique*s being built when we reached the Sporades.

Trikeri Scala to Skiathos town (August 28th to 29th)

We left in the grey dawn at 5.00 am next day. Very soon the island of Skiathos appeared ahead of us. Starting so early we seemed to have got up before the wind. Chugging hour after hour under engine, by mid-morning we were running along the southern coast of Skiathos at last. We stopped in a bay to bathe. It was a very inviting island, green and lush, with deserted sandy beaches all along the southern shore. We saw one set of terraces with olives growing, and vines, as if someone was beginning to develop agricultural potential now that at last the occupying forces had left and they were clear of the ravages of the civil war that followed. On the other hand, there was no sign of any road along the coast.

At anchor in the bay, an unfamiliar deep red butterfly landed on our boat - perhaps a distant relative of a peacock butterfly. I watched as it tested the surface of the thwart with its feet, using the sensitive soles to discover what kind of surface this was it had landed on. It was not impressed - after a brief rest it rose and fluttered off across the water.

We reached the main town of Skiathos in the early afternoon and tied up to the quay to go exploring. It was David's turn to be left with the boat. We crossed to the citadel, the Bourtzi, connected to the quay by a narrow spit of land. At the far end of the harbour front lay a spacious lagoon, separated from the harbour by a neck of land which formed the shipyard. Approaching the yard, I felt the ground suddenly soft underfoot, and looking down saw it was deep in woodchips. The place was a hive of activity. Sally in particular was interested in every detail, and astonished by what she saw, and by how primitive were the tools with which they built these huge boats. Here is her account in the log-book:

15.30 Moved to E. side of Skiathos Island, the caique harbour. Went to see caique-building: very grand 200 ton caique, 100' long, drawing about 12', clipper bow, stern with poop-deck and splendid bulwarks; planks about 5/8" lined the inside: keel and keelson comparatively light, but extra longitudinal timbers for bearing engine etc. Made with adze and clamps, only modern machine a band-saw.

Talked to builders who said lines had not altered with introduction of engines. This boat would go well under sail, doing about 10 knots in a good wind: she was built for a local man, as a cargo-carrier (and pretty roughly built in places too - v. short on iron fastenings by English standards). They said that before days of engines people also used smaller caiques (about 30 foot), with sail and OARS, crewed by 20 men. The boatyard makes up to 400 ton craft - this was 200 ton. They made such sizes also for sail only.

One of the *caique*s being built was for the regular run to Skopelos, a *caique* with a long bowsprit, sheer bow. People were at work on her raised stern - under its overhang on a bosun's chair swung a man who seemed to be setting in place magnificent scroll-work, which would doubtless be picked out in gold. A carved wooden balustrade ran around the lower deck, in the stern. She was to be named the *Pashkalis,* after her Skiathite owner.

At about midnight a sudden wind rattled the halyards and whistled in the shrouds. We would have a change in weather. Rain came, but stopped. When we woke the wind was less strong, but still fresh. Skopelos beckoned us - higher and more rocky than the rounded hills of Skiathos, and more primitive. Kosta had told us that the older men on Skopelos still wore a unique style of pleated indigo breeches - if we were lucky we would see some. We asked advice of the fishing boats near us as to whether it would be safe to go that day. They said that *caique*s were not going that day because Skopelos harbour was open to the north, and it was not a good anchorage in this north wind. But although we would not find a comfortable anchorage in the harbour, they said we could stop in a quiet bay on the western side of Skopelos, Panormos, instead.

Skiathos Town to Panormos Harbour on Skopelos (August 29th to 30th)

As we approached Panormos, which means "anchorage for all winds", it looked at first sight dubious shelter, even in fair winds - it was a wide pebble-fringed bay, edged with pine woods, not offering much shelter. Then we looked more closely and saw that at the southern end there was a long inlet, a bay within a bay, affording a quiet anchorage in any wind. There were two other boats at anchor, presumably fishing boats. Perfect. All that it lacked was a road connecting it to anywhere else.

Sally suggested that she and David set off on foot to see if they could reach the town. Robin was due to catch a train back to England from Athens in three days, and Sally offered to find out how he could get back to Athens. There were the ruins of an old jetty with a large old barn alongside that served as loading-bay, and we brought *Crab* alongside. Behind the whitewashed, red-roofed barn, a clear mule track led inland through the pinewoods. There was firewood stacked up against the wall of the barn, suggesting it was inhabited, and a haunting smell of pine resin. Further along the shore was a dilapidated cottage that showed every sign of habitation - a cheese in muslin hanging from a branch of a nearby tree, just as we had seen in the bay of Dessime on Levkas. There was also what seemed to be a home-made oven down by the rocks. A goat was tethered in the shade.

The hours passed. Robin and I had long finished the customary scrub-out and clean-up. We had had conversation with the men on the two fishing boats who wanted to know where we came from and where we were going to. We were both growing anxious. How was Robin going to get back to London? He would be in serious trouble if he arrived after the beginning of the school term.

As the sun sank towards the horizon a group emerged from the pinewoods and made for the cottage. We went to talk to them. There seemed to be a whole family. They were delighted to have strangers to entertain, and insisted we join them for the evening meal. They summoned the fishermen also. I brought food from on board - the meal I had made in readiness for Sally's return - and wine, and we talked long into the night. They were not Skopelos people, they said. They came from Alonnisos, a small island further to the east, to work all summer tapping resin in the pine forest and tending the trees. Those barrels on the jetty were full of pine resin, they told us. I questioned them as to what it was like living on as small an island as Alonnisos. "On Kyra Panaghia, to the north of us, it's even fewer," the resin-tappers told me. "There are only fourteen people in total - two monks in the monastery, some charcoal burners, and a herd of goats. Almost no water, these days." It was near midnight when we returned onboard. I dreamt a disturbing dream about the barren island with its two monks and its goats.

I was to spend nearly a week storm-bound on that barren island the following year.

As it grew dark, we decided that, as Sally and David had not returned, we should wait no longer. Robin had to make his way back to Athens or miss his flight. He packed his kitbag in readiness, and very early next morning we set off together, leaving the boat in the charge of the fishermen, and sharing the carrying of the heavy bag turn by turn. As we set off we passed an occasional almond-tree and lots of olive trees, already well-laden with green fruit. They were more or less kept clear of weeds and tended, though there seemed to be no village nearby. The dappled shade of the pines was a delight. Wafts of *rigani* met us as we struggled uphill.

Somewhere ahead was the clop of mules, and voices. And then through the pines I glimpsed a straw hat that I recognised immediately. Rounding a rock, we met up with Sally and David, each astride a mule, and the mule's owner, on foot. They explained they had brought the mules so that Robin could get to the port - one mule for him, one for his kitbag. They had found out that there was a Sunday morning boat from Skopelos town that would take him to Evia, and from there he could get a bus to Athens, arriving on Sunday evening. There was a quick round of goodbyes, Robin's kitbag was tied across the saddle of Sally's mule, Robin mounted the mule David had been riding, wheeled it round, and they were gone.

Panormos to Linaria, on Skyros (August 30th to September 1st)

David Edwards was also due to leave, so we had to set off if possible, whatever the weather. Under storm sails we left for Skyros mid-morning. But the wind headed us and we made almost no progress, even under engine. That evening we turned back and took shelter in Agnondas Bay. It took us two whole days to accomplish the relatively simple crossing. The following day we left at 5.30 am when there was likely to be less wind, and motored close inshore, in the lee of the cliffs, against a light north-easterly wind and a heavy swell. We continued most of the day under sail, heading for Linaria at the northern end of the island. At 4.00 pm the wind headed us again, and we resorted to the engine till the petrol ran out. When we finally reached Linaria we had to run in under sail. David was due to leave us on Skyros, where our next two members of crew were due to meet up with us.

Skyros was the largest of the Sporades, but not very thickly populated. This was the island with the waterside grave of the poet Rupert Brooke, and a bronze statue to him in the main square of the town (he died on St George's Day 1915 on board a French hospital ship, on the way to Gallipoli). David left on September 2nd. We saw him off on the *caique,* in the care of the proprietor of the local stores.

We had been spoilt, having two crew members as experienced as Robin and David for two weeks and more. The next two coming to join us were not experienced sailors, nor did Sally know them well. And they were joining us at a time when the weather could be relied upon to be difficult.

9. Rough Weather, Green Crew

Life on Skyros (September 3rd to 6th)

With the weather uncertain, Sally and I had no intention of doing any sailing till the new crew joined us, so the following day we caught the communal taxi from Linaria to Chora - Skyros village - and spent the day being tourists. The log describes being shown round a Skyrian house in Chora, and Sally's attempts to buy a length of Skyrian fabric so as to make a skirt:

...Nice carvings and lovely copper plates on walls but all for sale, rather annoying: finally bought goatskin off floor which surprised them a lot, so only paid 40 drachs [drachmas], and a roll of local material which I wanted dyed blue for skirt, the colour they wear here. But found a) dyeing would take a week, b) they dye them navy and it washes out over the years. So took it plain, and will try to buy pair of old trousers for a skirt, which will make them think us even odder. Returned to Linaria 15.30. Bought two more goatskins from an old woman who saw the one from Skyros and decided to try and cash in on our odd tastes. It rained in Linaria, not in Skyros, and wind and sea went down a lot: at sunset clear sky, but very cloudy at dawn. Today the most pronounced mackerel sky ever seen, gleaming rosy-pink like fish-scales, with low grey cumulus-clouds moving fast below it from the North.

08.30. Rain. Wind dropped. Saw church above Post Office with fine collection of old icons in dark corner of gallery upstairs, including ship with 3 masts, and two sails on each, + antemon on bowsprit (c. 15th century?)

These ikons had been successfully hidden from the Germans and saved from destruction in the civil war. How long would it be, now that there was peace, before they disappeared from their dark corner, carried off by a dealer?

In Linaria, Sally and I took the chance to spring clean the boat, paint boxes that were beginning to rust, and wash our clothes. At midday we watched a yacht coming into the harbour, the *Aralus*. That evening we were invited on board. She was owned by a Canadian Greek. Our two new crew members, Ian Morin and another David, arrived as arranged on the evening *caique* and were taken to the *Aralus* too.

The skipper of the *Aralus* questioned the two newcomers as to how they could be so foolhardy as to join us on *Crab,* especially at this time of year. He spoke of equinoctial gales approaching. Ian confessed that the only time he had sailed before joining *Crab* was after the Oxford Yacht Club dinner, to which he was invited as a guest. Traditionally after dinner there was a Backwards Race. Nobody remembered who won, they had drunk quite a lot, but at least no one was drowned. He had a vivid memory of having to hold the boom well away from the centre of the boat, pushing against the wind to do so, to increase their momentum. Ian's parents were both internationally known rock-climbers, and he had considerable experience as a climber himself, and Sally was confident he would soon find his feet on board *Crab*. He turned out to be the fastest learner we ever had on the boat.

An extract from a letter of mine (the first two pages are lost), describes our lotus-eaters' life on Skyros:

We had a magnificent feast with the grocer of the village and all his family before we left. I think he had a great fellow-feeling for us, because of having spent most of the war going from Skyros up to Thessalonika in a sailing boat, with oars but no engine. We asked them to Crab, but the party had to be in their shop because they could not close it and come to us. The grocer said again about Cyprus, how much Greece was bored with the fuss and did not want to behave that way. But if you were a mosquito and a lion was sitting on you, what else could you do?

During the night - our third in this harbour - it rained quite hard. We moved under the straw café shelter, and made a tent with our red sail and some tables. September seemed to be a month of almost unmitigated rain. But somehow we had to make the journey back to the Piraeus, if we were to lay up the boat where we knew it would be safe.

Skyros to Andros (September 6th to 7th)

Next morning we were uncertain as to whether or not we should set off. We asked the advice of our hosts of the night before, who kept the general store. They said the forecast was "changeable" and that we would be unwise to set off for Andros, but could make Kimi, which was nearer. When we did succeed in reaching Andros, the harbour to aim for was Batsi.

My letter describes the crossing. It was not till 11.00 am the next morning that we sailed into Batsi on Andros:

We left at midday on Friday [6th September] for the sixty mile crossing to Andros with storm-clouds coming up. We sailed two hours through the rain, which was gloomy. We laid bets on how long it would last. Sally's much the most optimistic, (and turned out to be right). We managed to cook supper, and just as we were about to eat it such a squall blew up that we dropped all sails and ran under bare poles. One of the crew was seasick and the other had diarrhoea, it being the first day either of them had sailed in Crab. I felt very scared that we were doing something silly, pushing off for a crossing, which Sally and I were used to and could stand – but with two people who didn't know the boat and didn't know how to sail. Fine for us, yes, and not at all fine for them. It's almost impossible to use the bucket on a rough crossing. We had very good luck in that the moon was full, so we could see the waves and steer to avoid them, and the wind was well aft [following us]. Sally and I did all the steering, and slept in the only dry bed. Towards morning we got into sheltered water off Euboea, and the other bed dried off. We couldn't let the others learn to steer…I don't much like the set-up of people being BOTH uncomfortable and useless – one can put up with a lot if one feels it is for the good, but just sitting idle is very miserable. Anyway by the time we reached Andros one of the crew had learnt to steer – quick going! We broke our spinnaker boom in the channel between Euboea and Andros, but otherwise arrived, at about eleven in the morning, in good order and fine spirits, and lay on the beach and slept the rest of the day…

Weather-bound on Andros (September 7th – 10th)

Sally wrote to her parents:

We are moored off a restaurant at the end of the beach, and after supper we went ashore to drink there, out of courtesy. First an American-speaking archaeologist dining two tables away sent us a bottle of white wine by the waiter, and then a huge paterfamilias, with a family of about ten, five minutes later sent us another identical bottle of wine and a huge plate of pickled octopus, with compliments to the captain. The waiter told us afterwards that he runs a big Marks and Spencer type of chain in Piraeus. It completely took us by surprise, and was rather embarrassing.

We took a great liking to the restaurant-keeper/waiter while we were there. He had tremendous nervous energy, always hopping up and doing something. He told us that in the winter he has a job in commerce in Athens. He and his family used to come to the house on Andros for holidays, but as the children grew up they felt there wasn't enough to do there, so they turned the house into a restaurant, and every year they extend it. After three years it has two outside dance-floors, a three-room hotel with sit-up lavatories with black plastic seats. The night we ate there, which was a Sunday, we had roast suckling pig…

Sally's letter was also full of gastronomic delights:

...friendly proprietor who talked French and let us sleep free in his hotel. *We had a marvellous party there on the night of my birthday – the others ate roast sucking-pig, and I had had a bit of tummy-trouble that morning so had red mullet, which was absolutely lovely. Then we sat and drank coffee and watched the locals having their Sunday night dance. Two of them came up and asked Penny and me to do the tango. P. refused saying she didn't know it, but needn't have worried as they only did the most elementary quick-step. The only blight was our two men, who were too shy to dance, so we had to take them off to bed instead of continuing the party.*

The log describes a lot of inland walking, as we marked time till the weather would become settled enough for us to be able to leave:

P. and S. walked to the monastery before breakfast – cold. Saw ancient books including 12th century gospel and very nice Byzantine stone carving of Virgin and angels, with triangular faces and archaic eyes, in room above church. Breakfast of cold roast pork, beer, and chips in café. Walked to Palaiopolis (2 hours, plus half an hour down to the sea). Bathed, but cold, and water too choppy to see much of underwater remains. Dig last year, also next year. Basis of temple visible, and columns built into all houses. Also inscription to Publius Venicius, from the "demos". Difficulty in explaining Roman Rule to our guide, who had not heard of anything between "ta archaia" and the Turks. Much wind all day, veering east, south-east, and then going back to north, during morning.

Batsi to Piraeus via Sunium (September 10th to 13th)

09.15 Left under storm sails, wind north, Force 4, seas steepish but not very high: advice from restaurant not to go. Speed 4 knots, rolling and shipping spray...

At midday, however, the wind dropped. An hour later we encountered a heavy swell, and an hour after that we were becalmed. We were fortunate to make Vourkarion harbour on Kea before nightfall, and had a peaceful night.

Next morning we got up early and fished, using a kipper as bait. We caught eight fish, two of which escaped into the bilges; we couldn't find them. We left at 11.00 am, passing Makronisi, the island later notorious as the place where the colonels kept their political prisoners. We reached Sunium, and anchored under the harbour master's office. On foot Sally and I went to look for the trireme slipway. This was two feet, six inches deep and three feet wide at the bottom. Sally was puzzled as to why the triremes were kept in so small a harbour, and not in the neighbouring bay. Perhaps it would be harder for a large enemy force to attack while they were still being launched?

It took us till Friday September 13th to make our way back to Piraeus, picking our weather and creeping from safe anchorage to safe anchorage. There was one other foreign yacht in Turkolimano, *Wayfarer,* a hundred-foot yacht. Sally talked with them, and discovered they were short of a crew. Since Ian had run out of money, she suggested him. And so within twelve hours of our arriving in Piraeus, Ian left on board the only other foreign yacht. We heard from him from the USA. The other crew-member, David, left as planned - by train - the next day.

Throughout the weekend Sally and I, the only ones left, worked flat out to get *Crab* done and dusted - or rather cleaned out and de-rusted - before I left by train to go back north, and Sally began her research residency at the British School of Archaeology.

What we learnt in that ten days was that the Aegean Sea is relatively small and well-endowed with islands, but *Crab* was so slow - especially in adverse conditions - that we were likely to run into danger. Looking back, I can see that as we two grew more experienced we began to take unreasonable risks with inexperienced crews. Sometimes we were lucky, sometimes recklessness led us into bizarre situations.

In Taormina we had told Polly and John Hope that we intended to reach Istanbul, and expected to get there before them. At the time we said it, it was just a boast - but the idea was beginning to take shape as Sally and I communicated with each other by airmail during the winter.

Corfu, manoeuvring in the harbour, close-hauled (Sally, Maggs)

Porto Gaio, Paxos – Early morning calm

Levkas – Café owner with us, bedraggled survivors

Dessime Bay, welcomed by a big family

Mesolongi, the house where we were given a gift of grey mullet
(reed roof, two flat-bottomed *monoxyla*)

Naupaktos, the fortress Byron dreamed of
capturing mid-winter from the Turks

Crab enters the Corinth Canal under engine

Lone man repairing walls of the Corinth Canal

Crab with a following wind, under storm rig

The temple at Sunium, framed by the shoreline and the mainsail of *Crab*

Gulf of Evia, lunchtime, David in venerable sunhat
(Sally, David, Penny)

Approaching the bridge at Khalkis (Gulf of Evia)

Crab demonstrating her storm sails, just north of Khalkis

Penny steering, in windy weather (Gulf of Evia, north)

Cave used as sheepfold, like the cave of the Cyclops Polyphemus

Crab moored outside the cave

Gulf of Evia, north: Paved steps down from Trikeri to the harbour

Trikeri harbour, viewed from the connecting footpath

The waterfront at Skiathos – Mule-transport

Fishermen mending their nets at Skiathos

Approaching Vathy, main harbour on Samos (Sally)

Samos, waterfront at Pythagorio, busy with *caiques*

Old man, resting (Patmos)

Patmos, two monks on the battlements

Patmos, the pilgrim path

Rhodes, square in the Old City with fountain:
Note the absence of cars – the only transport was bicycles

Rhodes, waving farewell to shipmates Roland and Roger on the ferry (Penny, with Tony Luttrell and Maggs)

Rhodes, inside the hospital of the Knights Templar

Interior of Evangelia's house, her dowry showing her *hochlakia* floor, array of copper pans on the wall, family lace and family portraits

Lindos: The steps leading to the fortress mid-afternoon, Penny studying the ship-carving

Astypaleia on the hilltop, with windmills along the ridge

A *caique* at Astypaleia

Zigzag path to Fira from the harbour below

Fira, on the rim of the crater, being rebuilt after the earthquake

Santorini: Sulphurous vapour rising from live outlet in middle of lagoon

Lower Fira: Owain, ready for more

4 Piraeus to Istanbul and Rhodes (1958)

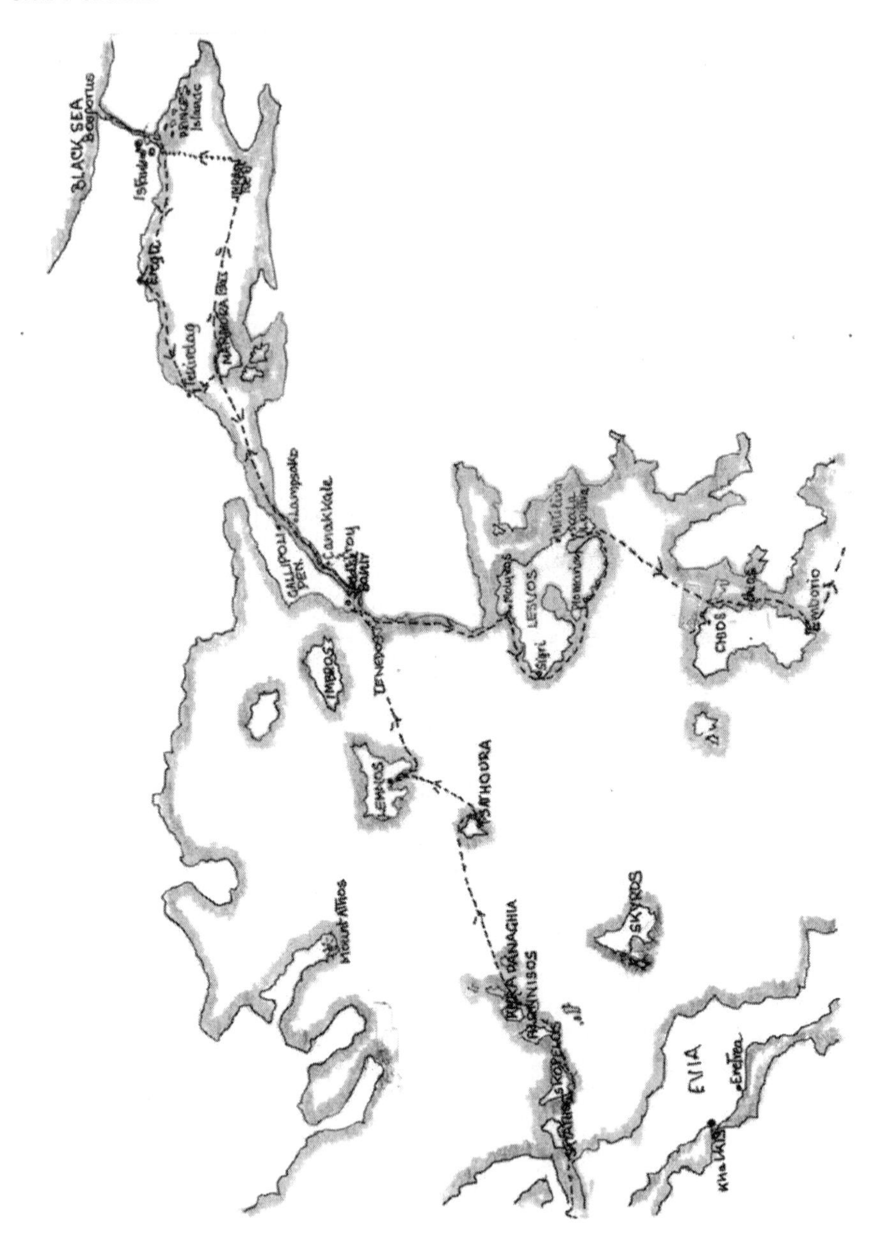
BLACK SEA
Bosporus
PRINCE'S Islands
Istanbul
Eregli
Tekirdag
Lampsako
Canakkale
GALLIPOLI PEN.
IMBROS
TENEDOS
LEMNOS
LESVOS
CHIOS
SKYROS
Mount Athos
KIRA PANAGHIA
ALONNISOS
SKOPELOS
EVIA
Eretria

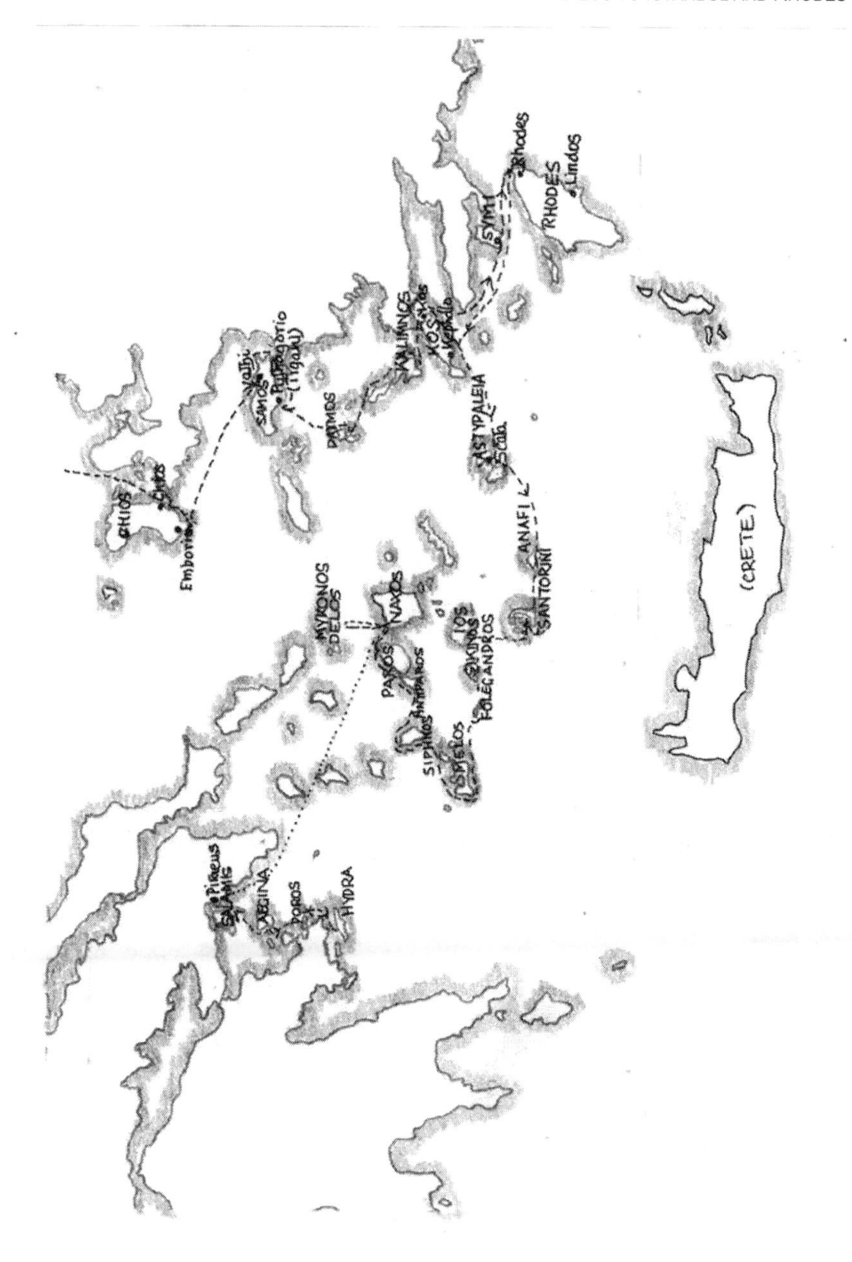
CHIOS
Chios
Emborios
SAMOS
Vathi
Pythagorio
(Tigani)
PATMOS
KALIMNOS
KOS
ASTYPALEIA
Skala
SYMI
Rhodes
RHODES
Lindos
MYKONOS
DELOS
NAXOS
PAROS
ANTIPAROS
IOS
FOLEGANDROS
SIPHNOS
MELOS
SANTORINI
ANAFI
(CRETE)
Piraeus
SALAMIS
AEGINA
POROS
HYDRA

1. The Big Friendly Giant Rejoins Us

Sometime during the winter months at the British School at Athens Sally read an article about Greek penetration of the Black Sea by Rhys Carpenter, a respected scholar, published 1948 in the *American Journal of Archaeology.* Why was it that, according to current archaeological evidence, there had been no penetration into the area beyond the Bosphorus during the Mycenaean period? Why was it that the development of Greek colonies along the Black Sea littoral was later than elsewhere? The answer in his view was that it was impossible for a merchant ship to sail up the Bosphorus against a permanent current of four knots, especially since the prevailing wind all through the sailing season blew down the Bosphorus, in support of the current, not the direction the boats would be sailing in. The Greek penetration of the Black Sea coincided, in his view, with the invention of the *pentekonter*, the fifty-oared longship, which could be rowed at more than four knots. Historians assumed this boat was mainly for naval warfare, but Rhys Carpenter argued it was also used a lot for trade. "Primarily, it was escape from the tyranny of the winds, on whose blowing from the proper quarter the sailing-ships had perforce to wait.[21]" Sally resolved to use *Crab* to test whether it was true that the Dardanelles and the Bosphorus were both a closed route for sailing boats that could hardly make any progress to windward.

Our planned route to Istanbul from Piraeus, after rounding Sounion, ran northwards again inside Evia, then north east across open water to Lemnos, then through the Dardanelles and the Sea of Marmora. Returning, when we emerged from the Dardanelles, we would sail down the east side of the Aegean to Rhodes, then westwards across the Aegean, following the traditional shipping routes for merchantmen. My younger brother Owain, who was fourteen, would travel out with Robin Minney and meet us at Rhodes.

Everything seemed to be on our side. When Sally had applied for her grant to study at the British School at Athens for a year, her application had stated, "We have a boat with all the disadvantages of an ancient

[21] Rhys Carpenter, "The Greek Penetration of the Black Sea," *American Journal of Archaeology*, 1948, Vol. 52, No. 1.

merchant-vessel, and would like to use it to explore trade-routes and merchant shipping in the eastern Mediterranean." This gave her funding, and a licence to spend four months of the summer on *Crab* - and we would need about four months to get as far as Istanbul, and get back again to Piraeus. I had received a 25% grant also - provided I gained practical archaeological experience as part of my assignment. We had scant funding, but we had time, and we had a clear purpose. It was an advantage that we were no longer bound by university terms.

And then the odds turned against us. Tensions between Greece and Turkey, and Greece and Britain, stemming from the crisis in Cyprus - the Enosis movement which wanted union with Greece - gathered momentum, aggravated by the British having sent Archbishop Makarios into exile. Even though Makarios had been released from detention and was settled in Athens, he was forbidden to return to Cyprus, and in the late spring of 1958 anti-British feeling ran high. Our parents were not at all in favour of our travelling in a small boat in the waters of the Eastern Mediterranean that summer.

Dates were not on our side either. One of the conditions of my travel grant from the Craven Foundation, which would help pay for the four-month trip, was that I should have a fortnight at least of practical archaeological work on a site in Greece. The British School was excavating in Cnossos, and because of other plans I would have to be there from the last week of May. So the first two weeks needed for our journey were also the time allotted for my spell of gaining practical archaeological experience at the British School dig outside the walls of Knossus.

Sally's letter to me of May 5th, from the British School of Archaeology in Athens, ended bluntly "with not much love, just now." She was painting the boat all day and writing letters all night, she said. To her parents she wrote more strongly:

I am pretty cross with her at the moment, and if I can think of any other heavy piece of equipment for her to bring out I shall probably order it!

Sally was preparing *Crab* in Turkolimano for four months of travel, and at the same time trying to gather crews to join us. She was nothing if not resourceful and determined. With my father Diccon and my friend Maggs as crew, she enlisted Sue Georghiou, an American sailing friend married to a Greek, to do the shopping and cooking till I could join the boat. Maggs would be arriving by ferry from the heel of Italy, joining the boat in Piraeus and coming as far as Istanbul, perhaps further, and my father, who only intended to come as far as the Dardanelles, being short of time, would also join *Crab* at Piraeus.

My father was now working on a long novel, *The Fox in the Attic,* which was largely set in 1930s Germany. His plan was that after the sailing trip he would go from Istanbul to Ulm, to stay with Bavarian relatives and research the early years of the rise of Hitler. To accommodate this Big Friendly Giant, one improvement was made while the boat was laid up. Sally had a pair of wooden forks fitted standing proud of the gunwales, in which the oars could rest, out of the way of people sleeping. Diccon had fallen out of bed several times during the night on his previous trip because the sleeping space which he had to share with the oars was so narrow.

Diccon's letter home dated June 2nd described vividly the journey by train across Europe, and the excitement of being in Athens for the first time:

After Munich the journey toughens up a bit: no more couchettes, and we were seven in the carriage the whole way to Athens. My behind actually got blistered, sitting on it for three days and nights! But my fellow-passengers were charming – very apologetic about their two squalling babies, and everybody solicitous to make everyone else as comfortable as possible, and to feed each other and so on – it couldn't have been nicer. On arrival one of them insisted on riding in the taxi with me to make sure the taxi took me to the right address – then wanted to pay for the taxi!

It was fascinating as we came south, watching the seasons change: Austria, dog-roses and chestnuts in full bloom, and the green barley nearly full grown, Yugoslavia, the golden barley being reaped (with sickles) and strawberries and cherries on sale, Greece, the stubble being ploughed over and the next crop even coming up, in places. Imagine countryside very like Spain, with its heat-shaped hills, but less red, and with more rocks, and much more rushing streams.

I arrived here [at the British School of Archaeology] at noon yesterday: Sally was out but the assorted collection of archaeologists seemed kindly disposed, and after I had had a bath and a few hours sleep took me off to supper in the Restaurant Bacchus, on the slopes of the Acropolis: a funny little place chiefly composed of flat roofs (so that one ate in the open air), and with highly bacchanalian murals. Then we went up into the Acropolis (it was a full moon, the perfect light for seeing it by) and stayed there till midnight came and we were thrown out. My chief guide was a young architect[22] *who knew Frank Lloyd Wright and Joe Brewer, and was very interesting about Clough's international standing as an architect, and about the great Lloyd Wright versus Corbusier controversy and all that…*

I saw Sally after breakfast this morning. Maggs arrives tomorrow morning early and we sail at once, meeting Penny at Chalcis on Saturday. She is flying back from Crete. We hope to reach Canakale (on the Dardanelles) on 18th June. So my address till 18th June will be Poste Restante, Canakale, Turkey. After that, British School again.

Piraeus to Khalkis (June 3rd to 7th)

Crab left Turkolimano, as it was then called, and headed south-east down the coast of Attica, making for Cape Sunium. My father's second letter was written on Saturday June 7th in Eretria on the island of Euboea, and describes the section of the voyage which I missed – the journey south-east to Sunium, and then north-west. It was posted in Khalkis:

…We left midday Tuesday in terrific heat, it was over 85° in the shade, and lolloped along the coast for a few miles, anchoring in a bay for the night so as to get everything stowed and shipshape. Wednesday we sailed about thirty-five miles: rounding the point of Sounium, where a huge white marble temple to Poseidon still stands on the brink of the cliff, glittering against the blue sky like salt. We put in for the night to a pretty horrible place, Lavrion, where the ancients mined silver lead and the moderns do too, so we moored in water that was half lead silt. We had to go there to get stores. But we were only too glad to up-sail and be off at 7 am next morning. By this time we were approaching the Euripus, the gulf between the mainland and the big island of Euboea. There was some light cloud all the morning, so it was not so baking hot as the day before, and beautiful coasts on both sides. We made a long day of it – 38 miles – and found on the Euboean side a deep bay with a cove turning off it at the end at right-angles, ending in a sandy beach between great rocks of marble, and thistles of many colours on the hill behind, and other wild flowers here are as brilliant as in Switzerland, but you see them against the bare burnt earth – there is no turf of course, and even the weeds have few leaves. This cove where we spent the night was absolutely deserted – indeed we have seen hardly any shipping – not one yacht, and the fishing caiques go out only at night. Not only was this cove lovely in itself and the perfect anchorage – the view out of it was lovely too.

[22] This was Peter Smithson, well known in the UK, who had participated in the Institute of Contemporary Arts Exhibition "This is Tomorrow" in 1956.

Yesterday we made not quite so early a start, and the weather was thundery: squalls from all quarters, and rain like a hot shower-bath: the sky most spectacular – inky black against a sea of turquoise as deep as night.

We were making for Eretria, but the harbour mouth is surrounded by underwater rocks and islets so we had to anchor outside for an hour till the squalls died down. Once Eretria ruled an empire –founded the first Greek colony in Sicily: now it is a pleasant, poverty-stricken (but not squalid) village, with a little fishing-harbour, with the ancient acropolis behind it, and a theatre almost perfectly preserved, and temples and so on. We spent the night there, and left this morning fairly late (Saturday) as we had only fifteen miles to go to Chalcis where we meet Penny tonight and I hope to post this. But when we were about an hour out, the main halyard suddenly broke, so we put in to a sandy beach, and found it so pleasant here – I am writing this in the shade of an olive-tree, surrounded by bamboos whispering in the breeze, and birds singing – we shan't go on till the afternoon…

Two strange things at Eretria: bats flying over the sea at dusk and at dawn the loud slapping of octopuses being beaten tender on the marble slabs of the quay...

7.30 pm Just arrived Chalcis. I must post this. Penny is not due in till midnight but we're tied up to the railway-station!

Love, D.

2. Rendezvous Khalkis

Khalkis (June 7th to 8th)

Sally had arranged with friends of hers living in Athens that they would meet me off the plane from Crete with their car and bring me to Khalkis when I had completed my two weeks in Crete at Knossos, gaining archaeological experience. It seemed I was forgiven.

We arrived in Khalkis with supplies for supper. It was not hard to spot the boat, since it was in such an odd place: it was tied up close against the railway station. We hailed Sally and somehow scrambled down onto the boat. Apparently they had tied up alongside the railway station because Sue Georghiou, who had replaced me on *Crab* as far as Khalkis, had only had ten minutes in which to catch the last train. We all had a brief supper-party on board. We had been joined also by Kosta Tsallis - he told me he had arrived earlier than me, and had been searching the waterfront for *Crab*.

After supper, as I walked with Sally's friends to the car to say goodbye, it began to rain. At first it was just large random splodges, but then came a downpour. I ran back to *Crab*, to find only my father on board.

He was sitting in oilskins in the stern, immobile, disconsolate, raindrops on his moustache, and the rain plopping down around him.

"You and I have been left to guard the boat - Sally and Maggs have gone off with Kosta Tsallis to a hotel for the night."

Crab lay almost six feet lower than the quay, so that he did not even have a view. Rain shone on the thwarts, gleaming on the new varnish of the stumpy little mast. Seen tied up to the railway quay, under the glare of the station arc lights, the boat seemed ludicrously vulnerable and small, an absurd way to travel. I sat down with legs dangling over the edge, and swung myself onto my stomach, feeling for the boat's gunwale till my feet found it. These quays were built for comfortable big coastal *caiques*, not for little boats with only eighteen inches of freeboard, like *Crab*.

Diccon and I shared out the tarpaulins between the two of us, swept the rain off the thwarts with our hands before spreading our blankets, and spent a night punctuated by the clanging of goods coaches being shunted.

Next morning, sticking my head out cautiously from under the tarpaulin, I found it had stopped raining. I heard the sound of church bells, and remembered it was Sunday. I woke Diccon and suggested he come with me to an Orthodox service. The sound of bells came from a church on the other side of the bridge, in the old *castro* district. I had had enough of guarding the boat – I reckoned it could look after itself, early on Sunday morning. It wasn't a high-risk time of day for thieves. I left a note for the skipper, saying when I thought we would be back. I knew the current was due to turn, giving us a brief period of slack water at 12.30, and that we would not leave till the tide turned.

We walked across the metal bridge and heard our footsteps ring out in the stillness of the early morning. The water was swirling past like a river. It is hardly surprising that the tide runs at great speed, with the gap between island and mainland at this point only forty-five metres.

I felt deeply drawn to these little Orthodox churches and their early-morning chanting and ceremony, the music hauntingly beautiful, the whole rich ambiance of the icons and their surroundings a contradiction to the hard glare of the midday sun, and to the grind of day-to-day work, with poverty the reality for so many we moved amongst in Greece. Later I read something written by Patriarch Alexis, Patriarch of Moscow, to his clergy in 1945:

In the church, everything is different from that which we constantly see around us and in our homes. The images are not the same as those we have in our homes. The walls are painted with sacred images; everything shines brightly; everything raises the spirit and removes it from the usual thoughts and impressions of this world. And when we see in a church something which does not correspond to its greatness and its meaning we are shocked. The Holy Fathers foresaw and ordained everything so as to create in the faithful a special spiritual state, so that nothing impedes their flight towards the heavens, towards God, towards the celestial world whose reflection a church should be. If in a hospital everything is directed towards the treating of the maladies of the body, and conditions are created which correspond to the needs of the sick person, so in a spiritual hospital, a church of God, one should provide all the things that are needed.

This was written when Russia was being utterly drained by the war with Germany, in that brief window when Stalin for his own purposes allowed the church a role in the country. He also wrote that the symbolism of icons is a reflection - though a very weak reflection - of the glory of the age that is to come:

God can be known to us in the same way as a man can see an endless ocean by standing at the shore at night, with a dimly burning candle. Do you think he can see much? Not much, almost nothing. And nevertheless, he sees the water well. He knows that there is an ocean in front of him, that this ocean is huge, and that he cannot see it all at once. The same is true of our knowledge of God.[23]

After the service we emerged from the church to find the wind was in the north and the sky was grey and heavy. We found Sally and Maggs back at the boat. Between 10.30 and 11.30 am it rained non-stop. As planned, we passed under the swing bridge at slack water at 12.30, but since the current was already beginning to head us, and would soon be running fast against us, we went for a long and leisurely farewell lunch with Kosta at a *taverna,* not setting off again till 5 pm. He teased Sally and me for so obstinately setting off at a time of year when no sensible yachtsman tried to sail. We had no alternative, we said, unless we gave up our plan of trying to reach Istanbul.

Khalkis to Trikeri (June 8th to 11th)

Diccon was now two years short of sixty. His sweeping grey beard and ample middle made him look more than that, in repose; in movement, his suppleness made him look far less than his years. The impressive feature was his skull - the back of his head so flat it was almost concave, while his forehead rose into an impressive dome. His blue eyes seemed often vacant, as if the owner was elsewhere, but little escaped them. It was surprising, really, that a man of his age should actually *choose* to travel in so small a boat.

The trip was hardly a rest-cure. A typical day on board would begin at 2.00 am, when there would be a sudden clatter and shouting as the fishing boats moored round us in the harbour loaded up, lit the great Tilley lamps that hung over the stern to attract the fish, and set off. This would be followed at about 4am by the coastal *caiques* starting up their diesel engines and departing. We ourselves would usually rise and be under way by 5.30 am, to make the most of the cool of the early morning. There were no sleeping bags to put away, for there was no room for such luxuries on board; we simply put sweaters and jeans on to sleep. Breakfast consisted of tea without milk, and bread - the delicious, tough

---

[23] St Symeon the New Theologian, one of the Desert Fathers, Oration 61, *Works* (Moscow, 1852), p. 100.

Greek bread spread with jam or honey - but no butter, as we had no refrigerator. Breakfast was usually eaten under way. At midday we would find a deserted cove where we could swim and eat, wash clothes and spread them on the shore to dry, and spread our limbs in comfort to sleep in the shade of a tree till the shadows began to lengthen again.

Diccon's enjoyment of this way of life was obvious, in spite of the discomforts. Once his ankles swelled up from the heat and the unaccustomed sitting, and one day when it was so windy that even he could not keep a hat on, the top of his head got badly burnt. But he never complained.

By no means every night was spent in a harbour moored among other boats. Lodged in my mind, unforgettable, is the memory of waking early, just as day was breaking, in a cove completely deserted except for one small house on the water's edge. Diccon was awake too, and we rose silently and waded ashore together. A fishing boat was just coming in, the glare of its Tilley lamp fading as the dawn spread. A very old man was paddling about in the shallows with his trousers rolled, his legs like beanpoles in the early grey light, casting a fishing-line. It was so still that smell and sound lingered on the air without dissipating - wood smoke from an outdoor oven, still gently smouldering from the day before, unseen but vivid-fragrant. There was a rustle of a cat climbing a vine on the veranda... Cocks answered each other distantly, and the hills were still waist deep in cloud.

On this particular morning the others were still asleep so we walked along the shore together. The sea's surface was so still it was like a clear glass to look down through. We left our clothes in two small piles and swam out into the bay. Ahead of us grey seas and grey sky merged so you could not see where one began and the other ended. Above the layer of mist the air was so still it was like a vacuum, so that the flight of a solitary bird, winging its way inland, seemed improbable in so limpid a medium.

We had forgotten that dawn was actually the busiest time of day, in those parts. A very old woman on a donkey, heading to the hills for firewood, passed close to our clothes at snail's pace. When finally we were able to come out and get dressed, we found the others ready to weigh anchor and be off.

At midday we passed the wide wooded bay where Jason was supposed to have built the *Argo*, in which he sailed to the Black Sea in search of the Golden Fleece. Two days earlier we had passed the Bay of Aulis, where Agamemnon had sacrificed his ten-year-old daughter to win from the gods a fair wind for Troy. We sighted the peninsular town of Trikeri, at the mouth of the bay, with thousand-foot cliffs plunging almost vertically down to the sea, where Sally and I had friends. The little town lay sizzling in the midday haze on the clifftop far above its harbour.

This year we had intended to bypass Trikeri and make straight for Skiathos. But the wind turned fluky and we had to take refuge in Trikeri Scala. We visited Iannis' wife - and the restaurant-keeper where we had eaten supper the previous year - and two brothers in the upper town that Sally knew, from a visit earlier in the year - and their father in the lower town. On our return to the harbour we were advised by a fisherman called Kosta to move the boat. After circling for an hour we tied her to a buoy and left her. We were then quietly warned by the wife of the sponge fisherman that Kosta and all his family were thieves, and that they had told us to move the boat to a more secluded place so that they could take our valuables. So Sally returned to the boat, while my job was to give a party on shore to well-wishers, among them the fisherman Kosta. Kosta kissed us both good night and asked if he could come on the boat as crew for a few days, next time she sailed in these waters.

Diccon's letter to my mother described the day's sailing, and the visit to Trikeri, and his amazement that *Crab*'s crew already knew so many people in the town, and that people were so friendly to us - he ends with a comment on his fellow crew:

Both Sally and Penny (chiefly Sally) had many friends there – indeed Crab's crew seems to have a husband in every port.

*

As soon as we were clear of the cliffs around Trikeri and approaching the open sea, far away to the north above the bare horizon loomed the dark cone of Mt Athos. For the next few days it was a constant presence on our port bow, as we headed north-east for the entrance to the Dardanelles. We had set our minds on reaching Istanbul to see for ourselves the problems presented to ancient merchant ships by the Bosporus passage.

3. Island of Monks

The Inner Sporades (June 12th to 14th)

The thundery, threatening weather was still with us. There was a mackerel sky and a disturbed sea, and a queer haze on the water, reducing visibility to less than a mile. But without any mishap we left the shelter of the Gulf of Evia and crossed the open sea to reach the first of the Sporades archipelago. Skiathos was like an Island of Eden after the bare Boeotian mudflats and the sterile crags of Evia. In the heat of the day the shade of pine, quince and fig was too tempting, and we landed and slept. We found that we were actually on the banks of a bee and crab farm. We were surrounded by thousands of edible crabs, and the buzzing of bees. Diccon remarked about Skiathos Town..."it seems strange, a thriving little modern town with no wheeled traffic at all. But of course on this tiny island there's nowhere for traffic to go".

In Skopelos we stopped to buy stores for the Aegean crossing ahead, and in oppressively hot weather visited some of the island's thirty churches. All night the *sirocco* wind swooped at us over the harbour, smashing plant pots in courtyards, and rattling the ornamental palm trees. We woke to find our canvas covering had been plucked off us while we were sleeping and blown away into the harbour.

Unknown Territory: Alonnisos and Kyra Panaghia (June 14th)

Beyond Skopelos, if we headed north-east, lay a few barren little islands and then open sea. We stopped at Alonnisos, where the resin-tappers Robin and I had met the year before on Skopelos had come from. Alonnisos had one or two villages, and we were able to restock our petrol. From there we set out confidently for Lemnos, some sixty miles away. But as we headed north-east, we found that a southward-setting current in the channel between Alonnisos and the next little island brought progress almost to a halt. The current was setting so strongly southwards that even with a brisk following wind carrying us northwards we were unable to make headway. Soon it would grow dark. In search of shelter for the night, we decided to stop at the island ahead – on the chart it was just called Pelagos; we learnt later it was also known as Kyra Panaghia, the island Robin and I had heard about the previous year from the resin-tappers. We made our way into a deep, forked bay with an islet at its mouth. Little did we realise how many days we would be trapped here.

There was already a fishing boat at anchor, and two more came into the bay close behind us. They must have been in search of shelter, like us, for there was no sign of habitation on the shore. After the hustle and clatter of the harbours we had spent the night in, this harbour was strange. Once we were moored to the skipper's satisfaction, in preparation for a windy night, we spoke to people from one of the fishing boats, who were lighting a small fire on the shore, asking them about the current. They shrugged, "Stay here tonight. Tomorrow go where you are going."

From the tone of voice we gathered that "tomorrow" was indefinite - and the outlook negative. The fishermen told us that there was a monastery on the island, with one monk and one lay brother in it, about ten kilometres away.

Time seemed to metamorphose while we were there, changing shape, now going very slowly, now very fast, as we waited for a fair wind so that we could leave. Perhaps it is against my better judgement that I have clearly delineated the five days we were stormbound. It might have been better to have left those five days as shapeless as they seemed at the time.

Kyra Panaghia SUNDAY (June 15th)

At 5 am I was woken by rain falling. I woke Diccon and we decided to set off for the monastery. It took two hours to walk to it. For most of the walk he was lost in thought. We entered the gate, which reminded me of the neat and tidy monastery on the foothills of Mount Hymettus, within easy reach of visitors from Athens. It was very well kept, surrounded with gardens full of hollyhocks and rosemary and fruit trees.

Diccon's next letter home told the events of that day:

Penny and I set off early Sunday morning, to get to the monastery for church, by a mountain path. It took two hours: when we got there, we found the service had ended at sunrise. The monks were giving lunch to a party of sailors who had just brought them a third monk, on a visit from Mt. Athos. The monks gave us Turkish delight, and cucumber salad, and wine from their own little vineyard. By this time the thunderstorm was about to burst, so the sailors took us part of the way round the island in their caique (we could see nothing for the blinding rain) to another bay where there was a charcoal-burners' hut where the necessities of life could be bought – oil, salt, cigarettes, axes. There we sheltered for an hour together with the charcoal-burners, the sailors, and a couple of goats, while the bread in the charcoal oven outside finished baking (actually the rain put the fire out so it had to be eaten half raw). Then some of the sailors decided they wanted to see Crab, so we set out in a party and walked the remaining three miles back to our own bay. Soon after it began to rain again, and there were no trees or caves or anything so we sat in oilskins round a myrtle-fire (myrtle has so much resin that it burns even when wet) and the fishermen boiled dried octopus in the ashes, and showed us how to brew an aromatic tea from a herb that grows there. They were as kind and nice as they could be, and as Crab has no shelter against rain, insisted on the four of us crawling under the deck of their boats to sleep, although that meant they had to sleep out in the rain themselves.

MONDAY (June 16th)

After breakfast we walked to a headland to look at the open sea. It was white with wave-crests whipped up by a fierce north wind. The seas were as high as ever. Everyone's food was running low, but the fishermen were used to this, and very cheerful in spite of it. We staved off hunger with endless sociable brews of camomile tea - for there was camomile growing wild all around us. The fishermen showed us how to dig a hole about ten feet from the water's edge and get fresh water. "Fresh" is too polite a name for it - it was the colour of weak beer, had the smell of peat-bogs, and the taste of water flavoured with Essence of Earth.

We had a visit from a skipper named Elevtheri, whose *caique* was on the other side of the island, and in the afternoon Sally and Maggs walked across the island with a bundle of charts, so that he could compare them with his own. His charts dated from well before the war, and he was anxious to know how much the banks had shifted since his charts had been made, for he was a deep sea fisherman, whereas the others all fished along the coasts.

In the evening we sat around the fire and talked. It is very pleasurable to be sitting by a fire in the darkness, aware that all around you the rain is falling, but that the heat of the fire is enough to cause it to evaporate before it lands on you. We talked, and after a while Diccon began a long folk story from Morocco, *Ishar the Fool.* Sentence by sentence, Sally translated. It was Diccon's only verbal contact with our companions on the island, apart from simple greetings, invitations and thanks, which was all that his Greek ran to. His personality seemed to come across to them very strongly as he told it. Because of his beard they referred to him as Pappas, the Priest, for foreigners with beards were still a rarity, and no one in Greece except priests wore beards.

"There was once a man round here," one of the men feeding the fire with myrtle branches began, "travelled abroad. Fell in love with a very beautiful woman. Her father was a big man. She left everything, and went away with him. Then he got back to his father's house, and after a time he tired of her...decided to get rid of her." There was something familiar about the story. I cast about in my mind, fishing for the memory. The story-teller went on,

"Jason wanted to marry a Greek girl, you see..."

That night, like the previous one, the fishermen insisted we should sleep in the hold of their *trechandiri*. They were from Trikeri, and knew Sally from a visit earlier in the year on a friend's yacht. The *trechandiri* from Alonnisos took advantage of a lull in the wind to slip away and return to their home till the northeaster had blown itself out.

TUESDAY (June 17th)

The wind continued to blow hard but it had stopped raining, and the fishermen occupied themselves with trying to catch rabbits for the pot. They caught them simply by stalking and pouncing like a cat.

The monk whom the sailors had delivered to the monastery was to be seen riding through the scrub from time to time. Their skipper, Elevtheri, said he was collecting male kids from the flocks on the island. He spoke bitterly about all the land owned by the church that had gone wild because of lack of use. The monks themselves he valued for their prayer, and the church also, but he was angry about the thousands of acres of wild scrubland and forest on Athos and elsewhere that with modern irrigation methods could become prosperous farms, if only it were not in the hands of the Church. This island itself was an "outstation" of Athos – the monks bred flocks of goats here and from time to time came to collect the kids because no female of any kind was allowed on the Holy Mountain.

"Do you believe in God, Diccon?" Sally asked, a propos the discussion about the monasteries.

"Yes – but God's existence is not something you can test and prove in the way you can test and prove scientific concepts. And it isn't self-evident either."

Our food was running out. We were reduced to collecting and boiling up winkles, so Diccon and I walked back up to the monastery with one of the fishermen. This man said he liked to eat one and a half *okas* of bread a day – an *oka* is just over a kilo, so he must have been feeling well-motivated to do the walk.

The long climb was a chance for talking with Diccon. The previous day, while the fishermen were hunting rabbits, I had noticed Diccon looking at *Crab*, lost in thought, and I asked him now if by any chance he remembered what he had been thinking about.

"I was thinking about the short story – I think it's by Pirandello – about a man who was a bitter misanthropist, who decided he would have a benevolent mask made for him to wear, to deceive everybody. When he reached the age of fifty, he would suddenly take it off, and reveal his true face. But when the time came, and he tore away the disguise, his own face had become like the mask, his expression kindly and compassionate," he said.

"You know, this boat is changing you and Sally. Both of you two spent much of your childhood in boarding schools, being groomed to win scholarships. You're both a bit aloof and intellectual – certainly Frances complains at home of the effect of all that on *you*. But this little boat is so unpretentious and friendly, people immediately react to you in a friendly way, they don't feel threatened, as they well might if you suddenly arrived in a gleaming yacht. I wonder whether when you get to the end of these four months of sailing, you'll find you are different people."

"Or whether we'll quickly revert to our old ways!"

"In Pirandello's story, the man found he *couldn't*."

Diccon was echoing something Donald had noticed when he was with us when we were storm-bound for nearly a week, and so kindly cared for, in the fishing-village of Pozzallo.

At the monastery we were loaded with onions, cucumbers and a great slab of bread the size of a small tombstone. Talking to Diccon as we walked back down the hill about yesterday's question from Sally, "Do you believe in God, Diccon?", I teased him for being for once somewhat tongue-tied. He said he had found it hard to formulate his thoughts in words.

"God exists in the same way as *I* exist – I can't *prove* I exist because I only know it from the inside. The basis of scientific investigation is number: you have to have more than one of a species before you can start making generalisations. But seen from the inside, I am unique. And God is unique – and all His actions unique."

I felt that for Diccon religious truth was of the same order as poetry - and his love for poetry was something private and passionate.

That evening there was a lull in the wind, and most of the fishing boats took the chance to get back to their homes. Since it was far too rough to fish, they would be better to be at home where there was work to be done. The only one to stay on was Eleftheri, the captain who had brought Diccon and me halfway round the island in his *caique* after meeting us at the monastery the first day. He remained in his small harbour on the other side of the island, insisting on waiting till tomorrow in the hopes that the wind would moderate enough for us to leave together.

Kyra Panaghia to Psathoura – WEDNESDAY (June 18th)

We rose two hours before dawn, motored round the headland in the teeth of the wind, and Eleftheri met us and took us in tow, telling us to ship the engine. The wind had dropped noticeably. But as soon as we ventured beyond the shelter of the headland, we realised that the seas were still high. By six in the morning the wind had sprung up again. Diccon's letter to my mother describes the next lap of the journey:

Again the wind proved too much, so we ran for yet another desert island. Psathoura is long and low, volcanic rock and sand, and here there had been no rain since January. The pilot-book says there is no harbour, and warns all craft away, but the Lemnos fishermen knew a little cubby-hole in the boulders with just enough room for two little boats like ours.

...So here we are on shore again, after a delicious second breakfast of sea-urchins and brown bread, lunch of what was left of the monastery salad, with winkles and crabs...sleep during the hot hours under an awning made of a sail...Penny is now cooking something for supper – heaven knows what, but it is sure to be delicious, and after that we start once more for Lemnos, and there really is no other island to stop at on the way now. But this is the day when I was supposed to have left Crab, in the Dardanelles, and we are still the wrong side of the Aegean!

Psathoura to Lemnos (June 18th to 19th)

We left Psathoura at 8 pm, hoping that by night the wind would be less strong. At midnight Elevtheri shouted to us to say that two should come on board the *caique*, so as to lighten *Crab*. Diccon and I opted to stay, as Diccon was good as a helmsman in such circumstances. Somehow, with amazing agility, Sally and Maggs transferred from *Crab* onto the *caique* in the dark, with both boats bouncing this way and that in the dark. Diccon and I, whose turn it was to be on watch, took turns at the helm as *Crab* butted into head seas in the pitch dark till our faces felt stiff from the salt spray and our arms ached from pumping. Just as dawn was breaking our two boats put in to yet another deserted island, Aghios Eustratios (Eleftheri had altered course for it at midnight). We rested till midday, then left again for Lemnos. And so it was not until four in the afternoon of the next day that we finally reached Lemnos.

This part of our journey had proved so slow that, had it not been for our determination to reach Istanbul, we would surely have given up and changed course. Far easier to thread our way south down the islands of the Eastern Aegean with following winds, and forget the Bosphorus.

That night we ate at a restaurant on the quay with Elevtheri and his mother, and that meal tasted like the finest *cordon bleu.* One thing troubled us. Elevtheri was too proud to accept money for all the help he had given us – the offer would be insulting. And so on parting Diccon gave him his pre-war German binoculars, one of the few precious possessions on the boat.

Lemnos to Çanakkale, Dardanelles (June 20th to 22nd)

The weather had changed; but what little wind there was the following day was still against us. In the late afternoon we put into a harbour on the north coast of Lemnos not mentioned in any of the sailing directions. The fishermen on the Island of Monks had told us of it. They said it had been large and flourishing in Byzantine days, but the coastline had sunk slightly, and the old harbour was submerged. Here, besides the natural silting-up process, there was a submerged mole, both inside and outside the breakwaters. But for a boat like ours there was plenty of water. It was good to be able to make use of so venerable a site.

We were now heading due east, and near to Turkey. We passed the island of Tenedos where Agamemnon's fleet had laid in wait till dark while the unsuspecting Trojans, thinking the Greeks had gone, had taken the wooden horse within their walls. Diccon's letter continued:

Saturday 21st June. Next day we moved to the last bay of all on the island of Lemnos, washed clothes, and made other preparations for the final crossing to Turkey. Lemnos is a strange, volcanic island.

Just before six in the evening we set out for the Dardanelles – we continued all night, passing along the south coast of Imbros (where we didn't land, for once), with plenty of lighthouses to guide us to the mouth of the Dardanelles. I steered most of the night, turning in for a couple of hours at half past five.

Sunday 22nd June. The Dardanelles are rather like a wide and turbulent river, with a strong current running out, but luckily we had a strong following wind.

We kept close to the shore as we moved up the straits, where there was a back eddy that would carry us northwards. The boiling effect where the two currents rubbed against each other made it easy to see the limits of our back eddy. We kept as far from the shore as possible because we were nervous of being shot at by the forts on either side of the straits as we approached Çanakkale. But in fact all that happened was that a little Sharpie dinghy with six Turkish youths on it came out from the harbour and circled round us as we sailed towards the narrows, which was humiliating considering we had got a sail like them, and they were no larger!

In Çanakkale we had trouble finding a space to anchor. Finally we had to anchor off the main pier. This was where Diccon was due to leave us and we were due to pick up a new member of crew. The GPO was surprised at the idea of *poste restante*, but produced letters in the end. Among them was a letter to Sally to say that her expected crew was not able to join us. But there was also one for Diccon from Bavaria, telling him not to come till after June 29th. With alacrity Diccon offered to come with us to Istanbul. He would have to leave us as soon as we got there, and from then on, there would be just us three girls, till the next rendezvous on the homeward journey.

I remembered how the fishermen had reproached us as we sat round their myrtle fire in the rain, "Poor old man! He ought to be allowed to sit and keep warm in an armchair, at his age, not be dragged around by you things." When we translated this to him he was much amused. I haven't been half as happy as this for ages!

The customs officers in Çanakkale must have felt the same way as the fishermen, for they invited him to spend the night on a spare bunk on the customs launch, and the sailor on the other bunk sprinkled him with rose water before he went to sleep. He slept for nine hours.

Chapter Four
Island of Murderers

Çanakkale to Marmora Island (June 23rd to 24th)

We passed up the Dardanelles Straits, stopping at the harbour town of Lampsaki to shop and buy petrol. A friendly Turk who spoke French guided us round the town after a crowd had taken us to his doorstep. I have a vivid memory of the blare of loudspeakers coming from every waterside café, but by means of gestures our guide asked the owners to have the good manners to turn them down till we were out of earshot, which they did. Just as we were about to leave, the police caught up with us. They had to ring Çanakkale for instructions, and then asked our excuse for stopping. "Ran out of petrol," we said. They told us that the whole coast on both sides was a military area, and no stopping was permitted. Troy was only a taxi-ride away but we could not visit it.

I half longed to visit Troy, but knowing that the city was a good deal further from the sea than it had been in the Mycenean Age, I decided it was perhaps better to store my imagined version of the Trojan War intact, untrammelled by mere facts. We left at 4.40 pm and pushed on right through the night and through the first half of the next day. There was a freshening south-west wind, backing to south. We decided to head for Marmara Island and shelter there. We anchored in Palatia Bay, on the north coast of the island, at 12.30 pm, and immediately fell asleep. Rousing ourselves at 4.30 pm, we went ashore and, to our surprise, found the people very_friendly, especially the mayor. Sally wrote in the logbook:

We were given little presents of all kinds, and loaned a table and chairs so that we could sit and eat supper on shore. One Greek-speaking old man, acting as interpreter, told us that the island used to be all Christians: it was deserted after the earthquake in 1935 and now repopulated by summer workers from Anatolia.

Marmara Island to Imrali (June 25th)

We left next day at 6.15 am and pushed on ruthlessly. When we were sailing such long distances each day, we all of us wanted to read when we were not at the helm. Fortunately Diccon had brought with him *The Brothers Karamazov*. Even more fortunately, salt water had caused it to swell and come apart at the seams. He shared the book out among the four of us, for the only other two books on board had long since been read from cover to cover.

Hour after hour we pushed on, mostly motoring, since the wind was light or nonexistent, though there was quite a strong swell coming from the north-east. But at 7 pm a strong north-easterly got up. We had already decided to take shelter in the lee of the western end of Imrali Island, which our Black Sea Admiralty Pilot recommended. At 8 pm, as it was getting dark, we dropped anchor. The shore was too stony to take a shore anchor. The wind continued all night. Sally and I got up from time to time to check whether the anchor was dragging.

Diccon's final long letter home (never in fact posted) tells a strange tale:

Constantinople, 28th June 1958

My dear,

When I found there was no way of getting from Çanakkale to Constantinople and decided to come on with 'Crab' I had no idea that the most fantastic part of the journey was only just beginning…Really! To wake up in the morning to find the boat surrounded by a deputation (in their underpants) waist deep in the sea, from a community of six hundred convicted murderers, proffering bouquets of carnations…

But I should begin at the beginning…

Sunday 22nd June: We reached Canakkale and spent hours tramping round from Customs to Police, to Medical Officer, and back again, and shopping in that rather dull and dusty little town: Troy only a taxi-ride, but no time to go and see it. That night a kindly customs officer invited us to tie alongside the customs launch, and I slept in a spare bunk in the fo'c'le.

Monday: We were in a part of the Dardanelles where landing is forbidden. Indeed, all the Western end of the Sea of Marmara, including the Island of Marmara, is forbidden landing, according to the charts. But with the current out of the Black Sea against us all the time the progress was slow, and on ***Tuesday*** *morning the wind sprang up again, so the only thing seemed to be to make for Marmora Island (we were more or less abeam of it by this time) to look for an anchorage even if we couldn't land.*

On the whole, the coast of the island was pretty forbidding: rugged limestone and marble cliffs, with few coves or beaches; and at the foot of the first bay we explored a Russian steamer piled upon the rocks, with only her stern above water, as a Memento Mori for all poor mariners like us. The next bay proved better, however, with a village at the end of it, and the whole hillside behind pocked with the marble quarries for which the island is famous. So we anchored in sheltered water at last, and rigged what shade we could against the heat of the day, slumbering and bathing alternately till about five.

Wednesday: we made an early start, as the next island lay forty miles ahead. This island, Imrali – called on the chart, Kalolimnos – was much smaller than Marmara, but outside the area where landing was forbidden, and only thirty miles from the Golden Horn. There was a flat calm, so we just chugged ahead with the outboard motor hour after hour, and reached Kalolimnos just before dark, just as a north-easter began to get up. The island has NO harbours, but we could at least shelter behind it, and this we did, in a shallow stony bay, where there was a garden shaded by planes and fig-trees, but no house.

Thursday: And then in the morning, that deputation with the carnations...the first thing that seemed really odd about them was that one of them seized our bottle of methylated spirits and drained it in a draught...then an imperious figure appeared on the shore and shouted at them and they scattered. He could talk some English, and explained that he was their school-master, and that the island was a penal colony. 'Six hundred criminals-guilty. All mens here and no womens for twenty-two years. All criminals-guilty. Too dangerous you remain. Killings with the knife, girl-stealings, very dangerous, but all good men, have no fear...'

So we and the 'good' men sat in the shady garden and discussed the situation. We couldn't stay there – that was clear. On the other hand, it was too stormy to put to sea. Finally the schoolmaster sent for the island's caique to tow us round to the artificial harbour on the other side of the island, where the settlement was: then the Governor could decide what to do.

Here we were interviewed by the Governor, a tall and rather exquisite young man, with fine, thin features. We couldn't remain for the next night: he was quite firm about that. But we couldn't, in that weather, put to sea – Sally was equally firm about that! A steamer bound for Istanbul was calling that evening, and we could leave in the steamer. But what about 'Crab?' we wailed. 'Crab' also must leave on the steamer.

At first Sally refused point blank to risk 'Crab' being lifted on board the steamer out of the open sea – for the steamer couldn't come very close in – but at last even Sally gave in, as indeed she had to. And so, when the steamer arrived, 'Crab' was towed out to it by the caique, and somehow, it did seem a bit miraculous, she was lifted out of the water by the ship's davits, and lashed outside the rail of the upper deck.

The log adds some details:

Ate lunch in the prison restaurant – milk, eggs, butter, bread, cheese yoghourt, cherries, and buttermilk! Packed boat for loading, took her out, with Sally steering and two convicts rowing – towed behind motorboat until we came alongside with much bumping. Altogether terrifying business. When they got her halfway up on the davits they began to bend, being only meant for one ton, and had to unload. Sailor who was put in boat to do so cut half our lashing-ropes before we could stop him... Eventually they failed to hoist her onto deck (in any case only place was on top of smaller boat which would probably have squashed), and lashed her to rail. Fortunately steamer very steady though quite large sea running. First officer spoke good English and very kind and friendly.

When we arrived in the port of Istanbul we tried to make arrangements to leave Crab and our belongings on board until daylight, but customs prevented us: made us unload her, and put everything back in alongside. Choppy sea and very dirty quay. Then kept us until 2400 doing passports and other formalities. Letter from Turkish counsellor helped, but produced it rather late. However, due to it we got our ride on the steamer free (having made a fuss about money-shortage at Imrali hoping to be allowed to stay, but merely made them offer to pay out of their own pockets, which we couldn't accept). Maggs and RH allowed to sleep on our steamer (s/s Gemlik) in First and Second Officer's cabins. Customs insisted on keeping passports till morning.

In spite of all the delays, we had reached Istanbul at 2 am on precisely the date Sally expected to arrive! Understandably, Sally spent a long time in the small hours explaining to the entry authorities how we came to be there.

5. First Impressions of Istanbul As Was

Istanbul – The European side (June 27th)

Early the next morning Sally and I woke to the particular thump of rigging and clatter of billycans that signified a series of waves from a passing big ship. A large oil tanker, heavily laden, was passing in the distance, disturbing us with her wash. This was something different, to be woken in the morning by passing Russian oil tankers! Diccon and Maggs had spent the night in officers' cabins on the steamer which had brought us. They soon re-appeared on the quay above. We shouted up to them that we wanted to move away from the Customs Quay, without waiting till we could have our passports. We would come back for them. Maggs and Diccon cast off most of our moorings, and then somehow scrambled down and joined us.

As we chugged northwards past the promontory with the Blue Mosque, Aghia Sophia, and the gardens of the Topkapi Palace, I was dumbfounded by the sheer scale of the waterway. At Istanbul the coast draws in to form the entrance to the Bosphorus Channel, which is not much more than a mile wide. At that time there was not a single bridge spanning the waterway. On our left the gardens of Topkapi Seray, and hidden below the greenery the palace itself, which for 470 years had housed the imperial headquarters, and between 5,000 and 10,000 souls - court functionaries and servants, scribes, guards and women. All that could be seen above the greenery were pointed chimneys and roofs, and a multiplicity of domes. The whole promontory was shrouded in a kind of haze - not mist or fog, nor traffic-pollution. It puzzled me.It was not till we took a tram into the centre of the city, later that day, that I saw what was causing that haze.

On the other shore we could just make out the hollow square of the Selimiye Barracks, and sparser buildings, with rolling green hills further northwards. This windswept, swift-moving waterway, dividing Europe from Asia, that now lay shimmering in the morning light, was once spectacularly crossed by the Persian king, Darius I, who constructed a bridge of boats so as to march his army across and lead them to the Danube basin. His successor, Xerxes, used a similar bridge of boats to get his army across the Dardanelles. In modern times, it was not bridged till the suspension bridges of 1973 and 1978. When the first was completed, it was the fourth-longest suspension bridge in the world.

We chugged on northwards, following the line of the coast, and crossed the entrance to the Golden Horn, spanned by the Galata Bridge. We were making very slow progress because of the strength of the current against us, so we had time to see under Galata Bridge, looking up into that vast natural harbour which divides the city on the European shore of the Bosphorus in two. We chugged on and on along the shore north-eastwards, trying to find somewhere to tie up that would be quiet. Finally we anchored just south of the ornate nineteenth-century Palace of Dolmabahçe - alongside a large cargo steamer loading rubble from a demolition site. Our new anchorage was not very calm, and there was the wash from passing ferries, but it was better than the Customs Quay.

Diccon had found a bit about Constantinople in French in Braudel's two-volume tome in French on the Mediterranean world in the age of Philip II, and had showed it to me the previous winter. Describing Constantinople in its heyday in the sixteenth century, Braudel writes:

Constantinople was not a town, it was an urban monster, a metropolis. Its site made it a divided city, and this was a source both of its greatness and of its difficulties. There were three separate cities joined together.' Of the three cities, Constantinople, or Stambul, or Istanbul, was the largest. It was the triangular area between the Golden Horn and the Sea of Marmara. In the sixteenth century it was an area packed with trees, gardens, squares with fountains, meadows, promenades. There were 400 mosques with lead roofs. Around each was an open space. The mosque of Suleiman the Magnificent, the sulaimana, was almost a city-quarter in itself, containing an esplanade, a madrassa, libraries, hospital, and schools and gardens. Finally, the most sumptuous of all, the Seray, at the southernmost end of the city, a succession of kiosks, palaces, and gardens. Istanbul was predominantly a city of Turks, their white turbans outnumbering the others…but here were also a number of Greeks with blue turbans, Jews with yellow turbans, as well as Armenians and Tsiganes.[24]

We had to go back and collect our passports. A friendly member of the crew had agreed to keep an eye on *Crab*. Our first stage of the journey was on the tram, which took us to somewhere near the Customs Quay. As we jolted through the city, it seemed as if it had been through a blitz. All around us we saw clouds of dust as bulldozers were pulling down

[24] Fernand Braudel, La Mediterranée et le monde Mediterranéen a l'Epoque de Philippe II, translated into English, 1975.

the old buildings. Doubtless they were rat-runs, crowded together so closely that there was no room for more than two donkeys to pass each other, but they were very picturesque, and they represented a way of life and neighbourhood that would be gone forever. It was devastating to witness destruction on this scale. We had no one we could ask the reasons for it.

Once we had collected our passports we rode back on the tram to the northern end of Galata Bridge. From there we went on foot, heading for the British Consulate. As we climbed, we stopped several times to check that we were going in the right direction. People were friendly, even when we found we had no language in common. But we found that young men were particularly keen to practice their English on us. I later learnt that this was because those of age to do their military service could get half as much pay again if they had proficiency in a foreign language, and many were strenuously teaching themselves English, using BBC World Service programmes.

As we walked we discussed our immediate plans with Diccon, even though he would no longer be with us. We told him we were determined to try and get *Crab* all the way up the Bosphorus, that nineteen-mile-long channel separating Europe and Asia, in places less than a half mile wide with a current always running north–south - on average at three knots, but in places it could run at seven knots.

"Do such small boats go up it?" he asked. Sally told him of her yachtsman friend Douglas Dixon (the ex-naval-officer whom she had met again in Greece during the winter) who had described to her the experience of taking his small yacht the *Dusmarie* up the Bosphorus. He said that the stream was often like a millrace, but even such small craft as his *Dusmarie* could work upstream by careful use of the eddies along the shores. He had not seen many other yachts - the world that passed by was mostly huge Russian oil tankers.

When we stopped walking uphill to rest and turned, we could see the Bosphorus below us through a gap between the high buildings. *Crab* was moored in an inlet so small the only other occupants were two local fishing boats and some ducks. But she was tucked in behind a cargo steamer loading rubble, and we could not see her.

At the British Consulate people were very helpful (and amused about our stop on Imrali prison island). They recommended a hotel to Diccon, who needed to catch his plane and travel to Germany, where he would join up with my mother. When we told them where we had left *Crab* they shook their heads – whether in disapproval or in sheer disbelief wasn't obvious. They told us that there was a yacht club at Fenerbahçe, on the Asiatic side of the Bosphorus, and we would do better to find a berth there. There would be shelter whatever the wind, and at Kadiköy, a taxi-ride away, there was a large shopping centre where we could get supplies. They warned us that the next day was a major Feast Day, a *bayram*, and all shops would be shut, both that day and the day after.

The idea of crossing to the Asiatic shore was alarming to me. This Bosphorus was not a backwater, it was open sea, with currents. On the other hand it had become plain to Maggs and me that on this side of the Bosphorus there was precious little welcome for a boat as small as ours.

"I can't see what you're fussing about!" Sally responded, "I was here, back in April, in a yacht owned by friends of Kosta Tsallis, and I know the Fenerbahçe harbour – I'll find it without problems. Of course it means that when we want to visit the Old City or whatever we will have to travel up the coast to the ferry terminal at Usküdar, and then take a ferryboat across the Bosphorus to the quay by the Galata Bridge. Too bad!"

Diccon mentioned he had seen signs close to Dolmabahçe indicating "Naval Museum" as we set out from the boat. He suggested that we should visit it together before he returned to the boat to collect his baggage and go to his hotel.

"I've been to the naval museum already – I'll stay with the boat," Sally offered.

Inside the naval museum, in a separate building, there was a collection of *pazar caiques*, the beautiful, long, narrow rowing barges used by the sultans for visiting their summer palaces. With two tiers of oars and oarsmen packed close together, they must have travelled at ten knots, we reckoned. The elegant, raised prows and poops, with their intricate woodwork, enchanted me.

"Are you going to be OK, venturing up the Bosphorus, just the three of you?" Diccon asked, suddenly and untypically practical for a moment. "Up until now you've had me, more or less keeping the engine working – and useful as ballast." I noticed he tactfully did not say he was also far more useful on the oars than we were.

"We'll soon find out, Diccon!" It was too complicated to explain to him that, judging by people's reactions to us two girls in Malta, one way and another help would be available if we got into serious difficulties.

"What on earth gave you the idea of trying to see whether you could sail up, against the current?"

I told him about the article by the rather brilliant American archaeologist, Rhys Carpenter, responsible for the American excavation of the Agora in Athens.

"You reckon *Crab* is like an ancient merchant-ship? She can't make good more than two knots against a head wind - probably not even that much. You want to see if you can get up all the same?"

"Exactly. It's nineteen miles long, and that isn't much! I don't believe all the imported goods and the colonists had to come in *pentekonters*, they are not suited for it!"

"Tourists don't usually go up the Bosphorus - or at least I've never met anyone who wanted to. It's the Blue Mosque and Santa Sofia, not a ride in a little coal-burning steamer they want. I wish I could come too!"

"If we had *YOU* with us it would be too easy! The engine would work, probably. And we'd have a good oarsman, if it didn't. You're not invited!"

By the time we three rejoined Sally on *Crab* it was already late afternoon. Diccon gathered up his baggage and we said goodbye. Sally and Maggs were perhaps relieved to see him go, and to have more space, but I knew I would miss him greatly. Naturally - he was, after all, my father. But he was actually the fittest - or rather the crew with most stamina and staying power - that we had had.

Still vivid in my mind was that morning on Imrali Island when we had sat in the shade of the plane-trees with the lifers and their schoolmaster, and talked and talked, Diccon brilliant at communicating in monosyllabic, broken English that could be understood. All his imaginative powers as a writer were brought into play in that conversation. His interest in them as people was self-evident: he leant forward, eyes alight. Since he thought of himself as a man with a life sentence as a writer, perhaps it was fellow-feeling for other "lifers".

I watched Diccon as he departed down the quay. When he had gone ten yards he turned back. "I've forgotten *The Brothers Karamazov,*" he said.

Reluctantly we each ferreted about in our luggage for the damp-swollen section of the novel we were reading, and handed the pieces over, and said goodbye again.

6. Exploring the Currents of the Bosphorus

To Fenerbahçe Yacht Basin (June 27th)

After saying goodbye to Diccon, we motored south-eastwards across the strait to find the yacht harbour, the current helping us on our way. Out in midstream I trailed my fingers in the water. There was something uncanny about the coldness and freshness of the water.

We made our way to the yacht harbour at Fenerbahçe, found somewhere we could berth for the night, set off that same evening for *Kadiköy*, where there was a big market, and had a taxi ride back to the anchorage. We found there was the useful system of the *dolmuş* - taxis taking several passengers at the same time. The following day we made contact with the commodore of the yacht club, named Kemal. He invited us to take tea with him on his yacht at the end of the day.

*

It was strange going down the companionway to a cabin, taking care not to bang my head as I went. Our host was dismissive at first. He said he was not sure whether we would be able to make progress against all the various currents, even with the Seagull outboard engine on full throttle - and we stressed that as far as possible we would try and do it under sail.

Gradually he began to warm to the paradoxical nature of our plan, and I began to like him more and more. He spread out his large-scale chart on the cabin table and showed us the Narrows, where the stream was no more than 7000 metres wide. It was marked by a fortress on each side of the Bosphorus. Here the current speeded up to four knots, and between Rumeli Burnu and Anadolu Hissari was known as the "Devil's Current", because it could run at up to seven knots. He showed us how there was a kind of "dog's leg", a sharp bend in the channel, at Kandilli on the Asiatic side. This sharp bend caused a fierce current to sweep across the straits, making a millrace where it hit the European side at Arnavutköy. He did not tell us where to tack, how to make best use of back eddies - we would see clearly enough, when the time came.

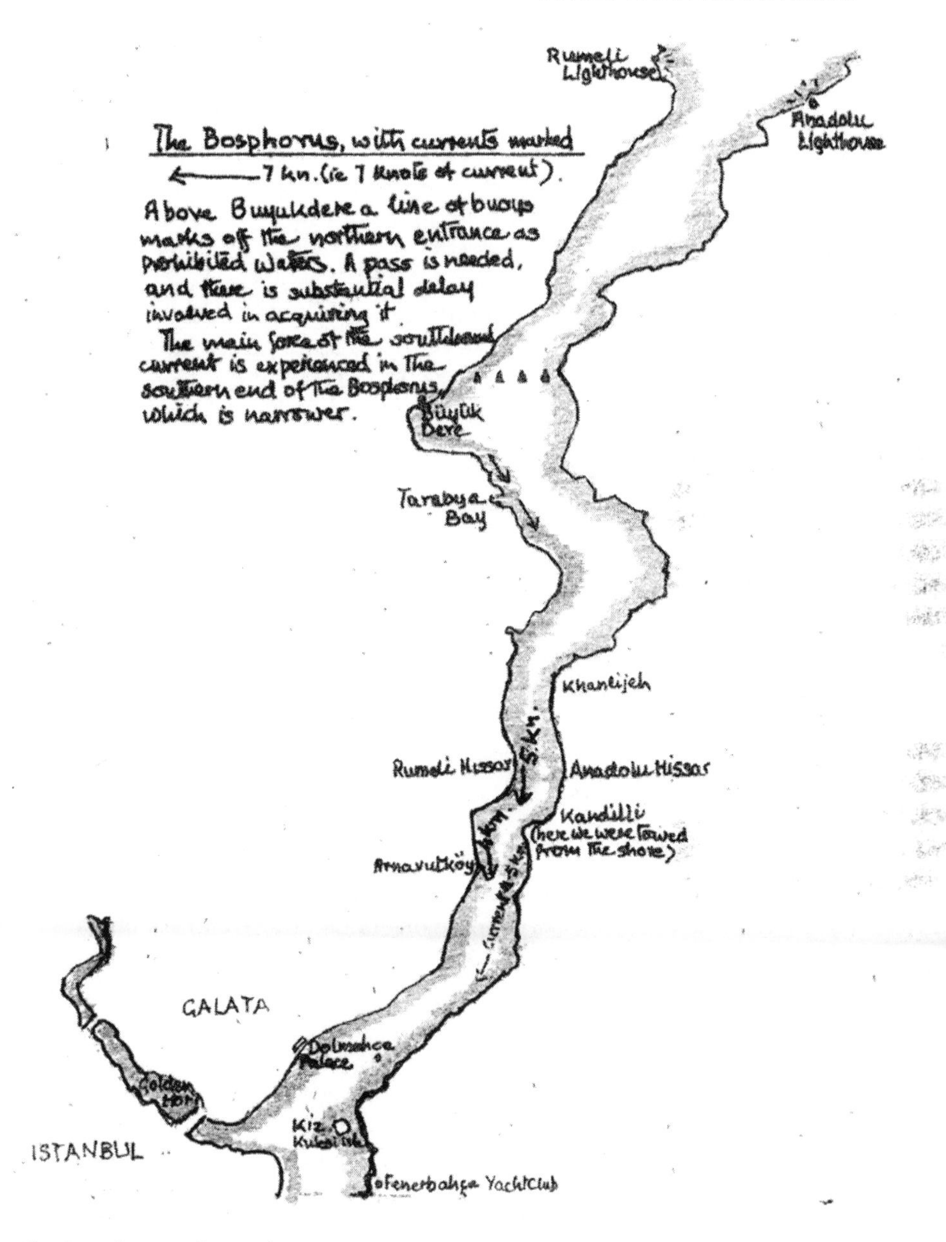

The Bosphorus channel

He did tell us that the rule was that up-going small boats hugged the two shores, while southbound traffic used the main current in the centre of the channel - bigger vessels kept on the port side of a central line, each way.

Arnavutköy itself, the Albanian village about halfway up the Bosphorus, was one of his favourite places. The seafront was lined with wooden houses. He told us to land and explore there, if we could. There were two Greek churches and narrow back streets. He told us that off the point the current ran so strongly that, according to the Renaissance traveller Gyllius, even crabs could make no headway, so they left the water and travelled overland. Their claws, he said, had left a perceptible track in the rock, proudly shown to visitors. Another of our host's favourite places was Tarabya or Therapia, where the foreign embassies had had their summer residencies before Ankara became the capital and all the embassies were transferred.

Kemal stressed that we would not actually be able to enter the Black Sea without a special pass, and it would not be worth our trying to get one. Sally already knew this, and knew that there was a line of buoys just north of Buyükdere beyond which passage was forbidden. He told us a little about the fortress at Rumeli Hissar, which was a good landmark. It had been built in 1452 to prevent ships from coming to the aid of Constantinople from the Black Sea when it was under siege by Fatih Mehmet. Once Constantinople had fallen, it had no further military use, so it became a prison, and the bodies of those executed would be tossed into the fast-moving current.

Journey up the Bosphorus – European shore (June 28th)

We set off under engine at 8.15 am. None of us three weighed much more than nine stone, and *Crab* rode high in the water, responding much more friskily than usual to sudden puffs of wind, heeling unexpectedly. We felt nervous enough, setting off to battle with the currents in this vast waterway, but her friskiness gave me a jittery feeling. We passed plenty of weekend fishermen, their small boats not so much smaller than *Crab*. Whenever a big ship or a ferry passed, like us, they were tossed about wildly. The big ferries all had their haloes of gulls. What amazed me was the variety among those gulls: the great fulmars and the little kittiwakes co-existing in this semi-urban, semi-nomadic life.

Close to the Asiatic coast, more or less opposite the entrance to the Golden Horn, is a little rocky knoll with a white tower on it, known to Westerners as Leander's Tower. To the Turks, it is Kiz Kulesi – Maiden's Tower. We chugged slowly past Kiz Kulesi at 9.05 am, and made our crossing back to the Palace of Dolmabahçe. As we crossed towards the palace we looked westwards towards the Old City, a magnificent skyline of domes and minarets, shrouded in dust-smog. It felt historic and forlorn.

To the north we could see the long waterfront of the Dolmabahçe Palace, downstream of which we had anchored on our first morning - a massive, westernising confection in greying marble that had helped to ruin the Ottoman regime. *Dolmabahçe* means "filled-in garden". Originally it had been an inlet, but one of the sultans had filled it in so as to make a park and pleasure gardens right on the water's edge, close to the heart of the city. It was not built on till the early nineteenth century. Just downstream of Dolmabahçe Palace I glimpsed the small inlet close to where we had moored on our first day. The entrance had been blocked by the cargo-steamer, which had now gone. Inside I could see ducks feeding, or spreading their wings in the sun, and two small fishing-boats, and I felt a pang of longing in my stomach for *small* things.

Finding that once again we had the current with us - a back eddy close inshore - we stopped the engine to cool it. This counter-current could be used by any boats small enough to go close, alongside the rocks. We continued northwards. I was at the helm, keeping only eighteen inches off the rocks with our fair-weather mainsail and the help of the back eddies.

The city lay on both sides of us as we sailed. The separate villages were linked to Istanbul at that time only by the bevy of some thirty coal-burning ferry-steamers. Some of these ferries plied to the Princes Islands, others zigzagged up the Bosphorus. About half simply linked the two sides of the strait. *Crab* was such an improbable craft in which to venture on that great waterway.

The Owl and the Pussycat went to sea, in a beautiful pea-green boat.
They took some honey, and plenty of money,
Wrapped up in a five pound note[25]

Prudent mariners compared with us three girl students, who had neither some honey as reserves, nor plenty of money.

Enjoying a following wind, *Crab* skimmed along. But now progress against the shore was at zero, and so at 10:45 am we re-started the engine. An hour later we had reached Arnavutköy Point, Akintu Burnu, where

[25] Edward Lear, "The Owl and the Pussycat," *Nonsense Songs, Stories, Botany, and Alphabets*. London: Robert John Bush, 1871.

the crabs opted to go overland because the current flowing round the point was so fast. Suddenly a formidable strength of current sweeping round the point confronted us. It would not help to cross to the other side: Kemal had told us about the race, the "Devil's Current", that could run at eight or nine knots at Kandilli on the Asian side, and about how the current swept across the Bosphorus to strike the point at Arnavutköy, where once again a tremendous race could develop. So this was the Devil's Current. We were in it! In addition, we had picked a time when current and wind were here in direct opposition, which made for plenty of spray. The engine spluttered and gave out - just as it had when crossing the Straits of Messina.

Under fair-weather sails the boat was slicing through the water at four knots, heeled hard-over, but against the land was making no progress at all. It was almost midday already. We decided to cross to the Asiatic side and see if we could find back eddies that would help us along. It was then that we discovered a flaw in Rhys Carpenter's argument that merchant ships could not get up the Bosphorus. His theory - that what triggered the opening up of the Black Sea to trade with the Mediterranean was purely and simply the development of the fifty-oared *penteconter*, a precursor of the Viking longboats - had overlooked the evidence on the ground.

The Asiatic shore

We crossed over to a protruding headland on the Asiatic side, and I at once noticed a path close to the water's edge and suggested I went ashore with a towrope. I found, however, that I hadn't the strength to get much leverage against the current. But then suddenly I found the weight taken from me. Unnoticed, someone had arrived from nowhere to help pull. Our log says that we were using both mainsail and oars, and also had one person ashore with a tow line, and moved upstream "with the help of a man on shore". As I read it, I remembered the scene. I later read, in Michael Pereira's book on Istanbul[26], that in the days before steam both promontories were impossible to negotiate in oared boats, but *yedekciler* - men to pull them round the headland with towropes - were on the towpath. One can well imagine a village springing up nearby whose inhabitants made a living by helping boats along. In this way the powerful southerly current off both points could be outmanoeuvred.

[26] *Istanbul: Aspects of a City*, Chaucer Press 1968.

Rhys Carpenter, a yachtsman himself, had conceded that much of the route could be negotiated by making use of back-eddies close inshore, but he had not allowed for the possibility that there would be a community who made their living by towing ships round the crucial headlands where the current was at its fastest.

Once past Kandilli we could relax a little and enjoy what was around us, here on the Asiatic side. *The Asian side is covered with fruit trees, villages, and the most delightful landscapes,* wrote Lady Mary Wortley Montagu[27] and it did not seem to have changed much since then. Inland were thickly wooded hills, with the darkness of cypress and copper-beech intermingled with a lighter green. At that time, when there were no bridges across the Bosphorus, the total population of Istanbul and the area lining the Bosphorus was half a million, whereas now it stands at 18 million!

Each village on the Asian shore had its own character; they were independent little communities with the mosque's minaret and a jetty visible. Presumably also there were a few shops. The villages lay two or three miles apart, the gaps plugged by *yali,* delightful wooden houses with carved balconies that jutted out over the water. No doubt these were summer residences originally, they now had the look of houses permanently inhabited. Each house had its own jetty, with a garden between it and the road - a road lined with trees giving shade.

At 12.45 pm we passed Anadolu Hissari (the fortress on the Asiatic side, opposite Roumeli Hissari). Forty-five minutes later we decided to cross back from Khanlijeh to the western shore, since against the land we were making no progress at all.

Return to European side

There was a fresh southerly breeze, which was just what we needed. But alas as soon as we approached the European side the wind turned westerly. As we passed the resort of Therapia, it was increasing by the minute. But we were determined to go on. We were determined to reach a point where we would have a clear view up into the Black Sea.

When we reached the south-east corner of Buyükdere Bay the wind was sweeping across the water in sudden squalls, darkening its surface, plucking the tops off the crests of the waves.

[27] *Letters 1709–1762,* published in London in 1906.

"Are those the spar buoys at last, the ones warning us to keep out?" I shouted to Sally, pointing to a row of black dots, topped by flags, leaning at 45 degrees to the wind. Sally nodded.

"Let's get as close as we can!" We decided we must change to storm sails. The wind grew rapidly stronger, lashing us with spray, and even under storm sails the boat heeled till her gunwale was within two inches of the water. Reluctantly we decided we would have to turn back – the wind was now too strong for us. At least we were now well in sight of the line of buoys that marked the point beyond which we could not go without a pass. Alas! We had hoped to spend the night in Buyükdere Bay, from where we could actually see the waters of the Black Sea. We would have to go into Therapia Bay instead.

The wind was directly against us, but we took down the sails and rowed up into the lee of what seemed to be a big block of flats on Therapia headland. Once we were in quieter water were able to start the engine. We then motored to the head of the bay, and dropped anchor among fishing boats. Mission mainly achieved! We had proved that even a sailing boat as slow and unwieldy as *Crab* could get up the Bosphorus – if it had not been for the prohibition on entering without a permit, we could have actually entered the Black Sea. If we had had a strong crew of four, as we had hoped, we could even perhaps have done the whole length of it under sail or using the oars. As it was, the engine had been out of action for the stretch known as the Devil's Current, although we had used it earlier, at the southern end of the straits.

The name *Therapia* means "Health Resort". In the days when Istanbul was the capital of the whole Ottoman Empire, the embassies of the Western powers used to migrate here from the city every summer from July onwards because it was the place nearest to the city where one could feel the cool breezes from the Black Sea. The resort stood in a small V-shaped cove, and once inside we found we had shelter from all winds. We were in calm water, and there was shade from trees. An embanked road ran round the cove close to the shore. The cove was surrounded by thickly-wooded hills.

We ate a celebratory supper. For my part I had hardly dared to expect that we would be able to work our way up the Bosphorus in *Crab* at all, let alone accomplish the whole journey in a single day! In the cool of the evening, Maggs and I went for a brief walk to stretch our legs after a long, hard day. There was a pleasantly fresh little breeze from the Black

Sea. How delicious it felt after the heat of Istanbul and the battering winds we had encountered as we tried to enter Buyükdere Bay.

Exploring on foot, we found that what we had taken for a block of flats on Therapia headland was actually a rather bleak hotel. Beyond it we passed the French and the Italian residences. The French residence was a large wooden building of the old style, painted in dark-red ochre. It had been presented to the French in 1807 by Selim III. In the distance we glimpsed the British residence, set back from the road a little in the fold of a hill. It had been accidentally gutted by fire in 1911, and still stood roofless. The walls and the imposing gate were still there, and there was a small whitewashed house belonging to the caretaker, apparently. There was even the glint of one or two flowerbeds. The German residence was situated on the far south side of the bay – too far for us to walk that evening.

When we returned to the boat we found that Sally, who had stayed, had been talking to local people, who turned out to be almost all Greek-speaking, and very friendly.

*

With my sister Kate, I returned to Tarapia in November 2013. It was no longer the sleepy fishing village with a once-famous esplanade, but had become a pricey summer resort. The building we had taken for a block of flats, in the lee of which we had found shelter on arrival, was now a five-star hotel with shimmering marble corridors, the *Grand Tarabya.*

*

Journey down the Bosphorus (June 28th)

Our good intentions of an early start came to nothing. It was a Sunday morning. The log says that at 8.00 am the starting cord got entangled with the throttle cable and broke it – a piece of crass incompetence. That would teach us to attempt a difficult journey with no one in the role of engineer, no one who was well-practised at starting the engine! Perhaps a hangover after our celebratory supper the night before was in part to blame. It was Sunday morning and all the local mechanics, being Greek, were having a lie-in, and we had to wait till 9.00 to get help. While we hung around people came to talk to us, and we received gifts of sugar, paraffin and petrol – all of which we had found to be in short supply. The Greek mechanic who came to mend the throttle cable refused to take anything other than cigarettes for doing it.

Eventually everything was in order and at 11.15 am we left under storm sails, and found as we reached the entrance to the bay that there was still a stiff breeze blowing. But this time the wind was from the north-east, which suited us exactly. Under storm mainsail, without even a jib, within an hour we were abeam of Rumeli Hissari – a stretch that had taken us three and a quarter hours the previous day.

As we sailed Sally told us about her visit to Istanbul the previous summer with Martin Lippner (the Martin who had been shipwrecked with us in the *Star of Malta*). The place that had excited her most was out on the western fringe of the city, a church outside the Justinian walls, known as "Chora". There were extraordinary mosaics there, full of life and movement, and more were being uncovered after restoration each year. Findings were being published year by year in the Dumbarton Oaks Papers. These frescoes and mosaics were contemporaneous with Giotto's work, and had the same dynamic naturalism. "But you would need at least half a day, to travel out there, and to enjoy them. Another time…"

We tied up in Fenerbahçe yacht harbour at 2.30 pm.

We had been invited to anchor alongside Kemal's yacht on our return. That evening there was a welcoming supper for us on board his yacht. We met at supper a fellow yachtsman who was a doctor, and who had a *yali* on the Asiatic shore. He had seen us trying to make our way upstream the day before and was intrigued as to where we came from.

Fenerbahçe Yacht Basin (June 29th –July 4th)

On Monday Maggs and I had the chance to begin to explore Istanbul, while Sally opted to join Kemal who was sailing to the Princes Islands. Next day we accepted an invitation to a regatta, and ate out on a neighbouring yacht that night. Sally woke up in the night feeling ill, and was sick all night. In the morning we called the doctor whom we had met earlier at supper. "I shall have to just wait for the doctor, and lie up for a day or two, here on the yacht," she said to us next morning, "the two of you had better go off and explore Istanbul while you've got the chance. You'll be able to see the mosaics at Chora." It turned out to be quite a severe bout of food poisoning, probably from a date-expired tin of stuffed vine-leaves eaten on board the yacht.

My letter to my parents was written early-morning from the yacht harbour the next day. It describes suppers on neighbouring yachts, news of Sally's friends the Dixons whom we hoped to meet up with, and then a visit by a journalist from *Cumhuriyet,* the Turkish equivalent of *The Times.* The journalist had been tipped off by someone at the customs quay who had watched *Crab* being unloaded (not by someone on Imrali Prison Island, as I thought). I wrote to my parents:

We had a party on the Commodore's yacht. We brought our primus, cooking as we came, and had supper with him, and then sat and talked, and all the harbour boatmen came alongside in their dinghies and came aboard and drank and ate with us. They told us how the Dixons had been. His wife they liked immensely...We met a nice young surgeon in his yacht here. He has a house on the edge of the Bosphorus, and told us he had seen us passing, under oars and sail.

All through the bayram the radio was blaring with protest-meetings about Cyprus, but there haven't been any riots that we have seen, and now things seem to have cooled down again.

We meant only to be here for three days, and here we are still.

Yesterday a newspaper reporter came to see us, having been told of our visit by someone on Imrali Island, and tracked us down. It is fatal staying more than three days in a place! But since coming down from the Bosphorus we have been completely abandoned by all wind, apart from one night of thunderstorm.

My letter ends with the words *Must stop and get breakfast.* With so much socialising the only way to get a letter written was to get up at dawn. The log says that what little wind there was blew from the south, which was no good to us.

As it turned out, the journalist was scrupulous, and even brought us the copy to vet before publication (it came out in their subsidiary *Hurriyet).* The article was to have surprising consequences on our next journey. And it even reached the eyes of our parents, after being translated via French into English.

ASRÎ ROBENSONLAR : İngiliz kızları teknelerinde (soldan sağa) Penelope Hughes, Sarah Hinchliff ve Margaret Whitehead. (Foto: Hürriyet)

Akdeniz'i 5 adımlık tekne ile dolaşan üç genç kız

Universite mezunu olan Ingiliz kızları Istanbula da eski eserleri görmeğe geldi

Malta adasından İstanbul'a kadar gelen dört metrelik tekneyi yaşları 23 olan üç İngiliz kızı idare ediyordu. İkisi Oxford'dan ve biri de Bristol Üniversitesinden mezun olan üç genç kız 1956 senesindenberi bütün yazlarını bu ufacık teknenin içinde geçirmekteydi.

(Devamı Sa. 5 Sü. 4 te)

Akdeniz'i dolaşan üç genç kız

(Baştarafı 1 inci sayfada)

Çanakkale Boğazından sonra sert rüzgârın sürüklemesiyle İmralı adasına gelip gece yarısı demir atan "Kavouri - Malta„ isimli teknenin mensupları ertesi sabah uyanınca kendilerini hep bir örnek elbise giymiş ağır hapse mahkûm kimseler arasında bulunca evvelâ hayret ve dehşet hissi duydular, fakat burada gördükleri müstesna misafirperverlikten sonra telâşlarının tamamiyle lüzumsuz olduğunu söylediler.

Kavouri - Malta teknesi üç sene evvel 90 sterline satın alınmıştır. Tam bir vazife taksimi ile çalışan İngiliz kızlarının bir aylık seyir ve yemek masrafı 52,5 sterline mal olmaktadır. Kaptanlık yapan Sarah Hinchliff mürettebatın Oxford mezunlarından birincisidir ve gene aynı mektepte arkeoloji doktorasına çalışmak üzere Londra'ya dönecektir. Ahçıbaşı Penelope Hughes da Oxford'da filozofi ve eski Yunan tarihi tahsil etmiştir. Teknenin lostromosu olan Margaret Whitehead, Bristol Üniversitesinden mezun olup Roma'da bir lisede tarih hocalığı yapmaktadır.

Üç senedir Akdeniz sulariyle mücadele eden Kavouri - Malta teknesi aslında iç içe geçmiş ve araları hava ile dolu bir cankurtaran filikasıdır. Yemeklerini teknenin içinde pişiren, karaya ancak alış - veriş ve İstanbul'un eski eserlerini görmek için çıkan üç amatör denizci, tekrar Akdenize açılmak için kuvvetli bir cenup rüzgârı beklemektedirler.

Photo explanation: The Contemporary Robinsons: The English girls in their boat (from left to right) Penelope Hughes, Sarah Hinchcliffe and Margaret Whitehead

Title: **Three young girls who traverse the Mediterranean with a five-foot[28] boat**

Subtitle: **Three English university graduates have come to Istanbul to see the monuments.**

Text: The four-metre boat, which came all the way from Malta to Istanbul was steered by three English girls. The three young girls, two of whom graduated from the University of Oxford and one from Bristol University, have been spending all their summers since 1956 in this small vessel.

[28] This is a direct translation of the Turkish term "five foot" which basically means "very small".

(Continued from page 1) The vessel "Kavouri-Malta" anchored on the island of Imrali after strong winds in the Dardanelles. When the ship's crew woke up the next morning, they were surprised and shocked to find themselves among people dressed in uniform clothing and sentenced to heavy punishment. Yet they said that considering the exceptional hospitality they encountered there, their worries were completely unnecessary.

The Kavouri-Malta was bought three years ago for 90 Sterling. The monthly expenses for the cruise and the food amount to 52,5 Sterling while the English girls work according to a veritable division of labour. Captain Sarah Hinchliff is the first of the Oxford graduates of the crew, and she will be returning to London to study for a Ph.D. in Archaeology. Head cook Penelope Hughes has studied philosophy and ancient Greek history at Oxford. Boatswain Margaret Whitehead has graduated from Bristol University and is currently working as history teacher at a high school in Rome.

The Kavouri-Malta vessel, which has braved the waters of the Mediterranean for three years, is, in fact, a lifeboat, whose compartments are filled with air. The three amateur seamen, who prepare the food in the boat and only leave to shop and explore the monuments of Istanbul, are now waiting for a strong southern wind to return to the Mediterranean.

Sally's bout of illness, followed by several days of adverse winds, meant that Maggs and I would have time to explore ashore. We discovered why the Old City was clouded in dust smog, and seemed forlorn. As we travelled through it on the tram as sightseers, the Old City seemed to be like a bombsite. It seemed as if it had been gutted by fire or had suffered a bombing raid. Except in the vicinity of the famous landmarks, there was rubble and demolition everywhere. From people at the harbour at Fenerbahçe we gathered that Menderez' government was dedicated to Modernisation, Mechanisation and Progress as the only way of salvaging Turkey's ailing economy. If people complained that the government had pulled down more than it could hope to rebuild, they would retort that there was no choice - they had started a process of modernisation that should have started two hundred years earlier, as it did in Western Europe. At least Menderez had left undisturbed - had in fact protected - those old wooden *yalis* that lined the Bosphorus on both shores.

At last Sally was sufficiently restored in health for us to leave, and the wind was light but from the desired direction. The engine had been serviced. We went to the customs office to seek clearance before leaving. Sally had to explain why we had arrived in Istanbul with a crew of four and there were now only us three girls. We were given a long list of the places that were forbidden as anchorages. On no account were we to stop at the Marmara Islands, which had been our mainstay on our way east. We were told that permission for this could be granted, but like permission to enter the Black Sea, it would take a long time. When we finally set off at 11.15am, we were under tow - a motor yacht leaving the harbour offered this, so as to conserve our stock of petrol.

As we moved away from the shore, towards the open sea, I remembered how the newspaper man who came to interview us for the feature in *Hurriyet* had said he wanted to lose fifteen kilos weight in two months, and did I think that if he came on *Crab* he would? "Yes indeed," we had assured him, "Come along! No one gets much to eat - and we need an engineer! Come with us to the Dardanelles! To Rhodes!"

7. Troy at Last

Fenerbahçe to Eregli (July 4th to 5th)

Leaving under tow gave us the chance to look around more. Upstream of us the lighthouse of Kiz Kulesi, which lies on the Asiatic shore opposite to the entrance to the Golden Horn, stood out briefly as a landmark. The European shore was as always shrouded in haze, through which we had a distant view of the famous skyline of minarets and domes. Quite quickly the vast city receded from our view.

Our plan now was to make for Rhodes, an island much further south, but almost as far east as Istanbul. In Rhodes we planned to stop and refit. Sally was quiet and turned in on herself, I sensed she was faced with decisions she did not want to share, any more than I wanted to share my own indecisiveness over Robin.

Our route from Istanbul was to take us along the northern shore of the Sea of Marmara. We soon reached the point where we must say goodbye to the yacht that had towed us. But there was no wind, so we motored most of that first day and, because stopping was forbidden, we had to continue travelling straight on through the night. It was a night with almost no wind at all. When there was a wind, it came from the west, and was right in our teeth. At 7.00 pm we filled the engine, again at 9.45 pm, and again at 11.45, and again at 1.30 am, and at 3.30 am. One person was on watch; the other two could try and sleep. We steered for a point between the two lights we identified as those on either side of Liman Burnu, near which was Eregli where we hoped to buy petrol. Dawn came at 4.00 am, with the eastern sky full of dark clouds with wisps like mares' tails along their lower edge. Approaching from eastward, the peninsula of Liman Burnu at first appeared to be an island off the coast. And at 6.30 am we anchored in Eregli. We were still less than half way to Çanakkale.

We expected to be met by officialdom of some sort, at that early hour in the morning probably someone particularly obstructive because of low rank. We expected to be grudgingly given permission to buy petrol, and escorted by a policeman while we did so.

To our surprise we found there was no grim-looking policeman, and the pump-hand at Turkpetrol was very friendly – he had read about us in

Hurriyet the day before. And we found ourselves invited to have breakfast with the mayor and his family. We had become instant celebrities.

"Is there anything you need? Anything we can give you?"

We suggested a kilo of fruit - it seemed a modest request. But it was not fit as a gift apparently, and we returned on board with a large and not too fresh loaf, and ten eggs. Finding a place to stow them was not easy.

Eregli to Tekirdag (July 5th)

After this interlude as celebrities we were on our way again by 8.30 am, still under engine. There was a freshening wind from the south-south-west, exactly from the direction in which we were heading. We set a westerly course for Tekirdag. We were still slogging on at 5.30 pm, when there was a sudden strong wind from the west, and it was with difficulty that we managed to claw our way to harbour under engine. Thanks to the newspaper article, we were permitted to stay the night. *Tied up in the lee of the pier. Choppy, dirty, but safe, at 18.30.*

At 10.30 pm, when all three of us had already been asleep for three hours, Sally was woken by the wind, and noticed a very ominous red moon. The wind was a *bora* - a north wind. Deciding to move the boat to a safer anchorage on the other side of the bridge, we got dressed again, took down the mast, and manoeuvred the boat through. But the threatened wind never came.

Tekirdag to Marmara Islands (July 6th)

Next day we considered waiting out the weather, since there was a fresh wind from the south. But we were advised to leave, "You'll never get better weather than this, if you wait two years!"

Since we couldn't get to our planned destination in such a wind, we decided to head south and make for Palatia, on the north-east side of Marmara Island, near the marble quarries. But the wind swung right round and that night we ended by anchoring under cover of dusk in a small harbour called Baba Liman - considerably further south than we had intended, and not a permitted anchorage. Sometime during the night a fishing boat entered Baba Liman, shone its lights and motored round the bay, and went away again. Two men sat on the beach and watched us in the dusk, but otherwise the place was deserted.

Marmara Islands to Çanakkale (July 7th to 8th)

We left again at 4.30 am, not taking any chances with officialdom this time, since we could not plead ignorance. A nice little north east wind had sprung up, and at 7.00 am we turned the engine off and went bowling along, taking advantage of the westerly current, under storm sails.

Now at last we were approaching the Dardanelles, beyond which lay the Aegean. I was looking forward to having a good strong current with us as we passed through the straits. The straits were twice as wide as the Bosphorus, and the current correspondingly less powerful, except in the channel between Kilitbahir and Çanakkale, where we bowled along in fine style. The European side was sheer and barren and rocky, with unexpected eddies of wind gusting down the gullies, so we kept to the Asiatic shore, avoiding the back eddies. One could clearly identify the edge of the main current by eddies welling up where the sea bottom shelved. The Asiatic side was composed of gently rolling landscape, cultivated with vines. Çanakkale was the starting-point for anyone who wanted to visit the ruins of Troy. And this time we planned to do it, by hook or by crook.

Approaching Çanakkale at dawn was bad planning. We passed but were unable to see the place where Xerxes had bridged the Hellespont with a pontoon of ships lashed together for his great invasion of Greece in 480 BC. It was 5.00 am when we reached Çanakkale and tied up near the customs house. From the officials we learnt that Sally's sailing friends the Dixons had passed through on Sunday - we had missed them. But we also learnt that political tensions had eased enough for us to be able to linger long enough in Çanakkale to visit Troy.

After breakfast Sally went off to the Çanakkale *poste restante*. She came back bringing a stranger, who was to join us later in the summer, as it turned out. She said that she had bumped into him in the post office. He was an unmistakeable Englishman Abroad - burnt by the sun darker than many Indians and Pakistanis, wispy sun-bleached hair to his shoulders, sandals much repaired, a small ancient khaki knapsack his only luggage. Unmistakeably Winchester and Oxford - and probably a capable sailor. From the ensuing conversation we gathered that he had completed at Oxford and then done his military service in the navy. They had taught him to sail. He had then done a term's English teaching in Ankara with the British Council. His name was Nicholas Woolley.

Sally was inviting him to join us. "Currently I'm on my way to Mount Athos," he said, "and I'll be there for several weeks. But how long are you sailing for?" We told him we hoped to continue till mid-September. He said he would come and join us at the beginning of September, after Mount Athos, and we exchanged *poste restante* addresses.

Troy at last (July 8th)

We found a a taxi to take us. I vaguely remember the road hugging the coast, and then climbing through vineyards, and remember reaching a place where there was a view of the River Scamander and Mount Ida. Sally's letter home describes it briefly: *Visited Troy which is rather terrific, much more so than I had expected. Lots of walls left, and splendid position commanding the plain, with a view right to the Dardanelles.*

Xerxes, as he set out to invade and annex Greece, visited Troy as he approached the straits. In Troy he sacrificed one thousand oxen to the Trojan Athena, and to the spirits of the great men who had died in the fighting there. Herodotus tells us the River Scamander was the first river to be drunk dry by his army. At Abydos, a Greek harbour city, Xerxes had a white marble throne placed on the hillside so that he could review his troops before crossing the straits - a crossing very different from the unseemly haste of his returning troops, defeated.

Contrary to the impression given by the *Iliad*, archaeology demonstrates that Troy - known now as Hissarlik - stood and prospered for many centuries after being burnt to the ground by the Greeks under Agamemnon. Troy was not a harbour town, it was not even on the coast. Nowhere in the *Iliad* is there mention of a Trojan fleet. It seems that Troy, like Corinth, in early times provided porterage. In the case of Troy, porters were needed for the merchandise brought as far as Çanakkale by sea-going vessels, and unloaded. Once it became possible, in the Classical period, for merchandise to make its way eastwards by sea through the Dardanelles, Troy declined. In Greece's heyday in the fifth and fourth centuries BC there seems not to have been even a minor settlement on the site of Troy.

A new city, called Ilion, was founded on the site in the reign of the Emperor Augustus, but in St Paul's day the centre of activity had moved from Troy to the coast, where the large city of Troas, only about four miles from ancient Troy, was the chief city in Asia Minor. It was there that Paul had his vision of the man of Macedonia begging him to come over to Macedonia and help them.

We sped back down the long road from Hissarlik to Çanakkale.

Çanakkale to Seddül Bahir, westernmost tip of the Gallipoli peninsula (July 8th)

The taxi dropped us alongside the boat. *Crab* left Çanakkale at 3.45 pm, under engine. We had to meet a deadline in Mytilene, and we had lost a lot of time. We travelled till six in the evening, when we decided to find shelter, and put in at the biggish port of Seddül Bahir, at the mouth of the Dardanelles on the Gallipoli peninsula. It had a fine ancient citadel to protect it.

The next day we would leave Turkish waters and be back in Greece. We had a journey of about fifty miles - it would take us sixteen hours or more. We were to change crew in Mytilene on Lesbos, and we had only two days left before the rendezvous. Maggs, who had been with *Crab* since leaving Turkolimano in Piraeus, was leaving to join a friend in Rhodes, and we would be joined by two young men - Roland, whom Sally had met briefly in Athens where he was working in an architect's office during the winter, and Roland's architect friend Roger. Sally mentioned Roland was tall.

8. Frontier Islands

Molyvos on Lesvos (July 9th to 10th)

We were back in Greek waters again, after more than twelve hours at sea! The sun was bathing the west-facing walls of the castle that dominated the harbour. Roland, Roger and I were walking from the bus station to the harbour front, our long shadows going ahead of us. *Crab* was anchored a little way from the quay, but I hailed Sally, who was alone on the boat, and she manoeuvred the boat alongside the quay.

Roland was six foot four inches tall, but he stepped on board without his weight causing havoc. On board, I settled down to peeling onions, while Roland began to unpack his gear to put it away. Engrossed in onion-peeling, I suddenly heard the loud protest.

"Sally, you should have sent me a scale drawing!" I looked up and saw that the thwarts were entirely covered in packages. Sally was telling Roland bluntly that he had far too much luggage for the boat's storage capacity. She told him he would have to post back to Athens his reserve pair of shoes and suchlike, because this boat did not have any storage space under or alongside the bunks- as the article in the Turkish paper put it, this was a lifeboat, and the compartments were filled with air.

"I didn't think you were serious, when you listed in your letter what was allowed!"

After supper I was fit only for sleep, as my day had begun with accompanying Maggs on a bus at 6.00 am to catch her ferry from Mytilene, and to collect Roland and Roger. But Sally was full of energy, and took Roland climbing up flights of steps, exploring the part of the town clinging to the hill topped by a Byzantine fortress. Next day we planned to sail as far as Mytilene, the biggest city on the island, which faced across the water to Turkey.

Roland was passionately interested in how differently people built houses in different places, and pointed out enough to Sally for her to have to allow her enthusiasm outlet in the ship's log, most unusually. *Very charming – houses with one storey and terrace on top of 100 ft wall on sea side: narrow streets roofed with vines: Turkish-style houses: castle perhaps XIII century*. She could have added to her list also the Turkish fountains, set among a profusion of flowers – a leftover from the days before the population exchange between Greece and Turkey in 1923, the days when over a third of the inhabitants of Molyvos were Turkish. They had formed an elite, building mansions down the face of the cliff with the living quarters on the top floor, and storerooms below.

Lesvos: Sigri (July 11th to 12th)

Roland and Roger had been allocated what ought to have been an easy journey, slipping from island to island, to Rhodes or beyond. But we had not reckoned on the strength of the *meltemi* in July. From about 10.00 am every day the wind blew hard for most of the remaining daylight hours. It was clear that the best time for travelling was before sunrise. So on their first morning we rose at very first light, and left our anchorage at Molyvos at 4.45 am, planning to reach Mytilene, about thirty-eight miles away. But, unusually, the wind was already blowing hard, and the proximity of mountains meant it came in fierce gusts. At 6.15 am we changed to our storm sails, and ran back to Molyvos. *Crab* was in need of repairs, and we were anxious not to push her too hard, in case her leak became worse before we could reach Rhodes, where we planned to beach her. We decided to go the other way round Lesvos, down the outer shore, and seek shelter in Sigri near the south-western tip of the island.

In Sigri harbour it rained. The log contains the terse note: *Rain in night. Fixed awning*. Apparently a feat achieved in the middle of the night, so that it would keep the rain off us, at least to some extent.

We spent an interesting afternoon at Sigri, visiting the petrified forests inland of the town. It seemed as if ever since leaving the Dardanelles we had been hurrying. Morning after morning we had risen at 4.30 am and immediately set off. Sally kept noting in the log that this was so as to benefit from the relatively windless early hours of the day. But it was also because she was keen to get to Rhodes where the boat could be hauled up out of the water for repainting, while she went back to Athens for several days to sort out some urgent matters. I was longing to get to Rhodes also. In Rhodes Robin would join us, and my brother Owain.

I liked the new crew. Roland turned out to be different from most of those who sailed on *Crab*. He had left school at fifteen, and by the time he was twenty-two he was a qualified architect. He must have had a lot of initiative, because after qualifying as an architect, and doing military service, he applied to join the firm of Constantine Doxiades in Athens for a year. Sally had met him at a party in Athens, and suggested he join us. I found him full of kindness. Sally found him a bit too serious – though like me she was absorbed by his fascination with small buildings as well as large ones.

Roland's close-cropped hair bristled as if embarrassed, and he was awkward when speaking, an introvert. But he was a very good listener, and I wanted to try and work out what direction my life seemed to be going. The previous summer, in the hills above Hidden Harbour, Robin had put to me a question. This summer when we met in Rhodes he was going to insist that I answer one way or the other. I was feeling a strong pull to join the Franciscans – I was already a member of their secular Third Order, and I felt the pull to a lifetime commitment within a community. I had recently spent an exploratory three weeks in a convent. But Roland had brought on board a book by Eustace Chesser, a book which did the work parents were supposed to do – and seldom did – in terms of sex education. As I read it I had begun to understand myself, and to realise that an unpleasant encounter I had as a child, when I had felt myself too small and weak to say No, had put me into a permanent funk as regards sex. I was grateful to Roland for lending me the book, and felt able to talk out the issues with him, which helped me recognise my fears, and be honest about my motivation to date. The important question now, as Roger pointed out, was "Do you love him?"

Lesvos: Sigri to Scala Loutron (July 1st to 13th)

We left at 6.00 am, and for once we were able to leave our berth under fair-weather sails. But as we moved eastwards along the southern coast of the island the wind began coming down the gullies in fierce gusts again. Lesvos has two deeply indented bays on its southern coast, the western one big enough to accommodate the whole British Mediterranean fleet. We spent the next night at Plomarion on the southern coast. In the second, much smaller bay the following morning we found the Dixons' yacht the *Dusmarie,* at anchor, in Scala Loutron.

We moored alongside. It did not take long to decide to move to a more pleasant anchorage which they knew.

Lesvos: Storm-bound in Scala Loutron alongside the Dixons (July 13th to 16th)

For the next three days the wind blew too hard for us to venture to sea. And at last I had the time to sit down and write a letter. I wrote of the meeting-up, much looked forward to by Sally. Dixon, Sally's first sailing instructor, was now beginning to show his age physically, but he was full of vitality and jokiness:

He must be nicer than he was when he taught Sally to sail, in Sweden. Then there used to be great ceremonies of breaking the colours at sunset, and ship's prayers, such as,

God grant me sympathy and sense
And strength to keep my courage high
And please a twinkle in my eye.

But woe betides you, Sally said, if there was a twinkle in your eye during ship's prayers…

The idea of having ship's prayers surprised me. Certainly not something we did on *Crab!* I greatly liked Dixon's wife, who responded thoughtfully and in detail to my questions about the political situation in the eastern Mediterranean. When we told her we were heading for Rhodes she said, "Try not to be there when the American fleet is in. It transforms the town, American sailors everywhere, looking for easy ways to spend their money."

Sally wrote to her parents a little later:

We stayed with the Dixons three days, nice lazy time, sleeping in their cabins, sharing the cooking, and reading all their books.

This was like being in the land of the lotus-eaters. Sally and I never wanted to leave.

Scala Loutron to Emporio, on Chios (July 16th to 17th)

On the third day, the wind had dropped, though the sea was still restless - a state when the surface is heaving and shifting but there are no wave crests - sailors call it lumpy. We left at 6.15 am. Now the winds were too light, and we crept along at snail's pace towards Chios. We had none of St Paul's luck with steady following winds.

Roland told us he had once had the chance to visit Chios before. Most interesting were the villages on the west coast of the island, each set several miles inland. From the Middle Ages onwards they had produced and traded mastic, a substance highly coveted by the Turks, a resin that was produced by terebinth bushes. It formed the basis of cosmetics, paints and medicines before the era of petroleum-based products, and was a great favourite of the Sultan's harem. Roland told us about the layout of the Chiot villages, with narrow passages and a baffling gridsystem so that strangers would very soon get lost. Everything was designed to protect against the risks of piracy or enemies - even the flat roofs of the houses were more or less the same height, so that the inhabitants could run from one roof to the next. He told us about the black and white geometric patterns that decorated the walls of houses in Pyrgoi. Apparently the walls were first decorated with a paste of black sand. Then a thick layer of whitewash was applied, and once fully dried, was scraped off in patterns that exposed the underlying black sand. The outer houses made a continuous line round the town, in lieu of walls.

"Roland, how do you know so much?" Sally exclaimed - all her knowledge was about the island as it had been in the classical era, before mastic had even been discovered.

"I left school when I was fifteen. You learn to use your eyes, and to ask questions of people, if you aren't being stuffed full of book-learning. My father worked all his life with his hands - he was a cabinetmaker."

Darkness came upon us as we reached the straits. Since it was too dark to go through, we anchored on the east side of a tiny island for the night, and set anchor-watches, since the anchorage was very exposed. But swell and wind got up from the north-west shortly after we anchored, and it was an uncomfortable night. At sunrise we set sail again, and passed safely through the straits. Roland told us that Chios was famous not just for the mastic villages but for Nea Moni - the eleventh-century monastery. We certainly ought to visit it. But when we reached Chios town, at 10.00 am, we found that the monastery was an expensive taxi-ride away, and Sally was desperate to stick with her schedule, in case of more bad weather. We left again at 2.00 pm, after posting the letters written while we were stormbound alongside *Dusmarie*. The night of July 17th was spent in Emporio on the southern tip of Chios, a Mycenean and Archaic site with the ruins of a temple of Artemis, and with a good natural harbour.

Vathy on Samos (July 18th to 22nd)

Another pre-dawn start at 4.30 am, and a fourteen-and-a-half-hour passage. For most of the time we had following winds, and for four hours we were bowling southwards under spinnaker, making four to five knots. In the evening we reached Vathy, the harbour on the north-east tip of Samos. We were looking forward to exploring Samos, one of the largest islands off the coast of Turkey, wooded and mountainous, and only a mile from the Turkish coast. And we had heard that there was a good local dry white wine, as well as the heady, rather sweet Samian red made famous by Byron.

In Vathy we discovered that there was still a British Consul, a person of local family - probably the post was hereditary. The anchorage was choppy, since there was a brisk north-west wind. In an open boat one does not really sleep in such circumstances. The night is spent trying to secure the awning spread over the sleepers, so that it doesn't blow into the harbour. Or it is spent trying to find better ways of wedging oneself so as not to fall out of bed because of the rocking of the boat. At dawn we rose. The north-west wind would see us nicely on our way, provided we could claw our way out of the deep bay. We folded away our blankets and the awning, and set off under engine. But the *meltemi* blew up, and quickly the sea became dark, flecked with white. The engine could make no headway at all against a wind that was right in our teeth. At 6.30 am we hoisted storm sails and ran back downwind, back to Vathy. It was frustrating not to be able to get out of the bay, since as soon as we were out the wind would be in our favour. We decided on the following morning that we would pay a local man to guard the boat, and would all take the bus to Tigani on the south coast of Samos to visit the temple of Hera. There we found a well-sheltered little port of great antiquity. It was an attractive place, the main street shaded with eucalyptus and mulberry trees.

The next morning Sally and I got up at 3.00 am to look at the weather. It was clearly no day for travelling, yet again, so we let the other two sleep. In the end we were stormbound in Vathy for three days. On the second day we were again able to leave the boat in safe hands and explore inland: with Roland and Roger I took a bus up into the hills to see the monastery of the Zoodochos Pigi (life-giving spring). The monasteries on Samos have the same lay-out as medieval English country houses - built round a courtyard, looking inward. Sally meanwhile took a bus south to Tigani again to try and see underwater harbour works.

Also sheltering from the *meltemi* in Vathy was a graceful French yacht, a vessel that could not have been at a more extreme opposite to *Crab*. She was a cut-down Twelve Metre - one of those large elegant class boats from before the war, with a towering mast, and originally with a boom which protruded far out beyond the stern counter. There would be a deep, well-weighted keel to compensate, and low freeboard, and a low cabin top, to avoid wind resistance. Simultaneously we invited each other to drinks on board at the end of the day. It was their invitation which prevailed - after all, they said, it might rain again! We spent a very enjoyable evening on board, and next morning we able to set off for the Samos Straits.

Samos: Pythagorio [also called Tigani, "Frying Pan"]

(July 22nd to 23rd)

We passed safely through the Samos Straits, with the wind behind us, and next night *Crab* was in Tigani (Pythagorio), tied up alongside the eastern pier after a fourteen hour journey. The following day we set off for another long day's sail southwards.

We were about to enter the Dodecanese, the islands of which lie close to the Turkish coast: so close, in the case of Kos, that with good conditions, you could actually hear a shout from the mainland. Because of this proximity to the Turkish mainland they became prosperous, and because they became prosperous they were coveted. For centuries they were occupied first by Crusaders, then by Turks, and then Italians. The Dodecanese only actually became part of Greece in January 1948, after a period of being administered by the British. There was a fascinating jumble of Greek, Western and Ottoman architecture, with plenty to interest *Crab*'s crew. Plenty also to outrage them, such as Mussolini's restoration of the temple of Asclepios on Kos, with pillars that gleamed as brightly as if they were made of fondant icing and only lacked a wedding cake to stand on.

Patmos (July 23rd to 24th)

It was late afternoon when we reached Patmos. It was on Patmos that St John wrote down the visions that formed the content of the *Book of Revelation*, and the island had the air of being immensely venerable, like Iona off the west coast of Mull, described as a place where the barrier between the seen and the unseen was as thin as tissue paper - a place permeated by centuries of prayer.

On the island of Patmos power had rested totally with the monastery for centuries. Looking at the top of the hill from the harbour I could see a great, grey fortress, with a scattering of little white houses like sugar-knobs around the base of the wall. This grey fortress was the Monastery of St John the Theologian, and the village Chora, which must have originated with the workers and craftsmen living round the base of the monastery's walls. Halfway between Chora and the port there was a large white building, below which was a smaller white building that is the Monastery of the Apocalypse.

We anchored off the pier. The only other foreign boat in the harbour was an eighty-two-ton Italian yacht, owned by a female member of the Feltrinelli family. Our two boats must have made a ridiculous contrast. Later I learnt that it was these Feltrinellis who the previous year had caused an international sensation by publishing *Dr Zhivago*. Banned from publication in Russia as being too hostile to the Soviet State, the manuscript of this, Pasternak's only novel, had found its way into the hands of this publisher, who had seen its potential, had it translated into Italian, and brought it to the notice of the world.

We scrambled up onto the quay from *Crab*. There seemed to be no street names, or signs, but we walked in a straight line away from the port, till we fell in with the paved zigzag mule track that led to Chora. We took a smaller path that went off to the left, a pleasant cobblestone footpath. Halfway up the hill we came to the Monastery of the Apocalypse, built around the very cave where St John had had his visions. There was a courtyard with flowers in every alcove and nook and cranny, and off it some tiny chapels, and some small cells. There was an intimacy about the whole setup that reminded me of the little monastery Diccon and I had walked to when we were stormbound in the Sporades.

The Monastery of St John the Theologian towered high on the hillside above this halfway house. The Turks had protected it because the Knights of St John paid their taxes, nor had pirates sacked it, and it contained a treasury of ancient manuscripts and vestments.

In the evening Signora Feltrinelli invited us on board. We talked mainly about where we had each been, and where we hoped to go. At that time, incredible as it must seem now, the only published guide for yachtsmen in the Aegean was the Admiralty Pilot. It was even the best existing guide to the Greek islands such as Rhodes, providing accurate maps and local information. It certainly gave more snippets of useful advice for small boats with local knowledge than do the more recent editions. Sally was pleasantly surprised to find Signora Feltrinelli much impressed by her local knowledge of the islands of the Aegean. Sally well deserved her approval - she was extraordinarily knowledgeable and prudent to have taken an open boat so far, with often very amateur crew. Later she persuaded the Hopes to sail with her in her little yacht *Gypaetos,* much against John's inclination. But his verdict on her was that she was a completely safe person to sail with - and that is the one thing that matters.

Kalimnos (July 25th to 27th)

We did not leave Patmos till after lunch the following day, July 24th. We stopped at Leros, with its impressive deep bay, then at Kalimnos Town and, when the wind blew up, put in to a deserted inlet further south on the same island. It was a very good sheltered bay, with a beach at the head of it, but shops were more than an hour's walk.

Roland and Roger went off to climb a mountain while Sally and I did some sewing. We had decided it was necessary to put reef points into the little storm mainsail, so fierce were the winds we were encountering. We had skated south with following winds, *like sliding downstairs on a tin tray* as I commented to my parents. Usually I would protest against Sally's restlessness to be always under way, but I was as keen as her to get to Rhodes. I had noticed that *Crab* was leaking more than was healthy, but there was nothing that could be done till we reached somewhere where we could beach and empty her, and give her a thorough overhaul. There were increasingly long sessions of pumping-out, morning and evening. I didn't draw this to Sally's attention, fearing it would stop her leaving for Athens till she had found the cause of the leak. I guess Sally and I were both feeling in need of beaching and an overhaul, ourselves - Sally said as much in a letter to her parents.

As we sat sewing, a deputation of children approached us along the shore. They were carrying something heavy in a bucket. Shyly they presented us with a whole bucketful of ripe figs, their skin green velvet. We transferred them into our own bucket, which was green canvas - the two such different greens together made ill bedfellows.

Kalimnos to Kos, Kos to Symi (July 28th to 30th)

We left next morning at 4.30 am, heading for Kos. We had read in Roland's *Guide Bleu* about the magnificent plane tree under which Hippocrates supposedly sat and wrote, and received his patients - the tree was the biggest plane tree in Europe, with a circumference of fourteen metres, and branches so heavy they had to be supported on pillars. But it was not because we were agog to see these wonders that we struggled awake before dawn to set off, but because it was still the only safe time to travel in *Crab*, the only time when the wind was gentle or nonexistent. Rounding the north-east corner of Kos in late morning, we anchored in the harbour among the other small boats.

Kos is second only to Rhodes now in terms of tourist popularity - the island groans with the weight of its visitors in summer. It was sleepy and poverty-stricken and refreshingly nondescript and cheap when we visited it. The most interesting remains seemed to us to be from the Roman period. Sally's log entry is unusually expansive:

Visited ruins by Phrourion (the fort) and Roman 'thermae'. Very good mosaics under sand, and houses (also very good mosaics: one especially fine Hellenistic one of very small tesserae, depicting 'fruits de mer'), and a Roman theatre. Also museum – disappointing. One Roman ship stern of type seen on coins, and mosaic of Hippocrates in a small boat of same type as Althiburus mosaic and same period.

Sally tended to rate museums according to whether she could learn anything new from them about ancient shipping. She comments also that the flowers and trees in the town were lovely. The proximity of Kos to Turkey meant that when we visited the office of the harbourmaster there was a lot of red tape before leaving, though they were friendly.

We left at 4.30 am again the following morning, hoping to arrive in Rhodes before nightfall and pull *Crab* out of the water. As we sailed, we took it in turns to read up about Rhodes in Roland's *Guide Bleu*. But at 9.30 pm that night we had still not reached Rhodes. Darkness was descending. We were not far off, skirting the coast of the little island of Symi. We tied up at the head of a small bay – from 4.30 am till 9.30 pm had been a long day's sail.

9. Rhodes and Lindos, Affairs of the Heart

Our journey was coming full circle - we had started from Malta, with its fortifications built mainly by the Knights of St John, and now we were approaching their most famous location of all. We rounded the north-east tip of the island and sailed southwards. As we passed a promontory with a substantial lighthouse, there opened up to starboard the sheltered, north-facing entrance to Mandraki, the yacht harbour, with statues of a deer and a fawn on the two arms of the breakwaters. At the far end of the harbour the Old City extended uphill, with its circles of walls and its ramparts. On the end of the outer breakwater was a fortress built by the knights.

As we approached Rhodes I thought of Roger's question to me. In Rhodes Robin would join the boat, and I would have to give him an answer. It would be embarrassing in the extreme to have to admit to family, some close friends, and a spiritual mentor that what I had thought was a strong vocation to the religious life was actually an irrational response to fear. I would just have to bite the bullet, and admit it openly. I also had another worry: certainly Robin loved me. But, leaving irrational fears on one side, did I love him? Was I capable of loving anyone? It seemed the best way forward was to put trust in myself - and in him.

The Order of the Knights of St John, which left so definitive a mark on Rhodes, was first founded in the eleventh century in Jerusalem to care for the physical needs of Christian pilgrims. They ran an infirmary. But gradually they found themselves defending the sea routes to the Holy Land as well. Defeated at Acre after a long siege, they moved first to Cyprus, then to Rhodes, where again they found themselves having to defend the pilgrim routes, and also commerce. The Knights' income derived from piracy against Turkish ships plying to Egypt, and anyone who wished to join the Order had to spend a sizeable period in the cramped conditions on board their galleys. Their sea power was formidable. The Turkish Sultan tolerated them because they paid all their dues, but clearly the time would come when he would find this rival sea power was becoming too strong.

That time came in 1480. The Sultan besieged Rhodes, but the Knights held out against him. After the Turks withdrew, money began to pour in from Europe - the Knights' success had made them very popular. Then came the second siege, when they were finally defeated after fierce fighting. They withdrew westwards and after a few years took up residence in Malta. There they thrived, and the Great Hall of their hospital was the largest room in Europe at that time.

We were now close under Fort St Nicholas, on the breakwater. The entrance to Mandraki was behind us. Nearby was a line of windmills in various states of disrepair. Within Mandraki, we glimpsed a very few tall masts - an unusual sight, for Greece. Beyond them we could make out a square building which was probably the office of the harbour authority. There was also a phalanx of local ferryboats, some of them on the move, stirring up a wash. Now we were passing the entrance to the commercial harbour. We did notice a prominent building labelled Customs, facing the steamer quay - too bad, we had already been carried past the entrance to the harbour, and fighting against this wind was not likely to be successful. It never occurred to Sally and me to wonder what our little craft, under storm sails, looked like to those on shore, or what *they* thought of *us*.

Once past the entrance to the Emporikos, the commercial harbour, we studied the shoreline carefully, and identified the boatyard. We dropped anchor by Psaros' slipway, intending to negotiate the beaching of the boat, and waded ashore. The boatyard asked to see our papers, puzzled over them, and then phoned the customs house. A letter to my parents describes the response:

...we had already unloaded half our possessions onto the shore ready for beaching the boat, when the first official arrived. "It is forbidden." He kept saying weakly, while all the boatyard men stood round him in a hostile circle, having helped us unload, and wanting to keep us. In the middle of re-loading, a second cousin of someone came bustling up saying, "Where are the two Germans who are trying to steal a boat and escape?" On the one hand all the fussiness of the officials, on the other the yard – but us very much favoured by the yard, which was a rough place, like Portmadoc, and very, very anti-officialdom... they had to send a launch round to tow us to the Customs House so that they could have a closer look at us.

The log narrates that the whole of the rest of that day was spent with the Port of Entry Customs officials. Roland and Roger went ashore, seizing the chance to see the Old City, and to get information on ferries to

Piraeus. Meanwhile the officials in the harbourmaster's office, highly suspicious of us, insisted that we provide a list of every place we had visited since leaving Piraeus in early June. It was not till 7.00 pm that they finally gave us clearance. When we got back to the boat we found Roland and Roger. It would be too late now to go to the boatyard. Wearily we pumped out yet again, and prepared for a night in Mandraki, tied up to the T-shaped quay among the local ferryboats. Roland, Roger and Sally all began to organise their packing, their elbows in each other's way, and an occasional clunk of heads as two people bent down at the same moment to lift something that had been stowed under one of the lengthwise benches. Sally wrapped up the ship's log and put it away.

That night I lay stretched out on my section of bench on *Crab,* full of misgivings. For five days I was to be living on my own on *Crab* – but not even *on* her. I would have to find somewhere nearby to spread my blanket and store my possessions. At night, would there be rats? After five days Robin and Owain would join me. I had to give Robin an answer, and I felt nervous about making such a life-changing decision, though I knew that my feeling for him was strong.

I was so much looking forward to having my young brother on *Crab.* Because of being responsible for him every spring half-term I felt a strong bond – but it was a mother-hen kind of bond, the last thing a resourceful fourteen-year-old felt in need of.

There was one piece of good news. Among the mail brought back from *poste restante* by Roland and Roger was a message from Maggs. Her good friend Tony Luttrell was studying the Knights of St John, and would be in Rhodes for more than a month, and she had joined him. She gave her address and a phone number. It seemed their lodging was within walking distance of the boatyard. There was also a brief letter from Robin, telling me when they would arrive by ferryboat. Originally we had planned to meet in Santorini, but had had to re-think, as we were behind schedule.

A colour slide taken by Roland next day from the ferryboat shows me with Tony and Maggs in a tight crowd, looking up from the quayside to wave goodbye.

Psaros' boatyard, alone (July 31st to August 5th)

A letter from me to my parents describes life in the boatyard:

I lived half the time with a family who lived down there at the yard in a little air-raid shelter. It was very snug, being built so much solider than most Greek houses – neither too hot in summer nor too cold in winter. The father worked at the steamer-quay. He was there when I met Robin and Owain, and had picked them out almost before I had. The daughter was married to a caique captain, and was due to have her first child in about two months. She lived in the family house which was her dowry, she being the only child, but she was lonely there when the husband was at sea, and lived down at the air-raid shelter too, so I got to know her well too. It was nice to know a family well enough to be able to explode occasionally, when everything was on one's nerves, and for them to be able to say bluntly, "If you come to church with us you will jolly well have to wear one of our skirts, and they're nice" and also to keep threatening to put me in the tub and scrub me all over, as soon as I had finished painting. We spent a lot of the day sitting under the caique in its shade, and just joking together, till R and O came.

Evangelia was a good friend to me. Once the boat had been emptied and cleaned, I identified a sizeable gap in the planking near the bows. I got that hole repaired in the yard, and then embarked on the re-painting, both inside and out, working flat out so that there would be the minimum to do once Robin and Owain arrived. I had found a place to sleep, on the rat-free foredeck of a nearby elderly *caique* on the beach, under the stars.

It was good to stay in one place for a change and to be able to make my own schedule. Often on the journey there were the rumblings of mutiny, even though we acknowledged Sally was a brilliant skipper. She had what is popularly thought of as a masculine ability to think things out, the capacity to strive for goals and overcome obstacles en route. She was also inclined to irritability – this she blamed on the fact that she was born when Virgo was at its zenith.

Now suddenly I was a free person. I spent a long evening at Maggs and Tony's lodging, listening as Tony Luttrell talked about the role of the Knights as the first *medecins sans frontières*, about their presence in other parts of the island, about their effect on the domestic architecture. Together the three of us went to visit a site at that time unexcavated, and Maggs and I held the other end of the measuring tape while Tony took endless measurements. "Wait till you see a place halfway down the coast where the Knights had a fortress, the steepest village I've ever been to," Tony said. He told us that when the Knights left, the Christians who remained moved down the coast to Lindos, the only other good harbour. The Lindiot sea captains took over from the Latin Christians, who had all left. Lindiot captains controlled the trade from Istanbul to Egypt, while the Turks controlled the coasts of Tunisia and Algeria, policing them with Algerian ships. We decided to leave the visit to that village till Owain and Robin were with us.

*

Psaros' boatyard, with Robin and Owain (August 5th to 12th)

The day came to meet Owain and Robin off the steamer. Owain had grown so much I didn't recognise him. He was excited to be abroad for the first time. Robin told me that he'd spent the whole of the night-crossing from Dover on deck, watching and exploring the ship.

I had high expectations of this young brother. At the age of eleven he persuaded a school friend of the same age to set out with him on a week's walk the length of the Lleyn peninsula, carrying a tent and provisions, a walk that took them across the foothills of Snowdon and finally to the port of Aberdaron. They crossed without problems to Bardsey Island but it was many days before the weather was calm enough for the boat to brave the makeshift harbour to pick them up again. It was an unusual feat for an eleven-year old - clearly he was cut out for adventurous travelling. They returned three weeks later without causing much concern to my father, who was supposed to be looking after them.

His other claim to fame was that single-handed he had salvaged a sailing dinghy that he spotted floating on the tide, and had been given £5 as salvage money. This young brother of mine was going to be a valuable addition, I reckoned.

My expectations were certainly high. Owain relates that on his first night on Rhodes, he had barely fallen asleep when I woke him and said I wanted to talk - wanted him to help me make up my mind between joining the Franciscans as a nun and getting married to Robin. He did his best, he said. I have no memory whatsoever of this.

Next morning, since Robin seemed to be biding his time, I reckoned I should take the initiative. We all went to a café together, and then I gave Owain the ship's purse, telling him to buy himself the best treat on the menu, and stay there while Robin and I went to the market.

To Robin's surprise, I think, I told him that I now knew my own mind, and if the offer was still there, the answer was yes. It was, and he was delighted. So the following night we went out to supper in a waterside café to celebrate our engagement. It was a place that catered mainly for American sailors. The girls who had come in the hopes of picking up a sailor must have seen that Robin only had eyes for me. Owain relates that they focussed all their charms on him, a fourteen-year-old, to his acute embarrassment.

Two days were spent repainting the boat, the final touch being the antifouling. While that was still wet we launched her, moored her a few yards off shore, and submerged her so that her timbers would swell and she would be watertight for the last lap of the journey.

Visit to the village of Lindos (August 8th)

The following day Owain came with Tony, Maggs, Robin and me to visit a little-known fort, Philerima, and then further south along the coast to the village of Lindos.

As the bus wound its way downhill, we caught a glimpse through the window of a bold headland jutting out to sea, topped by a castle. It reminded me of the castles built by Edward I along the coast of North Wales to garrison against the fierce Welsh. The connection was anachronistic, but the methods of waging war had not changed substantially in the years between Edward I and the Crusades.

The bus swept downhill and round a corner, and abruptly came to a stop. We found ourselves in the *plateia*. So this was Lindos. In the shade of the plane trees donkeys were tethered, waiting to carry tourists up the Acropolis - apparently the first year of this trade, judging from the competitiveness of the donkeys' owners. By the following year the mayor had decreed that no donkey was to work at this more than two days a week, since the donkeys were now the highest earners in the village. We declined to have a donkey, and set off to climb on foot to the Acropolis, up long flights of stairs that hugged the hillside.

Lindos was one of three original capitals of the island, before Rhodes had even been founded, but it was now just a village, with a spectacularly large harbour on the north side of the Acropolis, and another, St Paul's Bay, on the south side. Robin took photos, all duly listed with date and time of taking. Fifty-five years later, I keep giving thanks for his meticulousness, because with the help of knowing date and time I have been able to work out from Sally's log almost exactly where each was taken.

We were overtaken by a donkey carrying four heavy cans, slung onto the wooden saddle. Was it paraffin or petrol, we asked, and gathered that it was water - there was no running water in the village. Either you collected your own from the fountain in the shade of the plane tree in the main square, or you bought water from a donkey. We noticed there were no streetlights - presumably then there was no electricity.

The steps up to the Acropolis grew steeper. Alongside the final flight, near the top, is a huge relief-carving in the solid rock, almost five metres wide and more than five metres high, showing the stern of a ship, with lateral steering. There was the seat for the pilot, and the bridge, which jutted out for almost a metre. Owain was impressed.

Suddenly we had reached the top. The panoramic view was magnificent, especially for us sailors, who spent all our lives right down at sea level, in fact as low as we could reasonably be. From the top we could see up the coast almost as far as Rhodes City.

As we came down again from the Acropolis, Tony took us into a side-street to visit a house. "People refer to them as Knights' houses," he said, "but there were only twelve knights assigned to guard the fortress, helped by Greeks. And this house wasn't built till a hundred years after the Knights left Rhodes. But this had become the local style for building, by the time they left."

These traditional houses all turned inwards; there were no windows onto the street, apart from one small slit, and the door in the wall was small and unfriendly - the entrance to a courtyard, not a house door. Inside was an archway, and the floor was surfaced with black and white pebbles formed into patterns, the celebrated *kochlakia*. A house vine, trained right across from wall to wall, gave shade.

"When the weather is particularly hot they wet the pebbles, and that creates delightful coolness as the moisture evaporates," Tony told us.

At the far end of the courtyard was a big room, the *sala,* its floor also *kochlakia*. On the other side of the room, two steep wooden steps faced the door, leading to a platform about five feet above the general level of the room. Facing each other at the two ends of this platform were two beds. I was told there was a strongbox kept under the principal bed. A soaring arch divided the interior lengthwise. I noted a fireplace in the corner, not in the centre of the wall, as at home. It seemed that the whole family were born and died, lived and worked, in this one big room. The wall on either side of the arch was decorated, not with pictures in frames, but with rank on rank of painted pottery plates and the occasional copper pan. At the back was a very small window. Looking out one could see that the house had been built into the side of a hill. The lady of the house noticed me looking out. She opened one of the cupboards under these beds on the upper level - inside, to my great surprise, was living rock.

The lady of the house had things to sell, among them one or two cable-knit jerseys, made with rather scratchy, tough local wool, dyed to brilliant colours. We found that two colours - blue and lime green, for instance, or red and orange - would be twisted together to make a composite colour. The colours were glorious and subtle, but we could not find a single jersey that did not have one arm longer than the other or a change of wool colour two thirds of the way down one sleeve, or suchlike. I imagined these being knitted during the winter months, when supplies of any kind were hard to come by - especially materials for handicrafts.

From the little I had seen of this extraordinary village I had fallen head over heels in love with the place. If only I could live there! No mains electricity - but I was used to that at home in North Wales. No running water, however, was NOT something I was used to. The charm lay in the fact that the houses turned inwards, round a courtyard, with outside steps up to the upper storey. This was something really strange to me. Their pebbled black and white floors reminded me of the black and white patterns on the medieval walls in Taormina. I thought of Polly and John Hope whom we had stayed with in Taormina - where were they? Where did they live now? I remembered they were in a small studio flat in Chelsea somewhere. They should be HERE, for heaven's sake!

*

On August 9th Sally returned to us from Athens. She was relaxed and cheerful. Like me she had probably had to face embarrassment. But it was obvious she had achieved peace of mind. At supper on our first evening together Owain suddenly asked Sally:

"What is this place San Turin, where we two leave and you pick up the next crew?"

"Nothing to do with the Italian Turin," Sally answered, "...Pompeii maybe - both have had a massive volcanic eruption. It's not San Turin, it's Santorini. Have you seen a map of the island? It forms nearly two-thirds of the circular crust of a volcanic crater. I've been puzzling off and on this winter - surely there must be more to be found there, buried under the volcanic ash, if there was such a major eruption."

I wanted to chip in with what I knew of the legend of the lost Atlantis, but Sally continued with her train of thought, "Robin's *Guide Bleu* says the eruption was about 1100 BC. How are they so sure? Couldn't it have been earlier, in the late Bronze Age, contemporary with the end of the Minoan civilization? Remember that philology tutor, Professor Palmer, who taught us about the Linear B tablets? He kept linking the eruption here with the end of the Minoan ascendency."

I interrupted, "When the sea rushed in through the gap that had been formed, it would have caused quite some tidal wave... certainly it could have gone sloshing inland, even as far away as Crete."

"There have been three digs on the little island across the other side of the crater, Thirasia, and I want to learn all I can about what they discovered. Surely there must have been evidence the people were seafarers - and if so, what were their ships like?"[29]

[29] Note: It was not until 1967 that the Greek archaeologist Marinatos started digging down through the layers of volcanic ash on the shore near Akrotiri. He uncovered evidence that before the eruption there had been as many as 20,000 inhabitants on the island, besides uncovering frescoes that many people reckoned more vibrant and alive than those at Cnossos, among them a fresco of two large processional boats, with high poops.

10. Rendezvous on Santorini

Owain kept a daily diary, which he wrote up for a Travel Essay Prize at his school. I give the rest of our stay in Rhodes, and our journey westwards, through his eyes. In my recollection, the after-effects of this food poisoning incident dogged him throughout the holiday. But he makes light of it.

He had brought with him to Rhodes a serge jerkin instead of a jersey, reckoning it would be windproof and fairly waterproof. But it proved not to be sister-proof. It was bulky compared with a sweater, and in the sweltering heat of Rhodes harbour front in August I couldn't see that he would need it. Manoli's father-in law had helped a lot with *Crab*, refusing pay, and was Owain's size. So before we left Psaros' boat yard I insisted Owain give it to him. I couldn't have been more wrong about Owain not needing it.

August 11th

I spent all day asleep, as the tins from which we had taken our supper the night before were very rusty, and rust is the one food upon which I do not thrive.

August 12th

We spent most of the day packing the boat. This was fascinating to me as I could not possibly see how our vast pile of belongings, and us, could fit into so small a boat... I say that we had a vast pile of belongings, but each of us was only allowed an outsize sponge-bag full of clothes etc. However there is always a mass of things, from charts to food to spare sails and medicine.

At about 3 pm a friend who owned a trading caique offered us a tow north-west to Kos. We accepted the offer as the prevailing winds were NNW, and unless we were towed north, we could never make Piraeus. He explained that we would have to meet him some miles away from the harbour as there were 'complications' as he called them. We never discovered what form they took!

Saying goodbye we set sail for our rendez-vous. As we sailed out of the harbour we passed through the American fleet, which had been rushed to Rhodes to stand by during the Cyprus situation. Among the ships was America's largest aircraft carrier, whose deck would have made a good cornfield, it was so large. There were also four submarines which looked very sinister indeed.

Dusk was just closing in when the very heavily laden caique, about 25 ft. long, met us. She was carrying a cargo of tiles, the chief export of Rhodes. Very slowly we chugged away into the black of a cloudy night.

Kos (August 13th)

I awoke at about 2 a.m. to see that the sky had cleared completely and above us was a very dark blue, velvet dome with thousands of sparkling silver stars. As soon as my sister saw that I was awake she gave me the helm and went to sleep. We were gliding through a narrow passage between two islands, and although there was no moon, the stars gave us enough light to see the black shapes of rocks gliding past a few feet away. Once, the caique ahead lurched and groaned as she heaved herself over an extra high underwater rock.

The sun was just easing her stately majesty over the horizon when we rounded the fort of Kos, and stopped at the quayside.

We found that several hours in a cold wet boat had made Owain's diarrhoea worse again. He was not in a cheerful mood. A row flared up between Sally and me.

"We'll need to put him in a hotel and let him rest for twenty-four hours," Sally said. "Even so he won't stay put – I'll bet you. And it means yet more delay. Owain and Robin have got to get to Santorini by 21st August, to connect with their flights. And we've a rendezvous in Santorini, to pick up Nick and Mickey," Sally pointed out impatiently. "Oh, all right then let's go and be *tourists* – see the Asclepion…and the famous plane tree, the very tree under which Hippocrates sat to receive his patients, naturally... *And* the Italian restoration work that looks like a giant wedding cake decoration! We've got to kill time till we get the engine up and running, at any rate."

I sometimes grumbled to myself that Sally was on too short a fuse, she was always getting irritated, but I think that without Sally's irritability we would never have got as far as we did – perhaps would never have left Malta! Almost everyone else who came on *Crab* was a bit afraid of her. Harbour officials sensed a steely willpower and usually took the easy way out of the confrontation.

Owain declined both hotel room and bedrest. I continue the story as seen through Owain's eyes:

After a much-scrutinised night's rest, we decided to see Kos. First we went to see the very ancient and famous plane-tree of Hippocrates. All that remains of this tree, which is about 2,000 years old, is a vast shell of very thick bark, but strangely enough it still bears green leaves though from where it gets its sap I could not discover. After lunch we set out to explore the fort. This fort has thick walls with rooms and passages round the outside and a large open space in the middle with a small but strong keep. The open space was used for protecting citizens and their herds when the Turks made a sudden attack on them. I was walking down a dark passage with a torch when I suddenly noticed a square hole in the ceiling. Overflowing with curiosity I stepped directly underneath and looked up. There was a corresponding hole in the floor. Had I not caught myself with my elbows I would have made an abrupt descent some three storeys down!

Kos to Astypaleia (August 14th to 15th)

Before dawn we set off to try and round the northern end of the island of Kos, but we were soon headed by a very strong wind and it became very rough indeed. Turning round we were soon running before the wind so as to round the island to the south.

We had just finished breakfast when we were hit by a very sudden storm. We reefed down well, but found the wind too strong altogether for the fair-weather sail, and we hoisted the tiny storm sails. Kavouri was designed to roll rather than ship water. She did both! Luckily everything was so closely packed that it could not fall out, but we had to retreat into oilskins, hold on, and pump furiously. When a large wave hits you in the back it feels very soft and heavy. We were glad of our oilskins! As suddenly as it had arisen the storm died, and bathed in red early-morning sunlight we sailed into Kephalos, a tiny village on the southern end of Kos.

Kephalos is only inhabited during the summer months, and so the houses consist of only a bamboo frame with reeds interwoven. All the inhabitants are fishermen.

Very early the next morning we set off for Astypaleia. I feel the same kind of exciting thrill when going fast in a car as when we were doing a long crossing. For hours we just seemed to stay in the centre of a great disc of heaving waves, while the glaring Mediterranean sky made the waves an ominous dark blue. All the spray was so silver and sparkling that it hurt the eyes to look at it.

About seven in the evening we came rolling into the harbour of Astypaleia. The village is situated in a small round bay in the centre of which is a pillar of rock, crowned with a tiny, white church.

We get a different point of view from the skipper of that thirteen-hour journey from Kephalos to Astypaleia:

Astypaleia
August 17th

...We had a terrific day yesterday, doing a thirty mile journey with not much wind but simply enormous seas. Owain was a hospital patient wrapped up in sails and blankets to keep him warm. Robin was seasick, and I steered for about fourteen hours while Penny changed sails and pumped and fed me. Robin Penny and I all ended up soaking wet, but although it probably doesn't sound much like fun to you, Penny and I in fact enjoyed it very much, especially seeing how well the boat behaved in seas like that.

The weather is very odd round here as it blows like stink whenever you are near land and is often quite calm out at sea.

What was it that attracted us to this way of life? Maybe, quite simply, it was the fact that no day was like another. Maybe it was the surge of adrenalin that came when the boat heeled over as the wind freshened. One had to get the fair-weather mainsail down, furl it, and raise the storm main instead, bracing oneself against the pitching and rolling of the small boat, arm hooked around the mast all the time one worked. Or maybe it was the freedom to stretch full out on the lee side on the lengthwise bench and sleep when one was tired, a freedom still sweet even when one was cooled by a dollop of sea every five minutes. It was better than being confined at a desk in an office somewhere in a city. Or maybe it was the freedom from inhibitions - for example when one was trying to get the strands of a rope to form into a splice, or trying to untie a knot when the rope was swollen by being wet, one was free to vent one's anger with a fine range of choice language. When the *Tintin* books started to come out a decade afterwards, I recognised myself and fellow mariners so well in Captain Haddock.

Owain's diary continues:

August 17th

Although we had used the engine very little indeed it needed an overhaul so I spent the next day taking it to bits and polishing the inside. I took a heaped teaspoon of sediment out of the fuel-pipe! As the evening closed a wedding started. The service was a delightfully simple one. First the village priest placed a silver coronet on each head. These coronets were connected by a light chain. Then, in turn, each of the relatives swapped the coronets round, and when this was completed the priest, the couple, and all the relatives held hands round a small table in the centre of the church and walked round and round, singing hymns.

August 18th

Four o'clock in the morning had just struck on the church clock when we set sail for Anafi. As we looked back at the lights of the village we could still see the merry-makers dancing.

After a fairly uneventful crossing we sighted Anafi, but just at that moment we got into a mass of huge steep waves caused by contrary currents. 'Kavouri' would heel over, shoot skywards, waver on the top of a wave, and then tear down to the next trough which we would hit with a smack like a shot-gun report.

The end of Anafi which we had just reached was a sheer cliff face, 195 ft. high, below which it was 220 fathoms deep within 10 yards! We 'sailed' along, about 18" from the cliff, because the main current and wind were dead-ahead, but here there was a strong back-current.

August 19th

The 18th was completely devoid of wind, and so we used the engine to leave the almost uninhabited island of Anafi. The crossing to Santorini was very unpleasant indeed. The engine made a revolting smell and an even worse noise, and the sun was so hot that a rag had to be used to open the water-tank in order to avoid getting burnt!

As we motored, Sally showed us on the chart where she planned to anchor on arrival, Kamara, on the nearest side as we approached from Anaphi, a harbour about a mile north of Ancient Fira, which stood on a headland. "Ancient Fira" was not, in fact, that old – a Dorian resettlement planted almost a thousand years after the great eruption. From Kamara we could get a taxi to the town on the hilltop, Fira, and meet up as planned with our next two members of crew. In Fira Sally could find out about whether we could tie up directly below in the tiny harbour.

August 20th

Early in the morning two young Englishmen arrived to take our places, and while they sailed 'Kavouri' south round Santorini we took an ancient bus across to New Thira.

Santorini was originally a volcano, and where the land slipped away an 800 ft lava cliff has been left. Into this cliff houses have been cut, and also a zigzag pathway down to the harbour. This pathway is more like a tunnel, for it overhangs itself all the way down.

We soon found a cheap, cool room; the only difficulty was that it was cut out of solid rock just below a road, so that donkeys' feet echoed very loudly in our room.

In the evening we made our way down to the harbour and as we sat there in the shade we saw two pigs being loaded onto mules to go up the pathway. The wretched creatures' legs were tied together and were then used to hoist them, with a small hand-crane, so that the mules to carry them could be driven under them – enjoyment was had only by the men, and not the animals concerned. 'Kavouri' arrived later and we had a last supper on board.

Lower Thira (August 21st)

Early next morning Robin came and dismantled the engine, and instructed our new crew in its management. He found that the trouble was caused by specks of dirt in the carburettor. Such an insignificant thing to give Nick and Mickey two hours of rowing! Meanwhile Sally and I climbed the long zigzag path to Thira to do some shopping, passing small dwelling-places that had been hollowed out of the *tufa*. We also visited the museum. Many of the houses were empty – unsafe since the earthquake. Some people were living temporarily in a New Town built on the flat ground south of Akrotiri. Safest were the older houses that were half underground anyway, hollowed out of the *tufa*.

We decided that the anchorage at Lower Thira was too crowded. We would visit the nearer of the volcanic islands in the centre of the bay, Nea Kameni, which had only appeared in 1707, and then go and moor at Thirasia, on the opposite side of the bay. Both Nea Kameni and the smaller volcanic island, which appeared many centuries earlier, were still active. We said our goodbyes on the waterfront. Owain and Robin set off to explore Thira, before taking the ferry to Piraeus.

We went back on board. Sally's eye was caught by words painted across the stern of a rowboat near us. Translated they mean "What I am like is not your business. He who owns me wants me like this." To me it spoke for much about Santorini as we found it, only four years after the most recent earthquake.

When we reached Nea Kameni, we could not find the creek where we had been told to land. There were several *caiques* moored there, but no one was on board. We had been told that the local fishermen bring their *caiques* to this island, and tie them up alongside the island for two or three days, allowing the sulphur fumes rising from the sea-bed to suffocate all the barnacles clinging to the boat below the waterline. I learnt when I got home to Wales that Owain and Robin had hired a boat and visited it also.

We found somewhere where we could make the boat fast and landed. The jagged lumps of lava were hard under my worn sandals. I imagined - I've never done it - that it felt like walking on hot coals. Sally had bought new footwear when she was in Athens, and she and Mickey set off to try and climb to the summit. It was said that you could climb to the top of the island's little crater and look down inside.

Nick and I stayed and looked around rather nervously, as if we felt a stage devil was going to emerge from a fissure between the boulders. Nick's appearance was striking. Whereas Greeks all had short-cropped hair, Nick's hair, sun-bleached and desert-coloured, hadn't been cut for months and was on his shoulders. And he had a beard. No young man, apart from priests, had a beard at that time. His sandals had been repaired with twine. His shirt, like his hair, was a sort of desertish colour.

From fissures between the lumps of lava eerie columns of sulphurous smoke were rising, and the lava in places was smeared bright green. Nothing grew. The only sign of life was an enormous spider sitting in the middle of his web, waiting for prey.

Sally and Mickey came back after about an hour deeply frustrated. They reckoned that they should have landed on the north side of the island, since they could see glimpses of a path from the water's edge.

From Nea Kameni we crossed to the southern end of the island of Thirasia. But there was a swell coming in from the south-west, even though what wind there was, was northerly, and we found ourselves encircled by unclimbable steep cliffs. We moved to the side facing the hilltop town of Fira, and re-anchored in Thirasia Bay, below the picturesque village of Manoli. After we had eaten Mickey climbed the long uphill path to visit the village.

Thirasia, August 22nd

We woke to find we were encircled in a wet Welsh mist. There were beads of moisture clinging to the underside of everything horizontal. Our bedding was heavy with it. Visibility was down to fifty metres. It was an odd sensation, as if we had been suddenly transported back to chilly Britain. It was, in fact, the first intimation we received that the weather was becoming unsettled and unpredictable.

11. Idling Through the Cyclades

Offerings to Poseidon so far this year: one plate, two forks, one carving-knife, two petrol-tank corks, one air-intake cover, two identical blue cotton hats, five sponges, and a Red Ensign with staff. The second of the two hats, which Poseidon helped himself to yesterday afternoon while Sally was half-asleep, seems to have pleased him, since he gave us a sea as smooth as a pane of glass at sunrise for looking for the ruins of a submerged city off Anti-Paros. There were lines of shaped stones, right-angle corners, and what looked like a broad flight of steps, all about ten feet down. Sally had read about it in the winter in a report of a Greek dig of Bronze Age graves. (Letter to my father from Paros, September 1st)

Santorini to Siphnos (July 23rd to 30th)

We were now doing the part of the journey which, according to the schedule put together the previous winter, Owain had been due to do with us. Flat sea, islands fifteen miles apart instead of thirty to forty miles apart, and apparently no *meltemi*. It was ironic that when Owain was with us, we had the worst and longest crossings apart from crossing the Sea of Marmara.

We visited Nios, Sikinos, Melos and Siphnos. A conversation in the village square on Sikinos gives the flavour of those islands in summer. I had written to my parents as we approached Melos:

On these islands the town is always at the top of a cliff to be out of the way of pirates, and a stone-paved mule-road leads up to it. But in spite of the familiarity of the pattern they are all different still. We walked up to church at a little one called Sikinos on Sunday. We had been for a late moonlight bathe the night before, and our feet were full of sea-urchin prickles and we got up at six in filthy tempers, wishing that both religion and hills had never been invented. On the way we stopped and asked a woman standing at her door for water, and she gave us coffee and little biscuits as well.

After church we sat in the village square and had breakfast and the entire congregation sat there drinking coffee.

"Where are you going to next?"

"Folegandros."

"What a coincidence! We are arranging an expedition there ourselves, for today or tomorrow."

"Our boat is small."

"Never mind. All of you get into a rowing-boat, or more if need be, and we will tow you along behind us. Just stay a day or two here – at Folegandros there are good fish, but there are no partridges. Here there are partridges. When we have shot some partridges, today maybe, we will take them and go to Folegandros – it is only fifteen kilometres."

When we climbed up through the village, the road was so steep that we stood looking down on the roofs below us. I noticed that instead of the sloping pan-tile roofs which we had grown used to in the Dodecanese, these roofs were flat, built of closely packed tree trunks surfaced with baked earth - so Roland had told me, explaining that they put a layer of closely packed reeds, topped by a layer of dried seaweed, before they sealed it with clay-earth.

Anti-Paros (August 31st)

From Siphnos we sailed and motored to Despotiko, the best harbour on Anti-Paros. There we called at a house and asked about where to land in order to visit the cavern with the stalactites. We were directed to an inlet on the west side of the island where the *caiques* from Paros disgorged their cargoes of tourists, to be met by mules to take them up the long hill to the caves.

Mickey had already left us, and this would be a last port of call before Paros where Nick also would leave us, and we would pick up our next crew. I had hugely enjoyed his company; he shared my willingness to stretch legs on long treks to interesting monasteries or churches. On Siphnos the previous Sunday, we had had an hour's walk inland to find the church, but it had been well worth it.

I had read during the winter in Robert Liddell's *Aegean Greece* an account of these stalactite caves on Anti-Paros. Liddell admitted that he himself was something of a speleophobe - he hated caves. He related that on Christmas Eve 1673 the French ambassador to the Sublime Porte, the Marquis de Nointel had had Midnight Mass celebrated in the caverns. *He was accompanied by five hundred people; a hundred torches and five hundred lamps were lit in the caves, and there was an orchestra of trumpets, oboes, fifes, and violins – it must have been cold, stifling, uncanny, and magnificent. I should not at all have liked to be present.*[30]

Nick's *Guide Bleu* said of the cavern that Byron had signed his name on a rock, but that *La visite est assez difficile (corde échelles, éclairage et un guide nécessaires) et sans grand intérêt.* [The visit is quite difficult (rope ladders, lights and a guide all necessary) and not of much interest.] Rope ladders, bringing your own lights ... this was a challenge. If Byron could get there, then we could, even if it was a descent of two hundred and thirty feet!

Arriving in the little harbour, we anchored discreetly, with a line ashore, and sat to wait for the tourist party. They turned out to be almost entirely Greeks. It was a half hour walk uphill, with the option of riding on a donkey, which Nick and Sally took, Nick looking the part in his tattered sandals and beard. The view as we climbed was splendid, with a semicircle of islands spread out to the south.

At the top, the Greek ladies began pulling out woolly cardigans for their husbands, urging them to put them on before going in to the cave. It seemed they felt that winter was only a week or two away. Nick, Sally and I had no such luxuries. Sally overheard a Greek lady's puzzled or disapproving comment to her husband, with a nod in the direction of Nick, "Is Jesus Christ going into the caves just like that - nothing warm?"

To my disappointment there were no rope ladders, nor torches - solid stone steps and electric light had now been laid on. The stalactites and stalagmites were splendid if you were a connoisseur and knew about them, and about how long it took for them to grow.

Anti-Paros to Paros (August 31st to September 1st)

We left under tow by a *caique* bound for Kastro, the main village on Anti-Paros. From there we went on to Paros, main town on the bigger island, our petrol supply just lasting till we got there.

Our next crew were complete strangers to us all. From Paros I wrote to Robin on September 1st:

...Since you left, the engine has been teasing us almost daily – its latest game being to pretend that the carburettor was dirty, and make us take it all to pieces to clean it in mid-ocean, in the course of which we dropped the air-intake cover

---

[30] Robert Liddell, *Aegean Greece*, Oxford, Alden Press,1954.

overboard. Only afterwards did we discover that the air-vent in the petrol-cap had somehow got blocked so that the petrol couldn't flow down the pipe…

We don't expect the next crew [Simon and friend] till tomorrow afternoon so I have leisure to finish this in peace.

<u>*September 2nd*</u> *Leisure not at all! At six this morning we opened one eye, and saw on the quay by the boat two rucksacks, ENORMOUS. And up in the bows a letter to Sally saying, "We have news of Simon. Come to the café at the end of the quay." Sally put on her shoes and went, and came back with two strangers, whom Simon had sent because he couldn't come himself. Heavens I hope they enjoy it alright, I am most nervous….Simon, having tried all his friends in vain just went to Victoria station and sniped among the crowd about to board the train for Greece! He had never met them before. One is Greats Oxford, the other Maths Cambridge. Watch the headlines for dramas in the Aegean.*

*

In the afternoon we looked round the *kastro,* which was built of recycled chunks of pillars from a classical temple, and saw Nick off on the steamer for Piraeus.

The next major goal on our route was Myconos, favourite resort of Athenians at that time. From Myconos we would be able to visit sacred Delos. People didn't live on Delos, there was no graveyard there - it was farmed by families from Myconos. And if you visited it was wise to leave again without unnecessary delay, or you might find yourself trapped there for many days by the weather. To reach Mykonos we would need to set off from Naxos, which lay on our route.

The new crew's names were Keith and Jim. We had more bad weather in the ten days they were with us than for the rest of the summer put together. It was an ironical twist of fate that those who had had least experience of cruising - in fact of sailing of any kind - should find themselves in a situation where for the first time Sally and I were at our wits' end.

12. Caught in Storm Force 10

Paros to Naxos (September 3rd)

In Paros, Wednesday dawned grey and overcast, and it rained on and off from breakfast at 6.45 till midday. Breakfast eaten wearing oilskin jackets, with hoods up, is not a sociable meal. To watch raindrops pattering into your no-longer-hot mug of tea lowers the spirits. Our new crew members took it stoically, without comment or complaint.

At 10.00 am, after sheltering in the café in the hope that the day would brighten, we decided to set off, rain or no rain. There was a changeable wind from the north-east, strong enough for us to opt for storm sails. But the wind was fickle. For part of the journey there was no wind at all, and we had to get the engine started. This gave a vital role to the newcomers, at least. We crept along the north shore of Paros, heading for Naxos. Our plan was to make for the port of Naxos, and from there set off to get to Mykonos, an island famous for its local fabrics and its attractive port, with narrow streets and a magnificent view from the harbour. The town rises like the tiers of an amphitheatre, with a line of windmills on the hillside above. All four of us were keen to reach it, by hook or by crook.

It was late afternoon when we rounded the north-east corner of Paros and set out to cross the straits between Paros and Naxos, progress slowed by a fickle wind which now blew from the south-east, and all but headed us. The island of Naxos was astonishingly green - it must have a higher rainfall than any other of the Cycladic islands. It was also astonishingly high and mountainous, with some running streams visible on the slopes.

Crossing the Naxos Straits we were taken aback by how choppy the sea was - Sally commented that there must be a strong south-going current, directly in opposition to the south-east wind. Spray slashed on board every few moments as *Crab* thumped her way through the waves.

Naxos harbour lies at the northern end of the straits, and is easy to find. The harbour was crowded and we had difficulty finding an anchorage. Finally we anchored alongside a steamer called the *Naxos*. Walking along the mole, it seemed that the harbour defences were inadequate, as if in strong northerly winds the main breakwater would not be high enough to prevent seas from breaking over it, setting up a surge in the harbour.

The skipper in a neighbouring *caique* was of the opinion we would drown in a few days - or if we didn't, we certainly deserved to do so! We had grown used to this prediction when we were sailing off the coasts of Sicily and Calabria, but it was unexpected in Greece. Perhaps the Naxians were a people apart. Or perhaps their experience of weather conditions was other?

We discussed our plans for the next day with our new crew members. They were surprised to find we had no radio on board, and relied on neighbouring boats for a forecast: we told them our neighbours said there was a gale warning for tomorrow, but that gale-warnings were very frequent. To hedge our bets we decided to try and go first to Delos, and from there go on to Mykonos, since Delos was slightly nearer.

September 4th

We did not leave harbour the following morning till 10.00 am. I can only think this was because we were unsure of the day's weather, because though there was not much wind, the seas were lumpy, the water restless. We left harbour under engine, setting our fair-weather mainsail. Though the wavelets were small, their crests not breaking, the sea was certainly lumpy. Delos lay almost directly to north of us. We chugged northwards, motor sailing because the wind came and went.

This was only the second day that our two new crew members had spent at sea, and they probably found the disturbed sea almost more uncomfortable than if the waves had been larger but more regular. Lumpy seas, without rhythm or pattern, tossed and twisted *Crab*. I offered lunch but no one showed any appetite for it.

And then, at 2.00 pm, when we had been travelling for about six hours, a wind got up from the north, and started to freshen. Hastily we changed the fair-weather mainsail to the storm sail, and turned off the petrol, stopping the engine. The wind came in gusts, a dark shadow sweeping across the surface of the water, now east of north, now well to the west of north. The sea was very disturbed. Would we be able to continue under sail, or would the wind be directly in our teeth - that was the question. There was no question of trying to use the engine, the seas were already so steep that the propeller would be out of the water half the time. With difficulty Jim and Keith lifted the engine inboard. Within ten minutes of when the wind first struck it was blowing so hard we knew we must reef the storm-mainsail.

It was not easy to lower it and reef it. While I struggled, Sally at the helm was responding to the gusts and keeping way on the boat. As the wind settled more or less due north, blowing hard, she found that she could just point for the easternmost tip of Mykonos – Delos was now out of the question. Sally glanced at her watch and showed me – it was only twenty minutes since the moment we first felt the wind freshening. We had never experienced such a sudden change in the wind.

The wind continued to freshen. The waves were getting longer, the crests beginning to break into spindrift, and foam was being blown in well-marked streaks. Behind us, the sky beyond Naxos was very dark. We continued thumping into head seas under storm sails for another five minutes. *Crab* was heeling more and more sharply as she was hit by sudden gusts, and was hard to steer. At 2.45 pm Sally said, "We'll have to turn back. Come and take the helm, downwind is your speciality. And I need to look at the chart."

Even with a pocket-handkerchief of a reefed storm-mainsail we seemed to be bowling along at about four knots. Suddenly I felt the boat's response to the tiller become sluggish, ineffectual. I peered down at the rudder, and saw at once that the rudderplate had come adrift. The bolt that held it must have snapped. With the help of the two boys, Sally was just able to pull the plate on board. Fortunately, *Crab* did still answer to the helm although the response was slower. Sally made the boat as snug as she could. In addition to wrapping a rope around the furled fair-weather mainsail to stop gusts of wind from catching a loose fold, she lashed it down to the thwarts. Keith and Jim were occupied with non-stop baling.

"Steering is difficult. Without the rudder plate, I don't have enough leverage," I said to her, shouting to make myself heard above the roar of the wind, "And with as much wind as this we may get pooped." "Getting pooped" refers to what happens when a wave is sucked up astern by the boat's speed through the water, and then overtakes the boat, breaking on board. I had experienced it once at home on the estuary of the River Dwyryd, where the wind would blow up very suddenly. The boat had come close to sinking. "We had better shorten sail still more."

We took the mainsail off altogether, and rigged the jib in its place, a small triangle of canvas. We found that running downwind even under jib alone we were making as much two or three knots. A long journey lay ahead – at this speed it would probably take at least four hours till we reached shelter. A row between me and Sally flared. As waves kept flipping into the boat over the quarter Sally was constantly getting a small wave landing in her lap, but was obstinately insisting on not wearing her trousers, not wanting to make them wet. I was angry with her, knowing her tendency to be knocked out by diarrhoea if she got cold and wet for a long time. If we had a sick skipper, where would we be? In a fury I took off my own green cotton trousers and told her to wear them. Numbly she did as she was told. For the next half hour or so we continued in silence. Then Sally began studying the chart.

"It's all very well me saying we must turn back, but where do we go to? The harbour at Naxos won't be easy to reach. The wind will be blowing straight down the straits, and you will have to stop running downwind and steer across the waves to get to the harbour mouth," said Sally. She studied the chart as best she could, with the boat heaving and pitching. "There's Cape Procoupis, just beyond the town of Naxos, which is protected by a low-lying headland so that you don't get the howling winds which you get in Naxos itself, and if we are blown past that there's Kouroupa Point, an even better anchorage, but it's another seven miles at least down the coast, seven miles beyond the port of Naxos. Will we find it?"

"It'll be dark by then – let's try to go back where we were this morning," I said. A curious sense of numbness was creeping over me, giving me the feeling of being wide awake but somehow disembodied, unable to exert myself. I was still at the helm, and responding to the movement of wind and waves, but somehow things were becoming remote. Waves were certainly getting large – perhaps twenty feet high occasionally. Visibility wasn't good at any time because of flying spray, but there was certainly a big difference between when we were down in the trough of a wave, and all we could see around us was walls of water, and when we were on the crest, and suddenly had a king-of-the-castle view of Naxos' mountains.

I remember how, as we approached the port of Naxos, we could see waves smashing against the breakwater, throwing up great plumes of spray. I prayed we would not get blown sideways onto that breakwater. The water was disturbed, the waves here running in several directions and colliding, so that we had five or six foot peaks rearing up around us. But *Crab* responded still to the helm, and I was able to steer her past the breakwater, and round into the harbour mouth. It was not easy because it was only when we were on the crest of a wave that I could see where we should be heading. Within the harbour itself there was a big, sloshing swell, and of course as soon as we were inside the harbour we encountered a head wind. We hastily mounted the engine and tried to start it, but it would not start. We pulled out the oars and began to row, but it was clear we were not making headway against the wind. We were more or less holding our own, but the quay where we had anchored the night before was not getting any nearer at all.

Through the spindrift and the gathering dusk we could see people standing on the breakwater, some waving arms. So at least someone had seen us! All of a sudden we noticed that a small *caique* was coming towards us through the gloom. They threw us a rope, and towed us in. Numbly we put fenders in position to stop the boat grinding against the quayside, threw ropes to waiting hands, and made fast against the quay. We climbed the rusty iron ladder onto the breakwater, and stumbled, with wooden legs, along the quay.

Anchored in lee of 'Naxos', a tramp steamer, safe from thieves, and decamped to hotel, borrowing clothes from the Naxos, and being stood two lots of brandy and one of hot milk en route. Sally wrote in the log.

Naxos (September 5th – 10th)

For the next two days I simply slept, dreaming of that sea that rolled around us. I don't even remember waking to drink water or ask for food. Perhaps I was running a high temperature; perhaps it was the aftermath of hypothermia. Then one morning I woke feeling quite normal and wide awake. I put more clothes on and went to look for the others.

I gathered that by the time we came into the harbour at 6.00 pm the wind had been gusting sixty knots - we knew this because, as Sally had discovered, there was a local weather station on Naxos. Apparently there had been a waterspout off Naxos harbour mid morning - we had not seen it because the sky behind us was so black at the time. We heard also that three people had been drowned that morning inland. There had been a sudden cloudburst. A group of men were working on repairing a bridge that spanned a dry riverbed, when suddenly the riverbed had filled with a torrent of water. And the next morning the screen of the outdoor cinema had been blown out, another major event.

Two days later I wrote describing the experience to Robin, giving more detail than I would have to my parents, I suspect:

We made Naxos again only about an hour before dark. So we were lucky. It was alarming when we got near the breakwater, the seas were breaking over it to such an extent that the lighthouse on the end of it was being completely blocked from view. Seas about 20′ high. I have been afraid. Being afraid wakes you up and makes you do things better, but also when you see things are not likely to get any better for at least three hours you do feel a strong wish to just put your head inside a bag or into the after-locker and forget about everything. Perhaps my great grandmother was an ostrich. Provided I went on steering carefully, as far as the seas were concerned there wasn't much danger to life or limb.

We gathered from people last night that in the cafés after we had left they said,

"They won't get to Delos before the wind springs up."

"They'll make it to Paros."

"No they won't. With the wind as it is we shall see them back at Naxos sometime this evening." This was the verdict of a capetanios, and how right he was!

As a matter of fact we were in danger, though as usual it was from officials, not from the sea. When they saw us approaching, and being completely hidden in the troughs of waves, the Harbour Master wanted to make a little cargo-steamer in the harbour go out and help us. The Harbour Master panicked because if we had been drowned he would have been summonsed. But if the steamer had come out, it couldn't have towed us in those seas, and we should not have wanted to abandon ship, and anyway we might well have all been drowned if we had tried that, because the three others were dopey from cold, not having got on their oilskins till after they were soaked, and when you're like that you would rather just slip over the side of the boat and recline on the bottom of the sea and get a bit of peace! And you know how scatterbrained I am, if there had been an argument on board I would probably have joined in, instead of thinking about my steering, and in no time we would have been swamped or capsized.

I learnt that the evening we came to harbour the wind had been registering sixty knots, and the following day it had reached sixty-three knots, which is Force 11, Violent Storm, on the Beaufort scale. There was still far too much wind for us to be able to leave.

Sally came to see me, saying they had visited the museum, and in the evening the cinema, which had been moved indoors. The *Naxos* was about to leave, which meant that we needed to return to living on the boat in case of thieves at night.

I wrote to Robin:

It was nice sleeping indoors for a bit, though after three days I was glad to get back. I've rather got to the stage where beds are far too luxurious to be wasted by sleeping in them – one ought to take a detective story and read all night – one will be sure to be able to make up the lost sleep on a park bench or somewhere…

By the time I was up and about again it was our third full day of hanging about in Naxos, waiting for the wind to go down so that we could go to Mykonos. We were still in harbour a week later, once again tied up alongside the *Naxos*, which had returned to its berth. Someone came from the steamer to tell us that they were leaving again, this time for Piraeus – would we like to come too, on board the steamer? They could hoist *Crab* on board, using the steamer's davits.

As Sally and I worked at stowing everything on board securely, we found a new hole in the corner of our cotton bread bag, and a rat's teeth marks. "High time we left Naxos harbour!"

I went to say affectionate goodbyes to the couple who kept the Hotel Dionysia, where I had slept non-stop for three days, recovering from the storm. The proprietors had been so intrigued by *Crab*, and felt such affection for her, that they had treated us almost as family. I wrote to Robin that Poppy's husband said to me, when I went to say goodbye, "When Poppy has a child, we will write to you, and you must come back, and we will christen him Kavouri, after your boat."

13. Homecoming

Naxos to Aghia Marina on Aegina (September 10th to 11th)

Crab rode ignominiously on the deck of the *Naxos* to Piraeus, since we dared not venture to sea again with winds as strong as they were round Naxos. According to the *Mediterranean Pilot*, the ship's *vade mecum*, the mountains on Naxos, considerably higher than any other island in the area, seemed to have been a frequent cause of local winds being exceptionally strong.

As soon as we reached the Saronic Gulf, the sea became a flat calm. We arrived at 7.00 am. We had no intention of being holed up in Piraeus while we still had time to sail and a crew. So midmorning we left again, heading south-west towards the island of Aegina. The overnight journey had cost us 800 drachmae, more than we could easily afford, but it had at least put a good distance between us and the violent winds we had encountered day after day. We made for Aghia Marina, already a resort because of the attraction of the temple on the hilltop above it. We found a promontory with shelter for *Crab* among other shallow-draft boats, walked up to the temple, and had a good night's sleep in the harbour.

Aegina to Hydra (September 12th)

We left early, with a light north-west wind. It was pleasant enough, and we even used the spinnaker. But as we entered Hydra harbour, our planned destination, it began to rain. Then the engine stopped - probably it had run out of petrol. We rowed across the harbour, found somewhere to tie up, and sheltered in a café till the rain stopped. The two boys decided to clean the engine while I made the supper. It was then that disaster struck for the second time.

"Look at this! The thread that holds the carburettor in place is completely worn away! It is so lucky that the carburettor didn't just fall off and sink. But we're not going to be able to get a large Seagull spare part in this vicinity!"

Hydra to Salamis (September 13th)

It rained heavily during the night. We moved off the boat altogether, and made for the bigger café tables. As these were round, not rectangular, the best we could do was sleep with our heads in shelter, and our feet out in the rain.

Next morning our two crew members told us, apologetically, that they had had enough of waiting for it to stop blowing a gale, or pouring with rain. Their plan was to leave the boat and have the remainder of their holiday as originally planned. So Sally and I were left to bring the boat back to Piraeus. We accepted the offer of a tow from a *caique* as far as Salamis.

The *caique* towing us at first encountered head seas and made slow progress. But then the weather improved and the *caique* forged ahead at seven knots. Sally and I were pumping nonstop, as seas broke on board because of the unnatural speed. But at least the weather cleared up. We anchored in Salamis town at 6:00 pm. We had to pump vigorously before going to bed, and again first thing next morning. It was clear that after that riotously fast journey under tow, water was coming in everywhere along the seams.

"One of those two who were picked up waiting for the boat train on Victoria Station and persuaded to come and join us – I'm convinced he was a Jonah!" Sally said.

I replied with a scornful lift of an eyebrow. Sally was supposed to be the atheist, the rationalist – what was all this nonsense?

"Just as well there's some wind. With the carburettor almost falling off – the thread gone – we can't rely on the engine anymore," Sally muttered, more to herself than to me. The wind brought a whiff of *rigani* from the flanks of semi-waterless Salamis Island. I remembered sailing there in a keeled day-sailer with Kosta when I was nineteen, and carefree and wild. I would challenge him to see how long he could steer blindfold, relying on the feel of the wind on his cheek.

I felt sadness to be leaving the Aegean, and this nomadic life. This was our last day at sea. And it was clear that the Seagull outboard was no longer fit for purpose – the thread was so worn that the carburettor no longer screwed into place securely, and we would have to replace it. It had literally "lost the thread".

I remembered Sally as she was when I first met her: a well made-up face, slim and well dressed – clearly someone's only daughter. I persuaded her and another Somervillian to come and stay in North Wales during the first Easter holidays from Oxford. I suggested that when we got to the nearest station to the Welsh border we walked the remaining fifty miles, over the top of the Berwyns, and by the Roman road through the pass and down to Cwm Buchan. We would ask permission and sleep in hay barns on the way. Once we were within ten miles of home I phoned my parents and they came to pick us up in their Jeep.

Sally's memory was that as soon as we arrived we were sent upstairs to have hot baths. The bath was huge, almost six-foot long. And as we were luxuriating in the steam and warmth my father knocked and said he had brought us slices of my Mum's fruitcake. "We'll be down soon," Sally called back to him. "No, you eat it in the bath!" the voice protested, "You'll probably never again get the chance to eat fruitcake lying in a hot bath!" Her other memory was that she found my father had a proof copy of *Lord of the Rings,* which he had been sent to review. By reading through most of each night, she read it all. It was the first for her of many visits. My parents' Bohemian lifestyle was so different from her home life in Kent, where her father was the much-respected local doctor – I suspect it set her free to live as frugally as we did on *Crab,* so that we could sail for months on end.

It is amazing that our friendship has survived for a further sixty years. We have sailed together on the west coast of Scotland, where I was part-owner of a pre-war, German-built, six-metre. We sailed together off the coast of Turkey, and memorably took a bareboat charter yacht from Hankö in Finland to St Petersburg in the early 1990s – the first year Russia opened up to welcoming foreign yachts into its waters.

In Turkolimano we had cheerful reunions with friends. This little boat of ours would go anywhere, come through any gale – the only danger was of her being washed up minus crew. In our first year, *Crab* had carried us to safety off the south coast of Sicily through a storm so untimely that we had to beach her and not leave again till the whole village decided it would be safe to go. The following year she had brought us safely across the Adriatic. In this our final year she had looked after us on the long crossings to reach the Bosphorus. She had been our home for four whole months this summer. We rinsed ropes and coiled them away for the winter, washed sails and hung them up out of reach of mice, carefully greased everything made of metal. The plan was to try and sell *Crab,* since neither of us would have the leisure any more for such voyages. We had grown up.

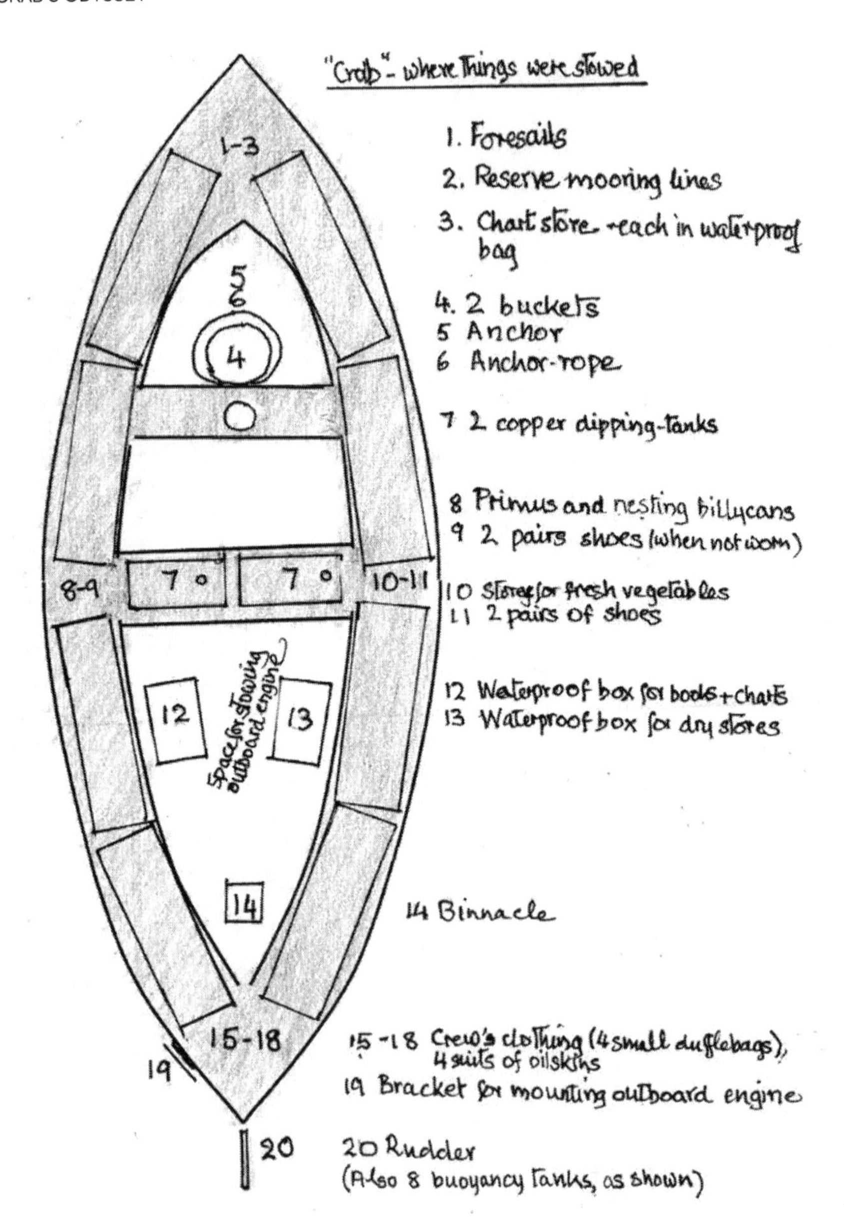

A Bird's-eye View of the Storage on *Crab*

Trips Round the Survivors

DONALD HOPE (*Crab's* virgin voyage, Malta to Sicily and back)

Memory, of course, is notoriously fallible, especially after the lapse of many years. Mnemosyne after all is the Mother of all the Muses, which should perhaps suggest that her office may be as much that of inventive improvisation as of a strictly factual recording. But two things stand out in Donald's memory - from the disappointingly enormous void of forgetfulness into which so much from that time seems to have disappeared - so clearly that he would swear that <u>they</u> at least must be true...

At what time of day *Crab* and her four sailors set out from the Gozitan harbour of Marsal Forn in the direction of Sicily, is for him one of the many things now long forgotten; but it was certainly well after nightfall, when they were far out into the open sea, that he was suddenly seized with an intense desire to pee. But perhaps due to the undulating movement of the boat, or to the embarrassment of the relative lack of privacy on board, or due to both such factors, he found himself painfully unable to do anything of the kind, either in the bucket provided for such emergencies, or simply over the side of the boat. So, mercifully, Captain Sally then suggested that a rope be tied firmly round his waist at one end, and equally firmly round some fixture - the base of the mast, or a thwart, or whatever - and he be encouraged to plunge overboard and try his luck in the sea; which he quite eagerly did, with welcome good results; so that, whether from the relative coolness of the water, or the relative privacy of his immersion, he was able to empty his bladder directly into the Canale di Sicilia with perfect ease - for this relief much thanks - and clamber on board again afterwards feeling much better.

(It's possible, however, that it was this unsailorly weakness of his that was later the reason why Captain Sally decided not to invite him again on any of *Crab*'s subsequent voyages; thus putting a disappointingly abrupt end to what he still remembers as one of the most exciting and enjoyable episodes of his youth.)

It seems to have been some time after this that it became clear that the *Crab* was heading rather fast, with a following breeze, directly into a small bay, with a fortunately sandy beach, on which a few small fishing-boats were drawn up; and on which the waves, not enormous but not inconsiderable, were breaking. While one of the girl sailors firmly held the tiller to keep *Crab*'s bows pointing straight ashore, to prevent her from veering sideways and thus risking being struck amidships by the waves, and possibly even capsized, her other occupants waited, a bit tensely, for the prospect of a rather abrupt landfall. But a few fishermen, busy about their boats, had suddenly noticed the rapidly arriving strangers; and four or five of them ran down the beach into the sea, and with the water up to their waists or higher, seized hold of *Crab*, on both sides, by the gunwales, and half guided, half rushed her up the beach and out of the waves.

Naturally, they must have wondered what on earth these four young foreign idiots thought they were doing, swanning about the Mediterranean in such a patently amateurish manner; but they only kindly and politely asked them where they were going. On being told, in rather halting Italian, that they were making for Syracusa [note: in fact it was Valletta], the fishermen kindly but firmly told them that they were to go no further at present, since the weather was extremely unpropitious for such a voyage; instead, they were to stay as guests in the house of one of their rescuers, until he told them it was safe to go on their way.

And so they gratefully did – for about a week, or nearly so, as far as this writer can remember – marvelling at the extreme kindness and generosity of such hard-working and quite poor people towards strangers whose irresponsible and fortunate lives they must hardly have been able to imagine; and who, thanks to their hosts' wisdom and experience and good advice, were then able to sail on in safety, owing to the essential camaraderie and fellowship of the sea.

Ojén, Málaga, September 2015

RICHARD DAVY (Syracuse to Soverato in Calabria)

Penny has asked me for my worst and best memories. I don't have any worst. My memories of the trip remain suffused in a glow of pure pleasure. I suppose there were a few mild negatives, such as a leaking boat, a recalcitrant motor, unfavourable winds, and failure to catch any fish up the entire east coast of Sicily despite following wildly contradictory advice from different fishermen along the way. But what were those niggles to put against the pleasure of sailing such lovely waters with two such brilliant girls? Nor was I impatient with *Crab*. Until then I had sailed mainly fast planing dinghies, so *Crab*'s stately and often crablike progress was about as great a contrast as one could imagine, but it gave us time to talk, admire the scenery and dreamily contemplate the water sliding by. A trip like that is not about speed.

A few highlights stand out: a magical night among the reed beds off Syracuse, the stop-off in Taormina, and the very Italian shrug of a bemused port official whom we persuaded to register an invisible boat after we had been blown down the coast of Calabria and were unable to make Reggio, so we took the ship's papers by bus. I also recall bowling along under full sail close to the steeply shelving coast of Calabria, so close that we could jump overboard, swim ashore and run down the beach to catch the boat again without it having to stop. I must have done it once with a camera because I took one of the few photographs of the 1956 voyage, reproduced in the photographs for that year in this book. My only regret is that I had to leave to return to a full-time job with *The Times*. I think I was invited the following year but by then I was working abroad and was even less master of my time.

I remained on *The Times* for nearly thirty years as a foreign correspondent, leader writer and foreign specialist, leaving only in 1984 when the Murdoch regime demanded that we adopt a very misguided attitude towards the Soviet Union. Then I spent four years with a consultancy in Oxford, four as a leader writer for *The Independent*, several years as a city councillor, all the while drifting crablike into pretending to be an academic, producing articles, reviews, book chapters, footnotes and the rest. I continued sailing in a variety of small boats out of Chichester Harbour, later with children, but nothing has dimmed my warm memories of *Crab*.

Oxford, 2014

DAVID WITT (Otranto to Corfu)

I can't think of any "worst" memory, but certainly the best, and well-remembered indeed, was the one voyage I was on, Otranto to Corfu, one night, navigated by the stars, and one day, with the stop on that island in between. I do remember the squid risotto, which I would have called "interesting" rather than "vile". And drinking *rezina*. And lots of Turkish coffee. Worth the effort of getting to Italy and back? Most certainly.

After Oxford I spent a year trying various things, then went back to Oxford to read a second degree in engineering. After that, the job I was hoping for, with the Atomic Energy Authority, building nuclear power stations, was held up when they discovered I had been on an Aldermarston March. So I took one offered by the engineering department where I had been studying, and was there for 40 years, until retirement in 1999.

How am I feeling? 82 feels different from 52 or even 72, but nothing drastically wrong. I did notice on a three-generation holiday in the Highlands last month, that my elder two daughters, now aged 42 and 40, very rightly did NOT invite me to join them on their climb up Ben Cruachan, but back in 2000 it was I who took them up the Cuillins!

Oxford, 2010

PETER THRING (also Otranto to Corfu)

I still have my own memories, which get refreshed from time to time when I dine out on the strength of them. The memories are pretty blurred and, of course, when I retell them, after a few drinks, they get suitably embellished. I tell how I helped these two beautiful girls sail an unseaworthy and unmanoeuvrable boat across the hazardous south Adriatic. I know this is a travesty of the trust; I certainly did not *help* anyone, let alone such competent people as you and Sally, not to mention David. I say how we had to run for shelter from the storm to an island, Othonoi was it? "Storm" is a considerable exaggeration, although I do remember spending an awful long time baling, while waves slopped over the bows. And then, of course, I tell how we sailed through the perilous mine-strewn strait between Corfu and Albania, under intermittent gunfire, only narrowly to escape being cast into prison on arrival in Corfu for sailing though waters that were closed to all shipping. Finally, there was the thunderstorm when, if I remember aright, some poor couple in a beachside cottage insisted that you and Sally should sleep in their bed, while they moved to the kitchen, and David and I slept on the floor at your feet. It all makes for a good story, if not entirely accurate, and, provided my hearers have also had a little too much to drink, it impresses the company. Truth and fiction have now got quite muddled in my memory and I should love to read the definitive account, when you finish it. I should also like to know of your other adventures on voyage from Malta to Otranto.

I hope that you never realised how naive I was in 1957 (or was it 1956?). The whole trip was a huge experience for me. I had had very limited foreign travel previously and just getting to Otranto was an adventure in itself; three nights and two days, eight trains (I think) and a ferry. I remember walking down to the harbour at Otranto on a boiling hot afternoon, wondering how to find you, and then coming across this tiny craft with two bronzed, semi-naked beauties lying beside it. At that stage I had not done much sailing on salt water, other than in Fireflies and in a minute cruising yacht called a Silhouette pottering around the East Coast and a single cross-channel trip from Dover to Calais and back with an incompetent friend of my father's. I thought you and Sally immensely competent; Sally I was always a little frightened of, but I fell in love with you at an early stage, love suffused with admiration. I do not remember being scared of being washed up on Albania's shore, although I do recall that someone on the Corfu coast fired a gun (at us?) (to warn us?) as we passed him. I had forgotten the food until you reminded me. I recall some fairly revolting squid and something that purported to be zabaglione but somehow failed to meet expectations. However, I am sure that we had many excellent meals as well.

Are you still sailing? I reluctantly decided to stop about four years ago; I was getting less agile and my sense of balance was deteriorating. I was getting increasingly nervous at falling overboard and I was realising that I was becoming less able to pull my weight. Most of my sailing in the last forty years or so until then has been on a variety of cruising yachts ranging from about twenty-eight foot to forty-four foot, mainly up and down the East Coast and in the North Sea, the Baltic and the Mediterranean, with occasional voyages along the South Coast and the west coast of Scotland. I have never owned my own yacht but I have been lucky with my friends. I miss the sailing now but I think that the decision was sensible.

Markyate, Hertfordshire, England, 2010

IAN MORIN (Skyros to Piraeus)

Looking back at my time on *Crab*, my two most interesting and adventurous experiences confronting the physical world have been in the mountains, whether climbing or skiing, and sailing. You and Sally and *Crab* gave me an original and very positive introduction to sailing in small boats, and the unique conditions on *Crab* have regrettably never quite been matched. And after that two-week induction you fixed me up with a job crewing the very large luxury yacht *Wayfarer,* just built in Bremen for the Rockefellers, so that in the space of a month I had some idea of the possible range of conditions and requisite skills, as well as a very varied foundation of happy memories of sailing in the Mediterranean, which also set me up for further nautical adventures. For all this I am really very grateful.

One possible regret is that I might have been able to contribute more if I'd been a bit more confident and less shy at the time. Oxford had been something of an academic and personal disaster, and shortly after Finals I had the socially stretching experiences of building haystacks to earn some money (worse for my mother, as she had to arrange transport and provisions at an early hour) and wearing a morning suit at my sister's wedding, trapped like a tortoise in its shell, able to rotate independently inside to some extent, but aware of the rigid constraints. Symbolic, perhaps! Another possible regret now is that I was so ignorant then of ancient Greece's extraordinary cultural achievements, a knowledge of which would have added depth to everything I saw and felt.

I do remember being slightly apprehensive when I travelled out: I was going beyond the familiar, and was unsure of being able to do whatever might be required. A couple of days in Venice, a Catholic procession in Brindisi with a saint's statue being delivered by helicopter high above the town, and the passage through the Corinth canal, all provided temporary distractions. The bus trip from Piraeus to a remote shore of the Aegean, with the prospect of an uncertain rendezvous with a small boat on a small island, felt like a committed step into the unknown. But I wouldn't have missed the whole trip for anything, and it has all left a deep impression which is an integral part of my overall experience, as I now look back on it. Any minor embarrassments fade with time relative to the mass of enjoyable memories of crewing for you and Sally on *Crab.*

Harlech, 2014

OWAIN HUGHES (Rhodes to Santorini)

I am floating in the Universe. When my eyes open in the night, I am engulfed in the vast heavens with their incalculable stars, clear and precise as tiny diamonds laid on a black velvet cloth. The vault above me is infinite, beyond depth. My consciousness swells just a little and I remember that this is the Mediterranean night sky. No wonder the Greeks were such great astronomers. Of course there were earlier southern civilizations that knew the stars as siblings, but this was the first time I had come so far South and could bask under such a clear canopy. My mind boggles at this infinity.

My sleeping bag, damp with dew, was already pushed down to my waist, for even on the water I was warm enough without it. Reluctantly I pulled my eyes from the sky and peered around, listening the while to the gentle slap of tiny wavelets against the hull. I was lying on one of the stem-to-stern thwarts, my head up near the stern post, my feet almost touching Robin's. The five-meter ship's lifeboat gave us each 2.5 x 0.45 metres of thwart to lie on, plenty of length but very narrow. Not that there was any danger of rolling off it in the night - the hull was packed with sails, cordage, water tank, food and our minimal possessions.

We are lying at anchor in a sheltered cove. Utter peace and stillness accentuated by the tiny slap of ripples against the hull. I turn my head a little and see the hulking great form of the small mountain whose flanks drop on three sides, perpendicular into the sea. It is a great dark mass against the bright night sky. My eyes leave the obscurity of rock and lose themselves again in the scintillating, bright night of the heavens.

Then dawn awakens me to the rising sun and the gentle splashing of two of my shipmates, swimming lazily in this perfect bay. Oh joy, I can swim and lounge in this warm salt water! I slip out of my sleeping bag and, grabbing a mask, plop over the side. The water is so clear that the fish stand out against the bottom of dark igneous rock with seaweed, interspersed by perfect white sand. For some reason, this was to be my only perfect swim that summer.

There is always something important to do, or we are in a harbour with fishing boats dumping fish guts and excrement into the clear water. Now I swim forever, my mask in the water as long as my lungs can hold out. I swim with the leisurely disinterest I learned from the small fish, just out for a stroll. Yet ready to put on speed whenever expediency required.

"Come aboard" cries the skipper, "perfect wind outside for our course." Oh bother, can't we stay all morning in this idyllic bay, on flat clear water? We could swim ashore and explore, sleep on the sand in the afternoon. Why move now? Do we have to?

The skipper is always right, even if she is an attractive Oxford Undergraduate in a bikini, burned black from months at sea. Robin (a graduate, working in East Africa, but at least another man) is my support when it comes to attempting mutiny. As the two of us haul ourselves up over the gunwale, he is grumbling about "just getting into the swim of things". But neither of us dares contradict Sally, bikini or no.

We unlash the sail (we only have a mainsail and a tiny storm sail), and Robin fills the little old 1930s Seagull outboard with petrol, primes and sets the choke and wraps the starting cord round the flywheel. He gives it a couple of huge pulls and the noisy, smelly thing bursts into life. I already have the anchor off the bottom and am stowing its line as I haul it up. In such a tiny boat, the anchor is perfectly manageable for a fourteen-year-old boy. Captain Sally has taken the helm and is pointing out of this sleepy bay towards the chaos of white caps surging outside.

Penny, my eldest sister, has already pumped, pre-heated and lit the Primus stove, which sits on the only piece of floorboard to be seen. She has devised a small well, carved out of the mass of equipment, so the primus is mostly out of the wind. To actually cook however, she is poised on her knees, her torso upside-down holding the frying pan in position, slightly below her knees. Yes, it would have been much easier had we waited half an hour so she could have cooked breakfast in calm water at anchor, but Sally is Captain and what the Captain says, goes. Penny is frying eggs and great hunks of stale Greek bread in strong olive oil. It smells a bit rancid, but that only enlivens my taste buds.

As she hands me my tin plate, *Crab* pounds into the very first waves and I start stuffing my face with food. I am incredibly hungry because I have had diarrhoea for several days now and vomited most of the food I tried to eat. It could have been food poisoning or, more likely, just sheer exposure. After all, when I had arrived three weeks before, my enthusiastic eldest sister, Penny, had pounced on my British Navy smock - made of a very tightly-woven heavy cotton that was designed to cut the wind. She gave it to an old fisherman who had been so kind and generous to us while we were all camping on the beach in the harbour of Rhodes, careening the hull of *Crab*. We had scraped, caulked the seams and repainted her in preparation for the long trip ahead to Pireus and Athens. The fisherman was ecstatic with the gift and I as yet did not know what it could cost me in health. On the sheltered beach in Rhodes, it had been warm and sunny, but once we were at sea, constantly splashed with spray, burned by the sun and yet frozen with the constant wind as it dried us between waves (à la *Kon Tiki*), it might well have been my saviour. But it wasn't.

I devoured my egg and fried bread before taking in the waves all around us. From the bay inside, the sea seemed a little agitated with whitecaps (so the wind was well over fifteen knots), but once outside, we were in a maelstrom of steep waves that crashed into each other like boys tumbling out into the playground - pommelling each other as they barged around, too hurried to let the others pass. Their breaking crests sparkling for split seconds as the sun played with their air-borne droplets.

The sail hoisted, the engine cut, we started the endless succession of climbing and falling down waves. With our gunwale only a few inches above the water, it seemed impossible that we could climb such vertiginous heights of water, nor slide down the other side, rather than be just simply swamped by each one. They looked much taller than our mast, but then, the loose-footed sail had no gaff and the mast was not high, about three metres.

We struggled forward, clambering up these vast water mountains, sliding down the other sides into their troughs where one was even sheltered from the wind. At noon, the sun was so intense that it devoured most colour. The sea became flashing patches of silver and black, the horizon a vague line interrupted by waves, far far away where the curvature of the Earth hid itself. From time to time a wave would slap the side of the boat and spray us heavily; at others, the wave might even come partly on board but we never risked being swamped - it was simply a matter of pumping from time to time. I must have slept. I took the helm for a while. I manned the pump a bit when needed. Away from the island, the waves became more organised; there was a direction to them. They came up behind us, raised high our pointed stern and then swept by under us. We could not see our destination. There was none. We were in the middle of the churning sea.

Ha! But now this is what's called sailing! Look at those sissies in their racing dinghies on the flat water of a lake, do they really think that's sailing? Or the yachties in their immaculate whites, sipping iced martinis on the poop deck in the setting sunlight? It was just that this very concept of waves being higher than the mast put me in my place. This is the Ocean doing what it does. Man has been trying to conquer it since time immemorial. The Ocean never invited Man on board. Man just tries to use it and often perishes in the attempt. It is a wild bull, you can try to ride it, but do not complain about the consequences! Let's face it and hand it to the designers: ship's lifeboats are designed to float like corks, come what may.

I imagine that I lost my breakfast soon after meeting these bullying, chaotic waves - as I had lost all other food, even on terra firma. I settled down with a piece of filthy old salt-stiffened canvas around me, trying to keep warm, yet burned by the intense sun overhead. We made good time that day, averaging almost a knot. Certainly better than lying at anchor. Sally was right, but Robin and I still yearned for that idyllic bay with its crystal-clear water as smooth as glass...

After that, I slept and only awoke as Robin started the outboard and we came putt-puttering into another strange fishing harbour. We found a space amongst the small fishing boats, most of them larger than *Crab*, and came up to a sea wall. The skipper and the cook called out to some men lounging on the dock, watching us as we came in, salt-soaked and burned. Our faces, feet and hands all cracked and split by salt, wind and sun. Bedraggled, but so accustomed to it, we'd be off again next morning for more!

Every morning as I listen to the news I am deluged with reports of still more desperate refugees drowned in the Mediterranean, trying to reach a land where they can live without being killed in their homes or in their villages, in search of a place where they may safely raise they families, earning a living in peace. What a contrast to our experience on *Crab*.

How very different was our youth! It was neither fear nor hunger that pushed us out to travel the world. Much later, I hitchhiked to Iran and back and earned my keep teaching English. I did have a few close shaves, but never really feared for my life.

When I arrived in Rhodes to "sign on" as a barely experienced foredeck monkey, *Crab* was bottom-up on the beach being scraped, caulked and painted. We worked on her together and we all knew exactly how sound a cockleshell we were trusting with our lives; stout, solid timbers held together with sturdy brass nails. This was no raft of driftwood held together with bits of wire and rope salvaged from old fishing nets, washed up on the shore somewhere. I can only imagine with no decent materials how flimsy the refugees' crafts must be. The contrast is really poignant.

CO-OWNERS

ROBIN MINNEY (Malta to Syracuse, Corfu to Skiathos, Rhodes to Santorini)

Anyone reading this is coming in near the end of a lifelong story of a wonderful friendship. In the cinema, you see the end of the "big picture", played as days or weeks or years later, and sit through the "shorts" to wait for the story's beginning. I've been instructed to leave out the shorts: how I first met Penny; why we wrote to each other when I was working in East Africa; and how it came about that by writing a cheque I owned a share in the little tubby lifeboat they called *Crab*.

For many of us looking back to the *Crab* adventure must be a memory, a recalling, even a reliving, seen and felt incompletely, even incoherently, through a long, long filter of many other adventures, other lives. For me, however, it seeded, budded and flowered and fruited in a continuing depth of love and joy, never wrecked or capsized through the swells and storms in our sixty year relationship.

Malta

I remember arriving in Malta in 1955, having flown from Nairobi via Cairo and Tripoli in Libya, when Malta was still a bastion for the Royal Navy. In 2016 I was back in Malta, our four-master holiday sailing ship moored next to a matt grey Russian warship. That was Gozo. The next day in Valletta we got on a tourist pleasure cruise round the many inlets of the harbour. I did not recognise anything of the harbour I had rowed *Crab* round in the dark in 1955, while the girls had abandoned us to go to a party. I was happy rowing alone, and Donald had gone to bed in the shed that was our temporary sleeping place. The contrast after sixty-one years was very marked: now Penny was with me and parties were shared. Streets were busy with cars and pedestrian tourists visiting shops and cafes, or buying tickets for pleasure boats. In 1955, not so long after the war, I bought a black Royal Navy belt which I still wear, and some little white clay pipes which sailors had smoked for maybe two or three hundred years.

Sicily

In 2016 our cruise also visited Sicily, harbours on both west and east coasts, but I did not see again the little bay where sixty-one years before two shepherd lads helped us secure *Crab* to the shore. As Donald could speak some Italian we quickly made friends. It turned out that one of them was a poet and he wanted to share his muse, so led us to a little hut not far from the shore. He unfolded his poem and began to look for his glasses. We had much amusement because we all could see his spectacles hanging by the curve of one arm from a hole in the back of his trousers.

Luckily he hadn't sat down in them. Or maybe he had. I don't think even Donald understood much of the poem in local dialect, but we were grateful and cheerful.

That night I was cold on *Crab* and thought I would go ashore and light a small fire, and then, shaping the sand, have a warm and comfortable night's sleep. But the fire, small though it was, attracted our shepherd friends. One climbed to a small cliff and pushed down part of a dry thorn hedge. The fire blazed, and the other shepherd called, "Christus! Christus!" Dry thorn burns up very quickly, so soon peace was restored and I got the calm and warm rest I wanted and needed.

The next day I had to get to a bus stop, then to Syracuse for my return to work in East Africa. When they learnt I was English, three men also waiting for the bus asked to see my passport, and admired the royal arms on the front. They told me they belonged to the "Partita Monarchista". I should have asked them whether they were supporting the recent king who somehow had survived Mussolini, or the more local pre-Garibaldi "Kingdom of the Two Sicilies" based in Naples.

The horizontal loom

It was probably in the Gulf of Corinth when we put in to land in the middle of the day on a quiet shoreline where a man came to meet us, carrying a rifle and wearing an official looking cap with a crown over the letter A. He was certainly friendly and I could see that the crown stood for the state (the King of Greece was in place then), and the A showed him to be a rural policeman *agrifylax*. He led us to his home and his wife, and they welcomed us with refreshments while their daughter worked at a horizontal loom. I took some photographs. When we said goodbye and thank you, he said, "We always thank God when he sends us good visitors."

Sailing by

Before the *Crab* adventure I had taught myself to sail in a small clinker built dinghy lent me by a friend of a friend who wanted it to be enjoyed. This was on the Stour estuary between Essex and Suffolk and a short cycle ride from home. The best thing about sailing alone is that if anything goes wrong there's no one to blame, so you really learn what to do. I sometimes practised sailing in a figure of eight round two buoys. The Stour estuary is muddy in places, so you do not want to be caught on an ebb time. Since then, most of my sailing has been with Penny, on *Joanna* off the west coast of Scotland, and particularly fun was a bare boat charter in the Adriatic on a short leave from Moscow (where we were working for some years after retiring in England). Sally was with us again, also Penny's younger brother Owain and another friend. Sally was skipper once more. One night we drifted and nearly tangled with a German yacht in the same bay. We got out smoothly as I could talk German and Owain handled all the needed manoeuvres.

Three eligible young ladies

Maggs, Penny's best friend from school, had already come when I joined the party at Corfu. So I had Penny, Maggs and Sally, all in their early twenties, and just me. Crab was an open boat and I saw envious looks from young Greeks and sometimes overheard remarks. But by that summer I had a definite plan and actually proposed to Penny a week or two later when we alone on a quiet island.

A storm

Is surviving a storm at sea a good memory or a bad one? Maggs said that fishermen had told her we should not put to sea that morning, but Sally said the crossing was short, and she was skipper. In the event wind and waves got up strongly and the only other boat we saw was overwhelmed and the man on board swam to shore. As Penny was the most experienced in steering with a following wind, she took the helm and with the greatest concentration steered to each wave while keeping our general direction. I am not clear where Sally and Maggs were, lying down out of the way I guess. Thanks to Penny, we shipped hardly any water, so most of the time I sat next to her and sang to keep spirits up. I know lots of songs by heart and this gift was really useful.

When we reached our harbour at last, I got someone to take a photograph, and this is I think the only one in which I appear. A small gold cross can be seen hanging from my neck, and I was wearing this the following year, 1958, when I came with Owain to Rhodes. The next day the family hosting us saw that now Penny was wearing it.

RICHARD HUGHES (Valletta to Syracuse, Piraeus to Istanbul)

Crab was only middle-aged and perfectly sound, but surely her sea-days were done! A writer spends half his life glued to a chair: as he ages he tends to get soft and the glue to get harder, so when "sixty" becomes the next leaf to tear off his calendar you'd surely think his (crazier) sea-days were done. Yet *Crab* took it into her head to sail to Istanbul, and the writer took it into his to sign on as cabin-boy even though she hadn't a cabin. Cabin? There wasn't even an awning to keep off the sun...

Everyone in Malta thought even Sicily rash enough, so nothing was said about going further. But that summer after I left them they worked up to Messina, across the stormy Gulf of Taranto and across the Adriatic, and on to Corfu...

The following summer (1958) I was at last free to join her again, and in the early afternoon of June 3rd we left Turkolimano, the purple island of Salamis dropping slowly astern as we chugged gently down the coast towards Sounion...

The fact was I had been working hard in my Welsh home on one book for three years and still hadn't finished it. Many writers take to the bottle when the nervous tension of writing grows intolerable; but instead, I had taken to *Crab*.

Naturally I wasn't as much use as a younger man. In a boat like *Crab* the helmsman ought to be able to leap clean to the forepeak, do something vital, and be back before she can luff. But one of the girls always got there before me. There was only one way I could earn my salt. Being older I needed less sleep: on a long night-passage I could sail her from sunset to dawn while the rest of them snored.

Harlech, 1958. [From an unpublished article written for *Sports Illustrated*. Diccon died in 1976.]

SALLY HUMPHREYS (skipper)

I am writing this in a *Crab*-like anchorage, a sheltered bay on the north-western tip of Euboea where we anchored at 8 am in flat calm after having motored all night from Chalcis. Differences: we are anchored in three and a half metres, and not right by the shore; we have seen two other yachts passing; the bridge at Chalcis is now opened only once every twenty-four hours, always at night, and the opening is preceded by VHF conversations about pilots for the larger vessels and the order in which we are to proceed. Also, we covered the distance between Lavreion and our present anchorage in twenty-eight hours, with a swim/lunch stop en route.

The reader of this book will probably have decided that I am a survivee – if the term exists – rather than a survivor, i.e. that being bossed by me was one of the hardships of life on *Crab*. Penny gave me *Life of Pi* when it came out; I assumed she had me figured as the tiger. Since my son, who grew up with his father and not with me, behaves very similarly on his boat, I attribute the tigrishness to DNA. It had its uses: one of the captain's jobs on *Crab* was to deal with port officials, a Father-William-like experience that equipped me with persistence and obstinacy helpful in later life for handling copy-editors and other obstructions.

This morning's anchorage is reminiscent of *Crab* in its peacefulness and solitude - on the other hand, yachts no longer arouse the curiosity evoked by *Crab*, nor the generosity. I especially remember one idyllic morning when someone from a nearby house asked for a container and brought back our canvas bucket full of ripe green figs. People invented their own answers to questions: "At night they open up the thwarts and there are beds underneath, with *nylon* pyjamas!" However, men in the Greek islands often worked on ships, and travel had made them tolerant of the eccentricities of foreigners. Whereas the Calabrians thought us mad - if we could't afford a large motor yacht, why not stay at home in wonderful England, which as prisoners of war they found a paradise in comparison with Southern Italy ("Ah, *Manchester*!") - Greece was different. When women exclaimed in horror about the dangers and discomforts of *Crab*, their husbands would just shrug and say "well, if that's what they like doing..." Very refreshing.

It was rare, in the fifties, to find Greeks who sailed. We talked to some men who had sailed small boats at night from island to island during the war, in search of supplies (movement was forbidden, and fuel unobtainable). Their advice was very useful. But outside the Saronic and (occasionally) Argolic gulfs we only met two charter yachts, one British (Sam Barclay's *Stormy Seas*, later owned by the underwater archaeologist Peter Throckmorton) and one American, owned by Hod Fuller (generally suspected, perhaps rightly, to be working for CIA), plus one private yacht owned by a Signora Feltrinelli. There were more sailors, and yachts, in Istanbul. Even in the post-*Crab* years, when I had a very small six-metre, *Gypaetos*, we met very few other yachts - and again the rare enthusiastic sailors were Turks. I had a wonderful conversation on the edge of the quay at Eski Foça with my harbour charts spread out and a Turkish yacht skipper pointing to all the best anchorages - no need for words.

Gypaetos had been built in Germany in 1909 and had won the Kaiser's cup in Kiel in 1914; she came to England after the war as part of a reparation payment. I don't know her history between 1919 and 1945, when Alan Buchanan found her in a mud-berth on the East Coast, replanked her bottom, cut down her rig, and added a cabin-top. There was just room inside for two pipe-cots and a Primus; the only person who managed to sleep in the foc'sle was my friend Noel Marshall, who was able to take off his artificial leg and leave it on deck (fortunately he couldn't understand the comments of the locals). My later experiences on his Halberg-Rassy 38 *Sadko I* in Japan and on the Mike-Pearson-designed *Sadko II* in Norway and Chile were much more comfortable.

Gypaetos was of course the opposite of *Crab* in terms of manoeuvrability (and twice the length, and narrower). Like *Crab* she had an outboard motor, mounted on a fitting beside the cockpit, which seemed safer than her long elderly counter; like *Crab*'s outboard, it could only be used in a flat calm with no swell. Like *Crab*, she acquired second-hand clothes; an old Dragon sail as mainsail, and *Crab*'s storm jib. She went to Fethiye and Marmaris, the year the Bronze Age Gelidonia wreck was discovered, north up the Turkish coast to Ayvalik, and thence home to Spetsai via Psara, where we were stuck for five days in September storms; and to the Ionian islands (scary tow through the Corinth canal, again like *Crab*). She now sits under a cover in the Mikro Limani car park, planks cracking; I hate to see her there. [Any reader who wants to restore a historic boat, please get in touch – though there may be legal problems – she had at least two owners after me.]

The most important change in the last years, from a practical point of view, is the introduction of the mobile telephone, which enormously simplifies crew changes. The worst change, in the Sea of Marmaris and round Ayvalik, is the spread of jellyfish, though fortunately those in the Sea of Marmaris don't sting. We never met one on *Crab*.

This year's cruise ended with a fine definition from Lefteri, our charter skipper, of a good Greek harbour: one where it doesn't blow harder inside than outside.

An anchorage on Evia, July 2015

Other books from the Taniwha Press UK

www.taniwhapress.com

A crippled boat and a lot of broken dreams. A broken marriage and a hunger to sail down into the Indian Ocean. This is both a love story about a boat, his beloved Tetranora and a story of a voyage out of love and into life. Along the way it explores ancient sailing routes from the Mediterranean to the Indian Ocean.

As his title suggests, Heikell is keenly interested in the exploits of those who sailed similar routes centuries ago. His narrative regularly quotes from Classical authors: Herodotus, Homer, Pliny (who died in the eruption of Vesuvius in AD79) and even the Acts of the Apostles. Long hours at the helm gave opportunity to reflect on how those early predecessors managed to arrive safely without the benefit of buoys, lights or binoculars.

... an engrossing account of an epic and redemptive voyage. *Cruising Association*

ISBN 978-0-9575849-3-8
Price £10.50 Also in kindle and epub

In 1976 Rod Heikell set off in Roulette, a 20-foot boat that should probably have never left the sheltered waters of the Solent, for the Mediterranean. Via the French Canals and Biscay, he somehow got to the Mediterranean and sailed to Corsica, Italy and onto Greece. It records the near disasters and highs and lows of a voyage which shaped his life in ways he never imagined. He became the accidental sailor and has led to a life-long love of sailing and exploring the seas. In 1987 he took a Mirror Offshore 18 down the Danube behind the Iron Curtain to the Black Sea and Aegean, probably the longest voyage one these tubby little craft has made.

A cracking read in the tradition of great cruising yarns. *Dick Durham Yachting Monthly*

They are charming tales that heavily reinforce the young man's mantra that the right time to depart on a voyage is right now. *Jake Frith Sailing Today*

ISBN 978-0-9575849-0-7
Price £9.50 Also in kindle and epub

When there is a knock on his door at night Douglas opens it to find a tall dark girl there. She gives him a package and tells him he must come to Greece. His brother is ill and needs him. Leaving his orderly, comfortable life Douglas travels to Greece where he becomes embroiled in a dark plot to destroy the manuscript for a book on a secretive neo-Nazi party that his brother has written. On his brother's yacht with the aid of Peter's friends Darcy and Europa he must out-run his pursuers through the Greek islands and try to piece together what is going on. He must also come to terms with his brother and their troubled early years. It is a voyage he is not ready for and one which will change his life.

This is a scary tale of the rise of the modern Greek national socialist party Golden Dawn during the early 21st Century, paralleling the 'Junta' years of the late 1960s and 70s. The possible suppression of facts, by destroying a manuscript due to be published, led to the sail from Naxos in the Aegean to Ithaca in the Ionian, to prevent this - all plausibly written with the ebb and flow of past and present well organised. The inclusion of some apparently unnecessary facts becomes clear at the end as the twist in the tail comes as an unpleasant surprise. *Cruising Association*

Fantastic read, drifting between fiction and non fiction, I did not want the story to end. *Amazon US*

ISBN 978-0-9575849-6-9
Price £6.75 Also in kindle and epub

If there is a back story to the *Odyssey,* then this novel by J. C. Graeme is it. Forget the return from Troy and a band of heroes voyaging the seas and encountering monsters and adventure aplenty while having their way with the local maidens and the odd goddess. In this story of Odysseus, he is a bar-fly in the Sunset Bar on Khios where he trades stories for jugs of wine with the bar owner Homer. He takes on a job for a local merchant on Khios to pick up some cargo on the mainland and while crossing the sea in his little boat he is blown off course along the coast of Asia Minor. On this adventure he encounters a whole cast of characters and maybe even a goddess or two, though they have little in common with the characters peopling the *Odyssey* as we know it. Some of them may even have been real.

J. C. Graeme vividly brings to life the goings on in the late Archaic period of Greek history and relates a more human epic where even the pantheon of Gods who have ruled over things for so long are being questioned, or at least defied, by mortals. Odysseus meets them all, the Anthropophagus, Circe, Calypso, and the Sirens, but not as we know them from classical literature. In the end Odysseus finds he is accidentally on a voyage that will lead to blindness and madness and even a vision of what the underworld is like. And he will find, despite the despair from all he encounters on his voyage and his descent into madness, that there was more wonder and excitement in the outside world than he ever found in a cup of Koan red in Homer's Sunset Bar.

ISBN 978-0-9575849-9-0
Price £7.50 Also in kindle and epub

www.taniwhapress.com